ADVANCE PRAISE

"As a forty-one-year veteran and lifelong practitioner of leadership, I am confident that the ideas in Changing Altitude will positively change relationships in any team or organization. Dennis and Greg have crafted a thoughtful and creative leadership model built around servant leadership, active listening, and consistent feedback. But Changing Altitude is not just for leaders. It will resonate strongly with anyone who wants to improve themselves, their team, and their organization."

—GENERAL (RETIRED) MARTIN E. DEMPSEY, 18TH
CHAIRMAN OF THE JOINT CHIEFS OF STAFF

"This book inspires the reader to dig deep inside their being to find the strength, humility, and courage to lead with honor."

—STEVE EDWARDS, PRESIDENT AND CEO OF COXHEALTH

"Greg has worked with me and my teams for a number of years. What sets Greg apart is his compassion and empathy for those whom he coaches, for the mission they are trying to accomplish, and for those who ultimately will be served. There is no question that Greg has made me a better leader, but I think he has also helped me be a better person—and that has had an impact on all of my roles. This book crystallizes what Greg has learned working with real leaders in the real world. The principles and concepts in this book are readily accessible, and I know, for a fact, they can make a great difference. Simply put, reading this book and putting the content into practice will make you a better leader and equip you to lead a more impactful and joyful life."

—DR. DAN CAREY, SECRETARY OF HEALTH AND HUMAN
RESOURCES FOR THE COMMONWEALTH OF VIRGINIA

"If your goal is to lead well and earn the enduring allegiance and respect of your team, O'Neil and Hiebert offer brilliantly practical and relevant advice."

—NORTON A. SCHWARTZ, US AIR FORCE GENERAL (RETIRED) AND PRESIDENT OF INSTITUTE FOR DEFENSE ANALYSES

"If your goal is to be a great leader, this is the book for you. I've been a leadership coach and speaker for more than twenty years, and I'm an experienced Air Force pilot—so I can say with authority this book will help you make an 'afterburner' climb—you'll soar to the highest levels of leadership.

Dennis and Greg have nailed it! If you want to lead and influence others, this book should be your flight plan—develop yourself and then others will want to be your wingman. You will all soar to new heights."

—LEON "LEE" ELLIS, US AIR FORCE COLONEL (RETIRED), BESTSELLING AUTHOR OF FIVE NATIONALLY ACCLAIMED BOOKS, INCLUDING LEADING WITH HONOR, AND PRESIDENT OF LEADERSHIP FREEDOM LLC (DBA LEADING WITH HONOR)

"While leadership books abound, few cover the critical transition between individual contributor and leader/supervisor, and no book does it better than Changing Altitude. Dennis O'Neil and Greg Hiebert brilliantly lay out practical next steps to become a successful leader in your demanding new role; take them up on their offer! Being charged with a leadership role is a 'make-it-or-break-it' moment in one's career, and Changing Altitude will ensure success at making it, not breaking it. Far too many people in leadership roles never take the time to deliberately develop the skills they need to succeed; Changing Altitude is a one-stop fix to ensure your leadership ability matches the demands of your role.

When you read Changing Altitude, you'll be stunned at how naturally unprepared you were to lead and enormously grateful to Dennis and Greg for helping you ease into a posture of success. Every potential leader should enter their first job with a copy of this book, whether a supervisor or not."

—THOMAS A. KOLDITZ, PHD, BRIGADIER GENERAL (RETIRED), FOUNDING DIRECTOR OF THE DOERR INSTITUTE FOR NEW LEADERS AT RICE UNIVERSITY, PROFESSOR EMERITUS OF THE US MILITARY ACADEMY AT WEST POINT, AND AUTHOR OF *LEADERSHIP RECKONING* AND *IN EXTREMIS LEADERSHIP*

"If you read Greg's first book (You Can't Give What You Don't Have), you have a richer and deeper understanding of the self-care and self-discipline necessary for leaders to master themselves so they can effectively serve and support their teams. You'll absolutely love the sequel, Changing Altitude, because it continues the challenge of mastery—this time to master connections with those you lead. In that same engaging, easygoing, and insightful style, he joins with Dennis O'Neil, another successful servant leader, to take us on a leadership journey that is other-focused, humble, highly self-aware, interconnected, collaborative, courageous and character-based."

—MICHAEL MONTELONGO, INDEPENDENT CORPORATE BOARD DIRECTOR AND 19TH ASSISTANT SECRETARY OF THE AIR FORCE FOR FINANCIAL MANAGEMENT AND COMPTROLLER

"Changing Altitude is truly a field manual that belongs in the hands of every leader who has taken on an increased level of responsibility. The authors offer more than just concepts—a true framework for leading yourself, your people, and your operating environment. New leadership roles can be a big adjustment, and this book will accelerate a leader's path to success."

—DREW SHAMBARGER, HEAD OF SALES AND CLIENT EXPERIENCE STRATEGY AT TRUIST

"As they always do, Greg and Denny have delivered a practical, introspective approach anyone can use to become an exceptional leader. Whether a first-time manager or a new CEO, it is the introspection that leads to *true learning and the understanding that comes from that learning that leads to exceptional leadership."*

"This is a first-day reading for anyone with new leadership responsibilities."

"Greg and Dennis approach leadership from the inside out—'know thyself'—and develop self-awareness in a constructive, yet brutally honest way. They focus on understanding the character and core values of one's own individual leadership style and how that is both a model and prompt to inspire leadership in others. Greg was the rarest student and the earliest during our years at Harvard Business School to deeply understand leadership in a human way. His compassion, authenticity, and deep understanding of human nature give him unique insights into what makes a true leader for a better world."

"Changing Altitude is a must-read for any leader who wants to soar to greater heights. Dennis and Greg make an excellent case as to why a leader must 'know thyself first.' Warts and all. Strengths and blind spots.

Exploring your psychological underpinnings takes courage and humility. This process is not easy, but it is necessary, and the payoff is huge. Read this book to improve your agility and mindset, so that you can successfully adapt and lead those around you."

"*For anyone who is serious about reaching new heights on their leadership journey, Changing Altitude is a must-read that provides a critical leadership foundation for military and civilian leaders alike!*"

—DATESTE EICKHOFF, THIRTY-TWO-YEAR MILITARY
VETERAN AND US ARMY COLONEL (RETIRED)

"*I know that this book is geared toward leaders in new roles, but Changing Altitude is a must for any leader! If you think you don't need this book, it is probably just the book for you.*"

—KIRK THOMAS, CHIEF ADMINISTRATIVE OFFICER AT GEISINGER
LEWISTOWN HOSPITAL AND GEISINGER WESTERN DIVISION

"*Greg and Dennis cover three critical areas Changing Altitude: Yourself, Your People, and Your Environment. They take a deep dive into each area to help you further understand, grow, and define success. This easy-to-follow road map provides leaders with clear directions on enhancing their leadership development no matter their title, responsibilities, or industry. Changing Altitude will equip any leader to soar in their role. The authors are trusted advisors, and live what they teach.*"

—JOHN BECKER, GROUP SENIOR VICE
PRESIDENT, STRATEGIC GROWTH, SG2

DENNIS O'NEIL, PhD
GREG HIEBERT

Changing
↑ltitude

HOW TO **SOAR**
IN YOUR NEW
LEADERSHIP ROLE

LIONCREST
PUBLISHING

CHANGING ALTITUDE
How to Soar in Your New Leadership Role

ISBN   978-1-5445-2564-8 *Hardcover*
        978-1-5445-2563-1 *Paperback*
        978-1-5445-2565-5 *Ebook*
        978-1-5445-2566-2 *Audiobook*

This book is dedicated to my ever-growing family. I love each and every one of you ten hundred!
—DENNIS O'NEIL, PHD

In order to meet the chaos and crises of the past several years, leaders have had to change altitude with greater speed than ever before. I continue to be inspired by the commitment, sacrifice, and compassion of the leaders who carried the burden of providing care, prioritizing justice, and finding ways to keep our economy operating during 2020 and 2021. I dedicate this book to them, with deep gratitude and reverence. May it serve you as you serve others.
—GREG HIEBERT

CONTENTS

INTRODUCTION

"Encourage us in our endeavor to live above the common level of life."

—FROM THE WEST POINT CADET PRAYER

It was not the weather forecast anyone would want to see just before getting on a plane. Sitting at our gate together at the Miami airport, we uneasily read the scrolling captions on the muted TVs: "Six inches of rain expected along the Eastern Coast in the next twenty-four hours. Eighty-mile-per-hour winds. This is a Category 1 hurricane..."

Out of the large windows, we could see the massive storm front moving in, already unleashing torrents of rain. Baggage tram workers sprinted from their carts to the plane's underbelly, the hoods from their yellow slickers covering their faces. We saw the large reader board update flights with new notifications in the adjacent terminal corridor: *Delayed. Delayed. Canceled. Canceled.* We had been to Miami often in the past six months to provide leadership coaching for a large hospital system—but we'd never experienced weather like this.

Finally, a voice from one of the flight attendants crackled onto the intercom: "Good news, folks, it looks like we're going to be the last flight out." As we boarded the plane, heavy rain pounded on the roof. With some trepidation, we settled in and buckled up.

The plane was able to take off, right ahead of the storm. The pilot took us seven miles above the earth's surface, flying high above the storm below. Up there, we sailed through the blue sky. It was calm and peaceful. But looking down, we could see a line of dark clouds, perfectly parallel to our aircraft. We could even see nonstop lightning strikes illuminating the darkness below. It was easy to observe all the misery pouring down—and yet, what we experienced 37,000 feet up was calm, smooth, and clear. The increase in altitude brought clarity and calm.

But changing altitude can bring its own set of challenges too, as we were quickly reminded. A woman sat next to us, reading Jim Collins' business bestseller, *Good to Great.* We commented on the book and mentioned that it's one we often reference in our work as leadership coaches.

"You're leadership coaches?" she asked, perking up. "What kind of clients do you serve? Big organizations?" We nodded. "Do you help leaders at lower levels," she asked, "or do you just work with the C-suite crew, the CEOs, the CFOs...?"

Yes, CEOs, we agreed—but just as often, leaders further down the organizational chain, as well: executives, directors, VPs, managers. "We build long-term relationships with our clients, and then over time, we help leaders at all levels of their organization improve," we explained. "We help them become more effective, more confident—essentially, our job is to help their people become the best leaders they can be."

She nodded, looking at us intently. "Can I pick your brain?" she asked.

The woman's name was Rebecca. She said that she had picked up Collins' book because she'd been promoted to a director role at her data analytics firm. But after six months in her new role, she was struggling. "In the last few months, I've realized that the scope of what I need insight into is enormous. My head is swirling with everything I'm responsible for. Honestly, I've begun to significantly doubt my ability to do this job. I miss my old life when I was just a manager."

Her previous promotion had been easy, she explained. As a manager, she'd worked with her former team, and they were all familiar with her skills in data analytics. They trusted her, and she knew exactly what she was doing. "I was confident; I was comfortable. I knew how to help my employees do their work well because I understood the ingredients for success. But it's a *totally* different situation now that I'm a director."

"How so?" we prompted her.

"It's a completely different job than what I've done before. I have all these new responsibilities, and I'm in charge of people who do jobs I don't understand. I'm supposed to get results—like everyone is looking to *me* to hit these benchmarks—but my team is not performing, so then it's presumed to be my fault. And because of that, I feel like I have to do everyone's job for them." She sighed. "It's exhausting. I'm working twelve- to fourteen-hour days, but it doesn't feel like we're getting anywhere. I'm starting to hate going to work." She looked at us sheepishly. "I don't think my employees like me. I feel annoyed with them. And I just feel *so much pressure*, all the time."

Rebecca's story was familiar to us. In our years of leadership consulting, we've learned that promotions like hers inevitably produce challenges. She was certainly not alone in the challenges she faced. You might be personally familiar with many of them.

THE STORM

When you "change altitude" like Rebecca, moving from your area of expertise to a much more significant supervisory role, the picture changes. New skills are required. Rather than moving from a storm into clear skies, moving upward can quickly feel like the reverse:

things felt clearer at a lower altitude. Now that you've gained in elevation, you might be flying in the storm.

It doesn't work to keep doing things the same way you did them before. Those skills may have gotten you promoted, but a promotion means a significant expansion in your responsibilities. It can be an enormous struggle to get on top of them. Many of your employees are likely doing jobs you don't have experience in, making it hard to mentor or motivate them. Perhaps you try to compensate by micromanaging or demanding more from your employees. Or, maybe you opt for a feel-good atmosphere at the expense of getting results. Turbulence can come from many problems: mediocre performance, poor communication, low trust, high stress—or maybe all of the above.

You need more tools, but you don't know which ones, and you don't know how to get them. You might feel like you're flying a plane without instruments. Things go relatively well, so long as everything is clear and it's blue skies ahead—but rarely do you have that level of clarity. Somehow, you need to learn how to utilize more tools to get above the turbulence. You need to see more. You need to know more.

You want an accurate appreciation, understanding, and perspective of your new responsibilities—which, all too often, are murky at best. You want to gain a deeper understanding of what's really going on in the areas you're leading. You want to make sure that your departments are functioning as effectively as possible. You want to enjoy the people you work with, feel a greater sense of fulfillment, and build a positive legacy. You want to feel less burned out, more energized, and with more purpose. But how?

GETTING OUT OF THE CLOUDS

It's no easy task. Rebecca had felt successful flying at a lower altitude; now that she'd been promoted to Director, she was trying to find tools to be successful at a higher altitude. But truly influential leaders must be ready to operate at a *range* of altitudes, depending on what their environment and people require.

Sometimes, you need to elevate your altitude to rise *above* the storm: you need to get clarity, revisit your big picture goals, and ensure you're flying on course. Other times, you need to *decrease* in altitude; you need to view in greater detail what's happening at the lower levels of your organization. Often, it's necessary for leaders to fly right into the thick of the storm, like when conflict inevitably comes up or a worldwide pandemic hits. In those instances, the pilot must utilize every skill they've got. They must trust the instruments, hang on amid turbulence, and reassure their people that it's going to be okay.

The task of leadership requires that you develop the ability and insight to navigate a range of altitudes with agility. This may feel like an overwhelming task, especially if you find yourself in a position like Rebecca, where the skills that helped you excel in your former position don't seem to translate to your new role. True, there's much to learn—but that learning process is precisely our passion.

> *Truly influential leaders must be ready to operate at a range of altitudes, depending on what their environment and people require.*

In conversations like the one we had with Rebecca and so many others, we've realized that leaders need assistance navigating the journey when the leader's roles and responsibilities have greatly expanded or when the context they are operating in has dramatically changed.

In this book, we've made it our goal to help shed light on what you may not yet know (or fully appreciate) and provide practical next steps on how to develop in critical areas, pivotal to your individual and organizational success. These strategies are research-based and have been honed throughout our decades of leadership development and coaching. They'll give you the momentum you need to change altitude successfully, get needed clarity, and lead an organization that excels.

CHANGING ALTITUDE: WHAT YOU'LL LEARN

As a leader, you're dealing with three key areas: yourself, your people, and your environment. This book will help you achieve a deeper understanding, growth, and success in each area.

YOU

- **Your leadership journey**: Good leadership starts with "knowing thyself." You'll be given strategies to strengthen your authenticity and credibility as a leader and provide you with much greater insights regarding your strengths and weaknesses.
- **The Seven Critical Characteristics of Leadership**: We'll define and defend the seven characteristics we've found to be most critical to effective leadership. We'll also provide questions to help you evaluate your performance in these areas.
- **The importance of feedback**: You'll learn the crucial role of feedback for growth, and we'll acquaint you with our valuable 360-Assessment tool.
- **Optimal altitude**: We'll give you strategies like energy management and a hierarchy of priorities to ensure you're investing in your self-care and performing at your best.

YOUR PEOPLE

- **Clarify collective values**: You'll learn how to create healthy group dynamics that will foster your employees' best performance. We'll also discuss how the health of your organization can be significantly improved by establishing behaviorally-based values that are embraced and practiced by team members.
- **Positive communication and active listening**: You'll learn how

to effectively employ active listening and reflection to promote efficient communication within your organization.

- **Leading change and exerting influence**: We'll overview the Comprehensive Change Model to help you effectively lead change, along with eight influence strategies to secure your team's full commitment and buy-in.
- **Empowering others**: We'll educate you on how to move away from micromanagement and, instead, empower your staff to perform at their best levels, ultimately raising up new leaders.

YOUR ENVIRONMENT

- **Understanding your environment**: In order to lead with agility, it's critical that you know how to read the proxies of your environment to excel within your unique context.
- **Conflict management**: Conflict is inevitable, but poor handling can rot an organization from the inside out. You'll learn strategies to minimize the harm of conflict and maximize its potential for good. We'll also discuss how to approach conflict with your boss versus your direct reports.
- **Paradoxical leadership and crisis management**: We'll explain the necessity of leading paradoxically and why that's especially important when managing a crisis.

In providing you with this roadmap, our goal is to give you a leadership development framework that will help you soar—enhancing your perspective, your development, and your success. We want to equip you to change altitude across the board. You will gain a higher level of confidence in your capabilities. You will see new levels of performance, trust, and cohesion across your team and organization. You will gain a broader perspective of the talent on your team. You'll also achieve higher levels of creativity, communication, and organizational health.

The psychological benefits will also be profound. You'll be refreshed by the positive energy and enhanced workplace culture you see as a result. You'll have a strong sense of peace and confidence that your organization is being set up to thrive well into the future—even beyond your tenure. You'll have a greater understanding of fulfillment as you see your legacy being built around you. In essence: flying at this new altitude will start to feel fun.

YOUR GUIDES

Since 2002, the two of us have developed thousands of leaders, from the CEOs at the top of multi-billion-dollar organizations down to the teams around them. We have formed deep, personal coaching relationships that have given us unique insight into the struggles and emotions that senior leaders must overcome. We understand what you're facing! The programs for personal growth and leadership development that we lay out in this book have been created, refined, and are proven to get the results you want.

We feel blessed and humbled to have gained the trust and confidence of our clients in supporting their efforts to build greater leadership effectiveness. Many clients have worked with us for a decade, asking us to continue our investment in their organizations' future by developing cohorts of future leaders. We've played a role in helping them build their legacies, and we remain their trusted advisors.

Both of us share a military background, and we've been privileged to be invited into some of the highest levels of leadership in Fortune 500 companies, the military, and the government. We're also close friends! Here's a bit more context about each of our personal leadership journeys.

GREG HIEBERT

My father was a career Army officer and ultimately inspired all six of his children to go into the military. I attended the United States Military Academy at West Point. After graduation, I served in an elite Airborne unit in Vicenza, Italy. Also, I served a tour with the 82nd

Airborne Division as an Infantry unit commander and battalion primary staff officer. After eight years, West Point asked me if I would consider returning to the school to teach. They offered to fund my graduate education if I agreed to sign on as a West Point instructor after completing my master's. The subject of leadership had always fascinated me. *What is it,* I'd wondered, *that causes people to follow other human beings with extraordinary confidence?* I was accepted to the Harvard Business School, where I had the transforming experience of learning alongside many intelligent, talented, and amazing people.

After graduating with my MBA, I returned to West Point and started teaching a variety of leadership and management capstone courses. Eventually, I also taught a capstone graduate course for experienced military officers. Teaching people who were just as experienced and often smarter than me was challenging but also exhilarating. Ultimately, that experience planted the seeds that would one day become leadership*Forward*, a company dedicated to helping clients build exceptional leadership.

During my time teaching at West Point, I met a great cadet, Dennis O'Neil. My wife and I, along with our three young children, tried to provide Dennis a home away from home and a means to briefly escape the spartan life of a cadet. After his graduation, we stayed in touch and ultimately became great friends.

Eventually, I came to realize I wanted to pursue a more active leadership consulting role with adults and made one of the hardest decisions of my life: I left the Army and joined the strategic consulting company, McKinsey. While McKinsey has experienced some reputational declines recently, it was a formative experience that taught me how to help clients improve their performance and build a firm of exceptional people. From there, my career led me to another Fortune 100 company and then to several high technology start-ups. I was consistently brought on as an executive, always in the area of developing leaders and honing organizational strategies.

Later in my career, I was recruited to a global executive search firm called Egon Zehnder International, headquartered in Zurich. We helped companies worldwide find C-suite placements and evaluated companies' top levels of leaders to determine if they had the leadership skills required to succeed in their roles well into the future for their organizations.

Finally, I determined the time was right to create my own leadership consulting company, leadership*Forward*, alongside a great colleague, Paul Litten, who shared a similar sense of purpose and passion for developing great leaders. Our first client was the CFO of the Air Force, which led to a five-year contract and opened up opportunities for other client work. Approximately five years ago, I also asked my old friend Dennis to join leadership*Forward* as an executive coach and leadership educator. I am privileged to work alongside him as a colleague—and now, co-author a book together!

Over the last two decades, we've sought to help leaders be healthier, more successful, and more fulfilled. I've had the privilege of coaching well over 750 leaders and working with over 120 leadership teams. I still can't believe that I get to do this work every day! I continue to feel enormously exhilarated by the work I do with clients. My wife, Claudia, says I'll never retire.

DENNIS O'NEIL

I grew up about twenty-five miles north of Seattle with two brothers and two amazing parents, Pat and Linda. My mom and dad were both educators and instilled positive values, a strong work ethic, a passion for studying and teaching, and a love of family and country. I went straight from high school into wearing a uniform at the United States Military Academy at West Point. It was daunting but also an opportunity that set the path for the rest of my career. While at West Point, I studied behavioral sciences at the premier leadership institution, met my future wife, Noreen, and set my path in the US Army into motion. After graduation, I commissioned as an Armor Officer and was provided with several leadership positions of increasing responsibility, including serving as a commander multiple times. Along the way, Noreen and I grew our family to include Nora, Katelyn, Megan, and Owen.

Like Greg, West Point asked if I would return to my alma mater to teach as an instructor upon completion of a graduate education. I received my master's and doctorate from Duke University in developmental psychology. Following this, I had the privilege of teaching at the bachelor's and master's levels at three institutions: West Point, the US Army General Command and General Staff College, and concluded my Army teaching at a master's level at the National Defense University as a full-professor of strategic leadership. While teaching, I had the opportunity to provide both emergent leaders, mid-career officers, and senior executives with the opportunity to expand their critical thinking and leadership skills. Rounding out my Army career, I served two combat tours in Iraq and Afghanistan, both in support positions and direct combat roles.

I've been fortunate enough to have also spent time with some of the most senior leaders in the Pentagon, working for three Army Chiefs of Staff[1] in a row: General George Casey, General Martin Dempsey, and General Raymond Odierno. I served as the Chiefs' speechwriter, researcher, and strategist. Eventually, I went over to work at the White House as the Executive Director of the Performance Improvement Council, working to enhance our country's performance management. Later, I took over one of the large budget portfolios under National Security in the Office of Management and Budget.

After retiring from the military and academia, I transitioned to the corporate world. I went to work directly for the CEO of a New York City-based Fortune 500 company, with a 60,000-person organization and an annual revenue of twenty billion dollars. As the Chief

---

1   In corporate terms, the Chief of Staff of the Army is essentially the CEO of the Army.

of Staff, I assisted the industrial manufacturing company through their de-merger from a single company with a 125-year legacy into two organizations.

Around that time, I heard from my close friend and West Point mentor, Greg Hiebert. Greg had founded leadership*Forward* and experienced great success since its launch. He was kind enough to affirm my skill set and background and invited me to join him in developing the company. I sensed it was the right time to return to my passion for teaching and leadership development, agreeing to make a move. Ever since, I've enjoyed this meaningful work alongside Greg. Together, we help the world's leaders become more effective.

I've been privileged to work at the highest levels of the military, the highest levels of the federal government, the highest levels of corporate America, and as a Professor in the highest levels of academia. My various experiences and skill set, across four distinct domains, have helped inform the many different environments I've coached. I have performed, observed, and evaluated leadership in many different contexts, cultures, and companies; because of that I've developed a clear sense of what works and what doesn't.

Together, Greg and I have developed a leadership brand characterized by servant leadership, active listening, consistent feedback, and achieving results. We both cut our teeth as leaders in the military, taught in higher academia, and have worked at the highest levels of corporate America. Our model of leadership development has been thoroughly informed by both research and our wealth of experiences. We're passionate about what we do—and we're privileged to share it with you.

SOAR

Over the years of our leadership consulting work, we've regularly seen leaders struggle at the point when they are promoted from direct to indirect leadership. In other words, when they move from an area where they used to have direct oversight—like Rebecca had when she was a manager with her data analysts—to indirect leadership, overseeing much larger teams and departments of an organization, some of which they have little understanding. The complexity and ambiguity of their responsibilities can create tremendous challenges, including losing confidence and feeling overwhelmed. In these situations, leaders can get into trouble when they try to do their jobs the same way they did before.

We're constantly reading literature about effective practices of leadership. Although there's a significant amount written about how to be a great CEO, and there's a tremendous amount written about your first leadership job, we haven't been able to find any books or even articles about making a successful transition from direct to indirect leadership. Yet, that move is a *crucial* shift in altitude. Doing it poorly can be catastrophic. Doing it well can lead to profound elevation gains in personal and organizational success.

We want to help you become adept at changing altitude. With this book, we're going to share timeless leadership principles that will help you ask the right questions, understand yourself and your organization more fully, and know where to pursue growth. We will provide you with tools and strategies to effectively grow in your efficacy as a leader. We'll also teach you to successfully empower those working for you, calling forth their engagement and best efforts. We'll advise you on key points to remember when leading others in a crisis, how to best manage conflict, and ways to build your own leadership resiliency.

You may currently find yourself in a storm—but you're not alone. Let's seek greater clarity together. Let's get out of the clouds so you can soar.

PART ONE

YOU

"If your emotional abilities aren't in hand, if you don't have self-awareness, if you are not able to manage your distressing emotions, if you can't have empathy and have effective relationships, then no matter how smart you are, you are not going to get very far."

—DANIEL COLEMAN

CHAPTER ONE

KNOW THYSELF

UNDERSTANDING YOUR OWN
LEADERSHIP JOURNEY

"We don't see the world as it is; we see the world as we are."

—FROM THE BABYLONIAN TALMUD[2]

A MOMENT OF TRUTH

Greg Hiebert narrates

The feedback had come in about a hospital CEO named Leon, and his leadership feedback was not positive. Leon's direct reports were unified in raising significant issues with Leon's leadership, noting that he was intimidating, often used fear as a motivation tool, was a poor communicator, was too withdrawn, and even seemed disengaged.

Before I was about to go into a meeting with Leon to discuss what his colleagues and employees had written about him, his chief opera-

---

2   Babylonian Talmud: Tractate Berakoth, Folio 55b, trans. Maurice Simon, ed. Rabbi Dr. Isidore Epstein, https://halakhah.com/berakoth/berakoth_55.html.

tions officer stopped me. She held my hands in hers and said, "Greg, I don't know what my colleagues put in their feedback about Leon, but I know what *I* put in there." She looked at me as though I was about to go to my execution. "Good luck. I'm praying for you."

I'll be honest: Even after all my years in the military, I was very intimidated by this man. When I walked into Leon's office, he did not look happy. We both knew what was in the report, and it was not good. I didn't know how he'd receive it. I didn't know how he would receive *me*. Knowing that I needed to lead from a place of strength, I calmly sat down.

Suddenly, I had an inspiration. "Leon," I asked, "I'm curious. You've been CEO of this organization for twenty-seven years. What do you think your legacy will be?"

He gave me a long look. Finally, he said, "Well, if it's based on what's in that feedback, it's not going to be a great legacy." He paused. "The only thing I can think of right now is that they'll say I worked really hard."

I asked, "Is that the legacy you want?"

He said, "Absolutely not. Frankly, that thought is incredibly disappointing." He sighed heavily. After another long pause, Leon finally looked up at me. I was stunned by what he said next: "We've got a lot of work to do, don't we. Let's get at it." I was amazed by his humble response and incredibly proud of him for being completely honest about himself.

Over the next several months, Leon threw himself into the hard work of transforming his leadership style. He made substantial changes in the way he interacted with his team and the feedback he gave people. There were certain aspects that he couldn't change—his personality, for instance. But by learning more *about* his personality, Leon's understanding of how to manage his team grew exponentially.

In his case, Leon fits the personality profile of the strategic thinker. He tended to be very dominant, reserved, incredibly challenging, and systematic. This personality type can be impatient and is quick to identify what's wrong in any given situation. They don't focus on relationships as much as they focus on results. Leon's personality was a big reason the hospital had been named one of the best in the country—but it was also a factor behind why his staff struggled to work for him.

When Leon realized that many of the people on his team were very different from him, he began to understand that they *needed* other things from him to perform at their best. In the past, his modus operandi had been to only provide feedback when things weren't going well. If he didn't give his staff feedback, in his mind, they should assume that they were doing a good job. *He* had never felt the need for verbal affirmation—why should they? But in learning more about his personality and those of his team members, Leon began to understand that many of them needed more positive feedback. He made a point to give his employees affirmation, and the morale on his team got a huge boost.

Leon had been a CEO since he was a young man. For the whole of his career, he'd focused on organizations, efficiency, and getting results. But Leon hadn't spent much time at all thinking about his *own* style of leadership. It was a profound moment of truth for him when he stopped to consider the legacy he was building. When he intentionally looked at the effect of his leadership on the people around him, Leon was forced to acknowledge some hard truths about himself. However, as he took a good look in the mirror, he began to learn even deeper profound truths. He worked until the day he retired to transform his competence as a leader. And when he did finally retire, his legacy was more than just "he worked hard." In fact, they named a hospital wing after him.

KNOW THYSELF: THE FIRST STEP OF EFFECTIVE LEADERSHIP

We believe the first and most crucial step to take in your leadership development is to *know thyself.* Why should this matter so much? Let's go back to the metaphor of navigating different altitudes in an airplane.

In any given plane's cockpit, there's a vast array of instruments. There's the altimeter, the airspeed indicator, the magnetic compass, the heading indicator, the turn indicator, the VOR, and NDB, the gyroscopic instruments, and many others.

Now, imagine that you're piloting this aircraft—and you don't know how to read any of them.

It's a scary thought, especially if you envision the plane being full of people relying on you to fly the aircraft successfully. You might be able to glide smoothly so long as you don't have to make flight shifts. But what happens when you need to land? What happens if a storm whips up? What do you do when all the instruments start giving you new readings, but you can't interpret them?

For leaders, it's just as critical to understanding *how you operate* as it is for a pilot to understand the instruments in a plane's cockpit. Think of this instrument panel on a psychological level, all informing your behavior as a leader: there are gauges related to your emotions, your stress level, your sleep habits, your cultural biases, your preferences, your personality type, your emotional triggers, your childhood experiences, and so on. There's a lot there, and every one of those factors impacts the way you lead.

If you're not deeply familiar with these personal "gauges"—if you don't know how to read your "emotional triggers" gauge, for instance—you risk endangering the people around you and the success of your organization. Just as a pilot is directly responsible for the lives aboard their plane, you as a leader influence the people around you—whether you intend to or not. You are taking your people *somewhere.*

So don't you think you should study up on your instrument panel?

The doorway to being a great spouse, a great parent, and certainly a great leader is the understanding that you have a limited view of reality. Your perspective is limited by your biases, your ethnicity, your background, your culture, your personality—all of the aspects that make you who you are. Therefore, if you want to change altitude—to soar high and fly far successfully—you must have the courage to study your operating manual. Knowing yourself is like learning how to effectively read all the instruments that can help to make a plane's flight smooth. It's the first step towards effective leadership, and it's a significant prerequisite to getting the best out of your team.

THE CASE FOR KNOWING THYSELF

Both the Marine Corps and the Army list the same first principle of leadership: "Know yourself and seek self-improvement."[3]

This principle of leadership is actually ancient. The emperors of Rome did not get a lot of good press, but there was one Caesar whose writing is still referenced to this day: Marcus Aurelius. Marcus Aurelius was one of the first historical leaders to articulate the importance of getting in touch with your giftedness and having the courageous humility to address your weaknesses. Aurelius wrote, "Look well into thyself; there is a source of strength which will always spring up if thou wilt always look there."[4] He also emphasized the importance of surrounding yourself with people who could bring strengths and talent to the areas you couldn't.

Why should self-awareness be such a key characteristic of great

---

3   United States Marine Corps Training and Education Command, "Marine Corps Junior ROTC: Leadership Principles," Marines Corps JROTC, accessed January 13, 2021, https://www.mcjrotc.marines.mil/About/Leadership-Principles/.

4   Marcus Aurelius, *Marcus Aurelius: Meditations*, trans. Christopher Gill (Oxford: Oxford University Press, 2013).

leadership? Self-awareness turns out to be the *foundation* for many other leadership traits:

- **Self-awareness helps you be more objective**. Every person has blind spots and biases that will influence their decision-making. If you know what yours are, you can account for them when you lead. If you don't know what they are, you have no idea if you're making decisions in an emotional, reactive way or in a thoughtful, objective way.
- **Self-awareness helps you be more effective**. By understanding your strengths, you can do more in those areas and pursue excellence. By understanding your weaknesses, you can better manage them. (We'll say more on this soon.)
- **Self-awareness is essential to motivate others**. In several of our later chapters, we'll talk about how good leaders provide purpose, direction, and motivation to their teams. If you don't have self-awareness about how people take what you say or do, it will be challenging for you to motivate them. If you want your employees to thrive in the workplace, you have to clearly understand how they respond to your leadership, which requires self-awareness.
- **Self-awareness is essential to empower others**. To develop others, you need to understand your own process of development. How can you lead employees in analyzing their own strengths and weaknesses if you haven't considered your own? You can deepen emotional intelligence in others by taking steps to deepen your own first.
- **Self-awareness helps you be more adaptable**. When you're not aware of your own biases and tendencies, they'll steer you every time—whether or not they should. But when you know what they are, you can think critically about the best response to any situation. You'll encounter new challenges with objectivity, enabling you to adapt effectively.
- **Self-awareness helps you be more creative**. If you're hung up on your own view being the only right one, you can't entertain new ideas. However, when you understand your own creative

potential limits, you can open yourself to ideas from your team and tap into far more creativity.

Self-awareness is the foundation for many other leadership traits.

And what happens if you're *not* self-aware? Well, your ability to lead will be compromised, and there's a good chance you'll look foolish. Remember the story of the "Emperor's New Clothes," which concludes with the Emperor strolling down the street in the nude after getting swindled by con-men, passing themselves off as tailors. It's an amusing story highlighting the dangers of not being self-aware. The Emperor did not see the world as it was; he saw the world through his delusion. As a result, *he* ended up looking like the biggest idiot!

The essence of self-awareness means that we clearly understand how others perceive us and are aware of our own strengths and weaknesses. Only from that position of awareness can we use our work to increase the good of the organizations we lead.

So how do you get that awareness? It often starts with a healthy dose of humility.

HUMILITY IS THE FOUNDATION FOR SELF-AWARENESS

If self-awareness is the foundation for most other leadership traits, then humility is the foundation for self-awareness. Leon would have never recognized his need to build self-awareness without humility. But *with* humility, he was able to look Greg in the eyes and say, "We've got a lot of work to do." And then—they got to it. His leadership transformed.

The leaders who most desperately need self-awareness are always the ones who think they *don't* need it. In those cases, the missing ingredient is humility. If you're reading this, thinking, *I don't actually need self-awareness*, then take a moment to check yourself. There's a good chance you are as woefully exposed as the Emperor with no clothes on, in full view of everyone around you!

If you want to know where you stand on this issue of humility and self-awareness, consider the "mirror and window" test. Imagine that in your office, there's a window that opens out onto the floor where your team works. There's also a mirror which hangs on the wall. Here's the test: When do you shout things out the window? When do you take a good look in the mirror?

The arrogant leader shouts things out the window when things go badly: "Hey! You guys are all screwing up out there!" When things go well, that's when they look in the mirror: "Good job, self. You did it."

The humble leader—the one bent on growth, the one who wants to pursue greater self-awareness—looks in the mirror when things go wrong. They probe that failure for meaning, asking, "What did I expect would happen? What did actually happen? How do I understand the difference? Where can I take my team from here?" When things go well—*that's* when the humble leader shouts out the window: "Thank you, team! Well done! *You* did it!" They show gratitude to their employees, acknowledging that many people were responsible for their success.

You don't just make yourself a better leader with humility—you also become a much better person to work for. American culture is filled with images of the lone hero on the horse who will save us all—but in reality, almost nothing gets done by one person. The humble, self-aware leader, on the other hand, embraces the idea of interconnected teamwork. They're able to inspire others and create safe environments to admit mistakes. They don't try to operate as a rugged, isolated individual—they're collaborators.

And life *is* a collaborative effort. Look at your own life: Who raised you? Who taught you? Who mentored you? Who were the people who reached out their hand to you during your own professional journey, helping to support you and lift you up? Most likely, there are many people you could name who all played a part in your leadership journey.

The two of us, in fact, make each other better leaders. When we work together, we often don't know where one person's ideas will stop and when the other's will begin. Because of the rich and different experiences both of us have, we're able to complement one another as leaders. Our different gifts also make us more well-rounded as consultants. When we're with a client who needs a blunt, direct message, we send in Dennis. When a client would benefit more from a softer, more subtle word, we send in Greg. We've learned our traits because we've both diligently pursued our own self-awareness over the years—and we're better for it.

The journey towards knowing thyself begins with the humble recognition that you need self-awareness. Are you ready with that humility? Do you want more self-awareness?

Good. Then your Leadership Journey can begin.

YOUR LEADERSHIP JOURNEY

When you commit to doing the self-reflection that we're talking about, you begin what we call your Leadership Journey. This journey starts with your reflection on several fundamental, "rooting" questions. Collectively, these questions will help you begin to articulate your leadership philosophy, your leadership story, and your strengths and weaknesses. We're going to discuss them one at a time, and we encourage you to reflect on each.

WHAT CHARACTERISTICS AND SKILLS DO I BELIEVE ARE ESSENTIAL TO GROW AS A LEADER?

On any given day in your role as a leader, you're projecting something. It may be positivity; it may be negativity; it may be inspirational enthusiasm or a dark, demanding cloud.

When you clarify your answer to this first Leadership Journey question, you help identify your priorities as a leader and consider what you're projecting to those around you. Consider the characteristics and skills you value most in your employees; reflect on the skills you believe are most important to your own leadership. Write those down—and then look at them. Are those the characteristics and abilities you genuinely embody as a leader?

You can improve as a leader by getting in tune with what you're actually projecting and what people are experiencing from your leadership. If you discover a gap between those two things, be encouraged: our following two chapters are devoted to helping you close that gap. We're also going to give you tools to accurately determine if there *is* a gap at all. Part of changing altitude is gaining a deeper, richer understanding of any gaps between the values you espouse and your actual behavior. You rise up by having the courage to face them and involving other people in overcoming them.

So consider this first question: What characteristics and skills do you believe are essential to grow as a leader? In what areas would you like to develop so that you can effectively accomplish your goals and best serve the people entrusted to your leadership?

WHAT KIND OF LEADER DO I WANT TO BECOME?

Often, there's a story behind why we value certain traits and qualities above others. For example, the two of us have come to appreciate humility enormously because of our leadership growth after going through extremely humbling experiences! (We'll share a number of those stories throughout this book.) Another example: Some leaders hate it when their employees voice disagreement, but we actually believe respectful dissent is a strength, and there's a story as to why. Both of us have benefited from military training and experiences in thriving organizations where healthy dissent was encouraged. Our values are rooted in stories and experiences that help explain why we've come to prioritize those ideals.

You, too, have a leadership story. It's been shaped by the values and strengths your parents emphasized when you were growing up. It's been informed by the people you respected most in your formative years. It's been defined by the skills which got you promoted and praised. But don't just look backward—look forward as well. Considering your future legacy is equally as important as reflecting on the story that got you here. When you are old and reflecting on your life's work, how do you hope people remember you? By considering your future legacy now, you'll help clarify the priorities and values you want to embody as you lead.

Recognize the formative experiences that helped shape your leadership story and cast a vision for your legacy as a leader. In doing so, you will plot a trajectory for leadership that is both authentic and focusing.

WHAT ARE MY STRENGTHS?

"Knowing yourself" means that you recognize that there are things that you do exceedingly well. You'll excel more as a leader when you do those things with greater frequency. Research says when we use our giftedness, we're happier.[5] And when we're happier, we are actually more successful!

We have so much to say about this point that we're going to devote an entire chapter to it. Our next chapter will help you evaluate your

---

5   Shawn Achor, *The Happiness Advantage: The Seven Principles That Fuel Success and Performance at Work* (London: Virgin, 2011).

strengths as a leader to lean into the areas where you are most effective.

WHAT ARE MY WEAKNESSES?

Certainly a dominant theme in this book is that it takes great humility to look in the mirror and recognize one's rough edges and flaws. However, by building awareness about the areas where you struggle, you can surround yourself with people who can help balance those weaknesses with their own complementary strengths. In other words, you can proactively manage your shortcomings rather than let them interfere with your effectiveness as a leader.

One of the most important but undervalued behaviors for good leadership is *being vulnerable and asking for help*. When you can ask for help, you're able to build deep connections with others. You recognize that you do *not* have to be all things to all people. You're more willing to challenge your assumptions and view of reality, which means you're far less likely to make a mistake. And you show the people around you that you value their ideas and opinions and that you, in turn, are not the sole source of truth. Asking for help can serve as a safeguard and can help you build bridges. Undoubtedly, it can help you gain altitude.

By building self-awareness about your weaknesses, your struggles don't need to get in the way of your successes. The self-awareness of your weaknesses can help you build trust in your team, increase collaboration, and broaden your understanding. It is important to note that there is a difference between one's weaknesses or struggles versus poor or wrong behaviors. A struggle might be having difficulty in staying organized if you have a strong preference for being spontaneous and creative. A poor or improper behavior would be to berate a team member for their lack of intelligence, either privately or publicly, or spreading malicious mistruths about a colleague to others. Great leaders work to manage their struggles and weaknesses; they rarely, if ever, display wrong and poor behavior.

When you are self-aware about your weaknesses, your struggles don't need to get in the way of your successes.

HOW DO I BEGIN TO ANSWER THESE QUESTIONS?

If you don't already have a clear sense of how you would answer these questions, we're here to provide you with the tools you need to build clarity. We're going to focus our next chapter on helping you learn more about your strengths and weaknesses. Then, in Chapter Three, we're going to guide you through a feedback assessment process so that you can get a "360-degree" view of your leadership from the people who work on all sides of you. Those 360-Assessments always end with a few open-ended questions:

- What are some things this leader can be proud of?
- What are some of the things this person should stop doing as a leader?
- What things should this person start doing?
- What things should they do more of?
- What things should they do less of?
- Does this leader have any patterns holding them back? Do any of these patterns have the potential to derail their career?

Before seeking feedback on these questions from other people, we'd invite you to start your leadership journey by reflecting on them yourself. Ask yourself: What are some of the things *I* should feel proud of as a leader? What are some of the things *I* should stop or start doing? These additional questions might help you begin the process of articulating your own leadership philosophy, strengths, and weaknesses.

CHARACTER IS YOUR COMPASS

Dennis O'Neil narrates

One of the finest leaders I have ever worked with was General Martin Dempsey. I had the privilege of serving with him on multiple occasions—when he was the Commander of the 3rd Armored Cavalry Regiment and again when he was the Army's Chief of Staff. More than anyone else I've worked with, General Dempsey had total congruence between the values he espoused and the way he actually lived; with him, there was no gap. General Dempsey saw the best in us while still making us feel challenged. We felt safe to be ourselves, but we also wanted to strive to do our best work. We gave General Dempsey everything we had because we knew he would treat us well. He was a leader who embodied integrity. His character was impeccable.

Before we go any further in discussing your growth as a leader, we need to hit one thing with resounding clarity—your character as a leader matters. If you want to change altitude successfully, you need to know where to steer the plane, and your values are like the guiding compass. If you consistently heed that compass, you're going to stay on course. If you ignore the compass—if you say one thing and do another—you risk getting wildly off track. Your character has a significant impact upon which direction the plane goes and its consistency in getting there.

A leader's strong character—or the lack of it—also affects everyone else on the plane. The values you demonstrate provide signals to all of your people when they're faced with an ethical dilemma about which direction to go. If they see you consistently lie and cut corners, they will heed that direction. If they see you always upholding strong ideals, they will align with that course. Your values are your "true north," defined by author Bill George as "the internal compass that guides you successfully through life."[6]

In future chapters, we will discuss how to articulate "true north" for your people by establishing healthy team norms and a team

---

6   Bill George, *Discover Your True North: Becoming an Authentic Leader*, 2nd ed. (Hoboken: Wiley, 2013).

covenant. Collectively, your organization will determine the direction it wants to go and the values it wants to uphold while getting there. However, if you do not have the strong character to uphold those values, there will ultimately be no true north for your people to follow. As your team's leader, you function as its magnetic pole. If you want your people to consistently uphold your organization's values, you need to set them on a course that leads to confident decision-making, guided by solid values.

This isn't easy. Greg and I were students at West Point at different times, but there was a strict and consistent honor code all students learned and were expected to uphold. The code was simple: "A Cadet will not lie, cheat, or steal, nor tolerate those who do." There wasn't much confusion about what it meant not to lie, cheat, or steal—but the word "tolerate" allowed for some wiggle room. Because of that, we received tremendous amounts of education on what "tolerance" looked like.

I remember our leaders asking us about a hypothetical scenario: Let's say I saw my friend put money in a candy vending machine, and the device malfunctioned, then my friend got angry and rocked the machine. Imagine that several candy bars then slid out—not just the one my friend bought, but several more—and my friend took them all. I would be bound by the honor code to turn in my friend for stealing. That was the level of rigor of the honor code when Greg and I were at West Point. It was strict—but it worked. We knew how to find true north on the compass, and our leaders consistently held us accountable for following it.

As a leader, you are responsible for identifying the true north and holding others—including yourself—accountable to follow it. Once again, we come back to the critical importance of "knowing thyself." You need to know what you believe in. Part of beginning your leadership journey and forming your leadership philosophy requires that you identify your core values.

How do you do that? Think of the question that Greg asked Leon: What do you want your legacy to be? Consider also: How do you want to be remembered? What character attributes do you want to define you? What characteristics do you want your organization to be known for?

Identify your true north.

After identifying your core values, it's time to think critically about whether or not you're genuinely upholding them. Granted, no one can perfectly uphold their values all the time—but good leaders recognize the importance of striving to live them out. Greg and I will continue to hammer on the importance of humility throughout this book because we believe strong character is fundamental to outstanding leadership. Without humility, you can't ever develop the self-awareness to admit that gaps may exist between the values you espouse and the choices you make. Without that self-awareness, you can't see those gaps and work to close them.

Strong character is something you work to develop over time by codifying your values, assessing your consistency in living them out, and closing the gap between what you say and what you do. Someone like General Dempsey has spent a lifetime closing that gap. He embodies truth north and provides a clear compass for his people to follow.

READING YOUR INSTRUMENT PANEL

Why do we believe so strongly that knowing thyself is the first step in growing as a leader?

Knowing thyself enables you to develop the self-awareness needed to lead your people with excellence.

Knowing thyself means you embrace humility so that you can pursue and model growth.

Knowing thyself means you authentically live out your values so that your character can serve as a guiding compass to others.

In building this crucial self-awareness, you will learn to read your instrument panel. That panel will equip you with critical information to fly smoothly, fly successfully, and fly true. That's the first step to successfully change altitude and soar—but it's only the beginning.

ACTION STEPS

Reflect on the following questions to help you articulate your leadership philosophy, consider your strengths and weaknesses, and codify your core values.

1. What characteristics and skills do I believe are most important for effective leadership?
2. How did I come to develop my leadership story? What stories and experiences from my life most inform my answer to question 1?
3. What are my greatest strengths that support me when I am most effective? What things should I be proud of? What things should I keep doing?
4. What are my greatest weaknesses that get in the way of being an effective leader? What things should I stop doing? Do I engage in destructive patterns, and if so, what are they?
5. What are my core values that I strive to live as part of my leadership story? How do I want to be remembered as a leader? What will people remember about how I impacted others? How will people describe my leadership legacy?

CHAPTER TWO

THE SEVEN CRITICAL CHARACTERISTICS OF LEADERSHIP

GETTING HONEST ABOUT YOUR STRENGTHS AND WEAKNESSES

"Mastering others is strength. Mastering yourself is true power."

—LAO TZU

DYSFUNCTIONAL OR DISHONEST?

The email we received from Sean, the CEO of a hospital, was full of complaints. After greeting us briefly and introducing himself, he explained why he was reaching out for our help:

> I have a team that's dysfunctional and low-performing. I could use some support and help provide an honest assessment of the team because, frankly, I don't think they're capable of performing at the level our organization needs. My COO is part of the problem. She's disengaged and passive-aggressive. The CFO is also a significant source of dysfunction. He undermines me and sabotages my work behind my back.

Sean's email was articulate and gave several examples to support each complaint. His view was that he was doing everything in his power to lead the organization effectively, but—because of the incompetence surrounding him—the results were floundering. He wanted our help to get his subordinate leaders to follow and respect him appropriately. If they wouldn't, he wanted our help in convincing his board to make some personnel changes. We agreed to help Sean and determined that we needed to complete a thorough assessment to evaluate some of the other "problems" he had identified at the executive level.

Our research revealed that there had been a terrible struggle for the past eighteen months between Sean as CEO and his team members. When one of his employees would initiate action towards a goal, Sean would second-guess them—and the team members claimed that they didn't know why. There was a critical lack of trust between Sean and his team. We kept coming across inconsistencies between Sean's report of the state of affairs and his subordinates' version. In a sense, everybody seemed to be flying in a heavy set of dark clouds, and each person's instrument panel read differently.

Over six months, we guided the team through many sessions to address dysfunction and assess the actual state of affairs. We had them step back, reflect on some of their differences, and consider communication patterns. We spent quite a bit of time discussing how to approach "crucial conversations"[7] in a healthy way so that conflict could lead to growth and healing, not relational harm. Finally, after six months of work, we got everyone to commit to a new set of norms that would reinstitute trust among the team. Here's an example of what they came up with:

- Rather than undermine our teammates, we agree to have each other's backs.

---

7   A crucial conversation is any conversation when the following three points are true: 1) two or more people disagree, 2) emotions are involved, and 3) the stakes matter. We will focus much more on crucial conversations in Chapter Ten, "Conflict Management."

- Rather than assume the worst about someone's motivations, we're going to give them the benefit of the doubt and assume positive intent.
- Rather than working towards our self-interests, we agree to work towards the betterment of our organization.
- When crucial conversations come up, we will communicate with respect, openness, and honesty to help restore trust and minimize harm.
- We will make sure we don't let issues fester, and instead, "when in doubt," we commit to talk things out.

As we formed this team covenant, you could see everyone begin to come around. They started showing real hope and enthusiasm that their team's dysfunction could be corrected. Everyone agreed that the session served as a much-needed "reset." By the time it ended, the group seemed to be on a high—it was the most positive session we'd experienced since we'd started our work with them half a year before.

The very next morning, Sean asked everyone to meet for a staff meeting at nine in the morning. His CNO—the chief nursing officer—arrived at 9:15. She'd been held up since seven in the morning with a crisis in the cardiac department and had only just been able to break away. However, Sean did not bother finding out about any of this. As soon as his CNO walked through the door, he exploded at her. He stood up and slammed his desk. He yelled, "We're going to have a crucial conversation about why you're late for my meeting! You are deliberately disrespecting me!"

In an instant, Sean's tirade undid all the work we'd done the day before. He assumed the worst about his CNO. He didn't communicate with respect. He didn't bother to see if she was serving the organization's needs; he was solely concerned about how her lateness impacted him personally. He indeed assumed the worst of intentions on the part of his CNO, and he used the term "crucial conversation" out of context, maligning the phrase and using it to justify acting like a jerk. The team covenant everyone had so carefully crafted only twelve hours earlier was essentially trashed. It was clear that their leader had zero intention of actually following it. In fact, Sean's explosion served as proof to them that he would never change and that the "reset" wasn't real.

The day before, Sean had enthusiastically agreed with all the values we'd recorded in the team covenant. He *professed* to have those values—but there was a massive disconnect between what he *said* he believed and what he did. No one could take him at his word. He could not command trust and respect from his subordinate leaders because he did not practice the values he demanded from others. Not only was he habitually dishonest with others, but he also couldn't be honest with himself. He had no real clarity about his weaknesses—instead, it was always someone else's fault.

In this chapter, we will discuss the importance of getting honest about your strengths and weaknesses. In getting honest with yourself, you choose to opt for health over dysfunction; clarity, over dishonesty; growth over stagnancy.

THE SAY/DO RATIO

Sean's struggle—and the struggle of many other talented people we've encountered over the years—was a massive gap in his "Say/Do Ratio." What do we mean by a Say/Do Ratio? Simply put: There is alignment between what you *say* and what you *do*. Even more simply, you do what you say you'll do. If you espouse values of collaboration among your team, you demonstrate that value in your actions. If you're not great at creating a collaborative environment, then the first step of closing your Say/Do Ratio gap would be to openly acknowledge that as an area of struggle, then pursue development in that area, strengthening your ability to live out that value.

To effectively gain altitude, you need to close the gap between what you espouse as your core values and how you actually live. The first step in closing that gap is to gain a clear and honest understanding of your strengths and weaknesses as a leader. It takes courage to take an honest look in the mirror and consider the disparity between what you *say* you value and how you actually live. Leaders with this self-awareness are not only healthy, open, and in a constant state of development; they're also gifted at building trust and confidence in their team.

> To effectively gain altitude, you need to close the gap between what you espouse as your core values and the way you actually live.

Once you achieve greater self-awareness about your strengths and weaknesses, the next step is to close the Say/Do Ratio gap through seeking development in the Seven Critical Characteristics of Leadership—particularly in those areas where you struggle. First, shed light on your strengths and weaknesses, then work to develop those strengths and minimize weaknesses to become the leader your team needs.

THE SEVEN CRITICAL CHARACTERISTICS OF LEADERSHIP

Why have we identified these particular seven characteristics as being so critical?

We've compiled these seven traits after poring through an extensive amount of research and after teaching leadership courses at four different universities at both undergraduate and graduate levels. We've collected feedback from thousands of leadership training participants and our own experiences working in the military, government, and at the highest levels of corporate business. The traits encapsulate more than twenty years of observation from our leadership training.

These seven characteristics highlight the themes that have continually re-emerged as being key to leadership development and success.

They address the most common leadership challenges that individuals and organizations face.

We're going to devote time in this chapter to defining and explaining each one. We'll also provide evaluative questions for your own self-assessment in all seven characteristics. Once you determine where you excel and struggle, you can clearly identify your next steps to gain altitude. The seven characteristics are as follows:

1. Inspiring Engagement
2. Advocating for Excellence
3. Planning and Implementing
4. Driving for Results
5. Leading Change and Innovation
6. Influencing Others
7. Practicing Teamwork and Collaboration

Let's have a closer look at each one.

1. INSPIRING ENGAGEMENT

President Dwight D. Eisenhower defined leadership as "the art of getting someone else to do something you want done because he wants to do it."[8] As a leader of many, you need to inspire the engagement of the people who work for you to actually want to carry out the objectives you give them. Your team needs to know *why* they should do what you've asked them to do, *where* they need to go, and they need to *believe* they can be successful in getting there.

There's good news here: Your employees want to engage. They don't want to slump apathetically at their desks and do the bare minimum; they want to communicate with you, share their ideas with their teammates, and work towards a better tomorrow. But they need your help with inspiring their engagement.

Leaders who excel in inspiring engagement do two things particularly well. First, they demonstrate an ability to connect deeply with their team members: they make their subordinates feel valued, cared for, and integrally involved. When people feel valued and seen, they want to contribute; that's engagement.

> When your team feels both inspired about the mission and cared for as individuals, they will move mountains for you.

Secondly, leaders can clarify the mission and secure people's buy-in to see how their work positively impacts that mission. This gives people the confidence they need to take risks and move the ball forward because they know where they're going; they understand precisely how they are a part of it and *want* to go there. When your team feels both inspired about the mission and cared for as individuals, they will move mountains for you.

---

8   Dwight D. Eisenhower, *Public Papers of the Presidents of the United States, Dwight D. Eisenhower: Containing the Public Messages, Speeches and Statements of the President* (Washington, D.C.: Federal Register Division, National Archives and Records Service, General Services Administration, 1958).

EVALUATE YOUR ABILITY TO INSPIRE ENGAGEMENT

Consider how you perform in the following areas of inspiring engagement. Check the boxes where you feel you can answer yes, and highlight any areas where you'd like to improve:

☐ **Are you a respected and approachable leader?** Are you aware of your biases and subconscious opinions towards others? Do you take ownership of your own mistakes? Do your employees show you respect and trust without you needing to demand it? Do you make it easy for others to challenge you and/or offer different perspectives?

☐ **Do you show your employees that you value them?** Do you practice active listening during group conversations rather than taking control? Do you act as a cheerleader and offer your employees appropriate affirmation, recognition, and encouragement? Do you appreciate the varying skill sets people bring to the team?

☐ **Do you foster psychological safety while also encouraging high achievement?**[9] Do you facilitate a culture where the team is encouraged to push themselves? Do you promote positivity? Do you give grace when a mistake is made? Do you give credit to others' contributions and ideas?

2. ADVOCATING FOR EXCELLENCE

Good leaders don't just make their employees feel safe and valued; they create high-performing units where high expectations and delivering on commitments are integral to the organization's ethos. Advocating for excellence starts with establishing a clear definition of success: your employees should know exactly what you expect of them. Goals should be focused rather than scattershot; you want your employees to be able to direct their energies at a specific target so that they hit it. Then you provide a roadmap on how people can achieve their goals. This might be provided through a strategic plan or some other document that provides a step-by-step route towards an end goal. Leaders who advocate for excellence clearly commu-

---

9   Psychological safety is defined as the belief that you won't be punished or humiliated for speaking up with ideas, questions, concerns, or mistakes.

nicate their expectations and standards that there is no ambiguity or confusion amongst team members. Instead, their people can put their focus and effort towards the mission and purpose.

> *Advocating for excellence starts with establishing a clear definition of success: your employees should know exactly what you expect of them.*

Advocating for excellence means you set the bar high, and your team members know it. You give them a clear, compelling, and ambitious vision and help them understand how their individual contributions will impact the team's overall effectiveness. When they do a job, you expect them to do it well, to the best of their ability.

Advocating for excellence means you set the bar high for yourself as well. How you live your life communicates volumes about this. Do you seek excellence in your own performance as a leader and hold yourself to the highest standards in modeling the values you espouse? You will inspire others to follow your lead by consistently striving for excellence in your own life.

EVALUATE YOUR ABILITY TO ADVOCATE FOR EXCELLENCE

Consider how you perform in the following areas of advocating for excellence. Check the boxes where you feel you can answer yes, and highlight any areas where you'd like to improve:

☐ **Do you provide clear definitions of expectations and targets for your team?** Do you promote high-quality outcomes? Do you plan effectively with your team to avoid mishaps? Are there clearly defined standards of excellence for the most critical tasks and functions of your organization?

☐ **Do you have systems of accountability in place?** Do you hold regular (annual, quarterly, etc.) reviews with your team? Do you have necessary policies and procedures in place and hold your group to them? Do you make sure to inspect what you expect?

- ☐ **Do you exemplify, personally, an attitude of striving for excellence?** Do you understand your job description and the responsibilities that come along with it? Are you effective with time management and make timely decisions?
- ☐ **Do you continually create a quality team culture?** Do you pursue professional development and encourage your team to do the same? Do those organizations that work with yours understand your deep commitment to excellence in everything your organization does, including how you work with them?

3. PLANNING AND IMPLEMENTING

Leaders who excel in planning and implementing ensure their teams have detailed plans for *how* they're going to achieve their goals. Planning and implementing are closely intertwined with advocating for excellence, but there's a key difference. Advocating for excellence *defines* success. It's like pointing to the top of the mountain and saying, "That's where we're going." Planning and implementing takes it a step further: it provides the resources to achieve the goal and the clarity of how your organization will structure, organize, and use those resources to achieve the goal. Furthermore, planning and implementing must include a means for tracking and communicating success; there should also be a systematic procedure for how necessary changes to plans will be initiated and coordinated.

> Leaders who excel in planning and implementing ensure their teams have detailed plans for how they're going to achieve their goals.

Provide measurable targets; identify tangible, specific outcomes; create enabling structures like plans and processes that will move your team from the current standard to the desired results. In other words, leaders who effectively plan and implement put mechanisms in place so that there's high reliability that your team can produce the desired outcomes over and over again.

If there's a shortage of resources—perhaps you don't have the necessary funding, time, or people to achieve the mandated outcomes—leaders should use their creativity to get as far they can. Then they should get candid with their higher-ups. You might say something like, "I agree that these are the right standards for excellence, but I've done the math, and we have insufficient resources to complete it. But, here's what we can deliver." Good leaders will welcome those conversations.

EVALUATE YOUR ABILITY FOR PLANNING AND IMPLEMENTING

Consider how you perform in the following areas of planning and implementation. Check the boxes where you feel you can answer yes, and highlight any areas where you'd like to improve:

☐ **Do you take a strategic approach to problem-solving?** Do you consider the long-term impact of your decisions? Do you lead your team by discussing complex ideas and concepts? Can you keep up easily in a fast-changing environment?

☐ **Do you consider multiple angles of your plan?** Are you comfortable dealing with increasing levels of complexity? Do you implement new strategies while taking into consideration the internal and external realities of your organization? Do you create contingency plans, especially for those areas that have a high degree of risk or potential uncertainty? Do you create safety for others to challenge your planning and ask the "What if" questions?

☐ **Are you personally dedicated to the strategy and mission of your organization?** Can you communicate an inspiring vision and articulate the plan clearly, so your team is motivated to follow?

☐ **Are you confident that the organization's plans have been communicated clearly and definitively to all those involved in implementing the strategies?** Are there mechanisms to allow members to give feedback to you that they are clear, committed to the organizational plans, and are confident of what they must do to implement the plan to success?

4. DRIVING RESULTS

Driving results means you hold your employees accountable for actually making progress towards the goals, outcomes, and standards of excellence you have articulated. You help them track their progress along with the roadmap. Going back to the metaphor of climbing a mountain, driving results is the process of actually *getting* your people to hike all the way to the summit. When they get tired and struggle, you have a conversation about what they need to keep going. When they reach a significant milestone, you celebrate. If they start to get lost, you bring them back onto the trail and point them forward.

> *Driving results means you hold your employees accountable for actually making progress towards the goals, outcomes, and standards of excellence you have articulated.*

Driving for results also means you steward resources wisely. You don't waste your employees' time with unnecessary meetings. You equip them with what they need to progress, getting them mentorship or professional development as required. After setting the bar high by advocating for excellence and then giving them a plan of implementation, you *drive for results* by effectively allocating resources and holding your employees accountable for their progress.

EVALUATE YOUR ABILITY TO DRIVE RESULTS

Consider how you perform in the following areas of driving results. Check the boxes where you feel you can answer yes, and highlight any areas where you'd like to improve:

☐ **Do your employees have all the necessary information to be successful?** Are you transparent with deadlines? Do you have measures in place to track employee performance, and do they know what they are?

- ☐ **Do you hold employees accountable?** Are you willing to hold people responsible for decisions and actions they make? Do you take the time to appreciate those who go above and beyond in delivering results and meeting objectives? Are you willing to fire or take action against those who hinder team performance? Is it clearly understood that when you fall short of performance expectations, you have a responsibility to address the gaps with thoughtful and thorough improvement plans?
- ☐ **Do you effectively steward resources?** Do you manage time well to make sure meetings are as efficient as possible and refrain from holding meetings that could have been a simple email? Do you recognize when individuals need personal or professional development and help them get it?

5. LEADING CHANGE AND INNOVATION

When Apple came out with the iPhone back in 2007, the then-CEO of Microsoft, Steve Balmer, ignored the new device. He claimed that the iPhone would be a "flash in the pan," and it wasn't anything that Microsoft needed to try to compete with. Four years later, Apple's sales of the iPhone by itself exceeded *all* of Microsoft's annual revenue. In hindsight, it's clear that the Microsoft CEO grossly underestimated the iPhone as the game-changer it was. He also neglected to take critical steps to *innovate* Microsoft's current offerings and lead change.

Why must leaders innovate and lead change? The essence of human endeavor is progress. High-performing teams and organizations know that if they are to embrace this notion of progress, they need to constantly examine their organization's current state. These thriving organizations regularly ask: What needs to improve, what needs to get better, where do we need to grow? Every question gets at the same essential root: How can we progress and change? This is why leadership is also so necessary. Most of us crave certainty and being comfortable. A leader's fundamental charge is to challenge that complacent certainty and take their followers to a better place.

> *High-performing teams and organizations know that if they are to embrace this notion of progress, then they need to constantly examine the current state of their organization.*

We do not subscribe to the statement, "If it ain't broke, don't fix it." Actually, effective leaders intentionally create an environment that promotes discontentment with things as they are. Good leaders should always be challenging the status quo to push the organization to be better, continue growing its markets, continuing to grow its ideas, and continuing to push its people to grow as individuals. Take a lesson from evolution: "According to Darwin's *On the Origin of Species*, it is not the most intellectual of the species that survives; it is not the strongest that survives, but the species that survives is the one that is able best to adapt and adjust to the changing environment in which it finds itself."[10]

This isn't just a practice that's needed to thrive—it's a necessary practice for survival. Psychology has taught us that the greatest seasons of stress come during periods of major life change. Given that change is inevitable and hard, good leaders must stay ahead of it by proactively leading change. Doing this requires a thoughtful process to understand where you're at and where you want to go. Once again, you must get above the clouds. Seek clarity about the true, current state of your organization and your targeted destination. We'll focus a large part of Chapter Eight on how to lead change effectively.

EVALUATE YOUR ABILITY TO LEAD CHANGE AND INNOVATION

Consider how you perform in the following areas of leading change and innovation. Check the boxes where you feel you can answer yes, and highlight any areas where you'd like to improve:

☐ **Do you continually question the status quo?** Do you encourage your

---

10   Leon C. Megginson, "Lessons from Europe for American Business," *Southwestern Social Science Quarterly* 44, no. 1 (June 1963): 4.

team to do the same? Are you willing to take appropriate risks? Do you hold a compelling vision for change and engage others in that vision?

☐ **Do you actively lead efforts to drive innovation and change?** Do you communicate the reason behind changes to your employees? Do you effectively persuade others of the need for change to secure their commitment and buy-in?

☐ **Do you invite others to suggest innovation?** Are you willing to adapt to change generated by others? Do you seek your employees' input when changes are made?

6. INFLUENCING OTHERS

If you want to change altitude successfully, you must be able to influence others effectively. Why? Because your new role requires that you get tasks accomplished *through other people*. Influencing others is at the heart of leadership. With each advance in leadership, you need to expand your repertoire of influence strategies so that you can increase your capacity to manage more complexity and responsibility. Embrace versatility! By learning various influence strategies, you can call upon the best one (or multiple strategies) in different contexts to effectively secure your employees' commitment. You also pave the way to empower your employees to develop as future leaders. We'll discuss eight strategies for effective influence in Chapter Eight.

> *With each advance in leadership, you need to expand your repertoire of influence strategies so that you can increase your capacity to manage more complexity and responsibility.*

Consider: Who are the people working for you? Do you know their values, their drivers, the things that matter most to them? Do you have a sense of how motivating factors might need to shift as the environment shifts? As a leader, think carefully about which influence strategy will maximize the best results while also taking the best advantage of the capabilities and talents of the people with whom you work.

EVALUATE YOUR ABILITY TO INFLUENCE OTHERS

Consider how you perform in the following areas of influencing others. Check the boxes where you feel you can answer yes, and highlight any areas where you'd like to improve:

☐ **Are you a flexible leader, seeking to influence others based on their needs, rather than imposing your own preferential leadership style?** Are you able to "read a room" and adjust your approach according to different variables? Would most people consider you to have strong emotional intelligence? Do you align your decisions with business priorities rather than your emotions?

☐ **Are you the kind of leader that others want to follow?** Do you understand your own strengths and weaknesses? Do you understand that positivity on the team stems from your example? Are you self-confident? Are you thoughtful with your words, displaying honesty and respect at all times?

☐ **Do you demonstrate integrity and trustworthiness?** Can you be trusted with sensitive information? Are you transparent with your agenda and don't conspire to take action in secret? Are you willing to stand up for what is right even when it is difficult to do so?

☐ **Do you demonstrate trust in your employees?** Do you prefer to keep people challenged and stimulated? Do you encourage employees to take on leadership roles?

7. PRACTICING TEAMWORK AND COLLABORATION

Influential leaders can unite people under a shared vision. They make all of the team members feel that they're part of something bigger than themselves. More than one person accomplished almost every great success in human life. Our American culture places great emphasis on the rugged individual, riding in on the horse to save the day, but life is a team sport in reality. Great leaders can get people to work together in harmony and unity.

Influential leaders can unite people under a shared vision.

This doesn't mean great leaders promote homogeny or uniformity—part of successful collaboration recognizes the value of seeing things from multiple vantage points. There's research that shows that the more complex the task is at hand, the more diversity is required.[11] Good teams are not those that defer or eliminate conflict; they work *within* conflict to get to better ideas and outcomes. Effective collaboration requires that you appreciate the unique capabilities of everyone. Ideally, you also *understand* the different individuals you work with, remembering that each person will be motivated differently. By seeking to meet the individual needs of each team member, you can motivate them towards teamwork.

EVALUATE YOUR ABILITY TO PRACTICE TEAMWORK AND COLLABORATION

Consider how you perform in the following areas of practicing teamwork and collaboration. Check the boxes where you feel you can answer yes, and highlight any areas where you'd like to improve:

☐ **Do you continually strive to build and cultivate a talented team?** Do you set the standard for the quality of work expected and hold others to that standard? Do you step in to help when an obstacle is in the way of the team?

☐ **Do you value and understand the diversity represented among your team?** Do you assess the skills of the group in a fair and positive manner? Do you coordinate tasks based on the skill sets of others?

☐ **Do you invite collaboration?** Do you involve employees in the decision-making process? Do you believe collaboration benefits all parties involved?

PUTTING IT ALL TOGETHER: AN IDEAL LEADER

When we think of a leader who embodies most of these leadership

---

11   Lisa H. Pelled, Kathleen M. Eisenhardt, and Katherine R. Xin, "Exploring the Black Box: An Analysis of Work Group Diversity, Conflict, and Performance," *Administrative Science Quarterly* 44, no. 1 (March 1999): 1-28, https://doi.org/10.2307/2667029.

characteristics, we think of a woman named Lynn Miller, a retired executive for the Geisinger Health System. Lynn was a driver personality and very results-driven. She was determined to get things done and had a propensity to see what was wrong quickly. She advocated for excellence constantly and held her staff to a high bar. She was tough and demanded nothing but the best from her people; they all knew that they'd better not show up unprepared to a meeting with her.

At the same time, Lynn's hard-driving leadership was balanced by her incredible ability to invest in her people. She mentored literally hundreds of people and was able to remember personal details about each of them. Before getting into business with one of her team members, Lynn would lead with a question like, "How are Nora and the baby doing? Is she getting better sleep?" She knew her people well enough to understand what they were dealing with, and as a result, people felt cared for and seen. That made them committed to Lynn's vision and eager to push themselves to achieve her vision. When a leader within the organization was feeling tired or burned out, we would often hear them say, "I need to get some Lynn time." Once they had met with Lynn, they felt refreshed and motivated to get back into the throes of work. She was able to help them reframe their difficulties and provide strategies that would make their challenges more workable.

Lynn was a master at inspiring engagement, influencing others, and cultivating strong collaboration and teamwork. She also advocated for excellence, drove for results, and constantly looked for ways to lead positive change. Lynn most certainly hadn't begun her career as a consummate leader—but with discipline and an attitude to continually improve her leadership, an ideal leader is exactly what she became.

THE CASE FOR AN HONEST SELF-ASSESSMENT

How did you do in your own self-assessment? Are you the consummate leader who excels in every critical characteristic of leadership?

If you said no, that would be a healthier response than if you had said yes. Growth requires humility. If you recognized that you are not yet a "perfect" leader, that's a sign you're taking an honest look at your strengths and weaknesses, which is the first step towards excellent leadership. You *can't* be all things to all people. But you can constantly learn and still be highly effective.

There's a wonderful story told by the historian Doris Kearns Goodwin about Abraham Lincoln. It begins before he became president when he was a young attorney in Illinois. In 1855, the famous lawyer Edwin Stanton came to Chicago to try a significant law case. He'd heard that an up-and-coming lawyer named Abraham Lincoln might have some insights about the judges in Chicago and directed his staff to reach out to him. When Lincoln showed up at Stanton's office after considerable preparation, Stanton was disgusted by his disheveled appearance. He told his staff, "We have to lose this long-armed ape." Lincoln's work was never looked at, and he was humiliated.

Despite the humiliation, Lincoln spent the entire week listening to Stanton plead the case. He was ultimately so inspired by Stanton's capabilities that he determined to pursue further education to become a better lawyer. He wrote, "I'm going to become even more than I was."[12]

Lincoln could have remained stuck in bitterness, but instead, he had the humility to let the experience with Stanton act as a catalyst for his growth and transformation. He moved beyond the temptation to be petty, jealous, and selfish to choose the harder right over the easier wrong. As a result, he grew as a lawyer, leader, and human being.

---

12 David M. Rubenstein and Carla Diane Hayden, *The American Story: Conversations with Master Historians* (Waterville: Thorndike Press, 2020).

He also found the right people to surround himself with during one of our country's most volatile times.

One of the healthiest things you can ever do as a leader is recognize that there are certain things you do exceedingly well—and other things you don't. The items you do well: do those with greater frequency. Gallup has determined from years of research that we tend to be more engaged when we get to use our greatest strengths in our work.

In the areas where you struggle, surround yourself with people with complementary strengths. When you are mindful of the places where you struggle, they are less likely to hold back your success. You can work on them in your own professional development, by strategically building your team, and by asking for help—one of the most undervalued behaviors for building deep connection and good leadership.

In this chapter, we've tried to equip you to assess your own strengths and weaknesses. But to get a truly clear view of your capabilities, you need to collect feedback from the people around you. In fact, we think this practice is so critical for excellent leadership that we're about to spend an entire chapter addressing it.

ACTION STEPS

Go through each of the Seven Critical Characteristics of Leadership and use the evaluative questions to identify your top strengths and your key areas of growth.

CHAPTER THREE

THE IMPORTANCE OF FEEDBACK

RAISE YOUR ALTITUDE BY BUILDING SELF-AWARENESS

"How noble and good everyone could be if, every evening before falling asleep, they were to recall to mind the events of the whole day and consider exactly what has been good and bad. Then, without realizing it, you try to improve yourself at the start of each new day; of course, you achieve quite a lot in the course of time."

—ANNE FRANK, *THE DIARY OF ANNE FRANK*

THE FIRST 360-ASSESSMENT

Greg Hiebert narrates

Higher engagement and higher performance. That's what I was aiming for in launching a 360-Assessment online. When I first used the tool, I worked as an HR executive for the phone company Bell-South Telecommunications. As part of my role, I was trying to change the way human resources was viewed—not as an obstacle and barrier, but as an enabler of high performance. I came up with the idea of using leadership assessments as a tool to create an environment that was all about learning and continuous improvement. These assessments, I reasoned, could be a means to hold leaders accountable for the kind of behaviors that we thought would drive up performance and increase engagement. If it worked the way I was hoping it would, we could use the assessments at every level of the organization.

The 360-Assessment questions evaluated leaders on the Seven Critical Characteristics of Leadership and were meant to be filled out by *all* the staff people connected to the leader being assessed—their subordinates, colleagues, and their bosses—hence, a "360-degree" view of the leader's performance. Each leader was also supposed to self-assess themselves. I received support from my higher-ups to launch the first 360-Assessment at Bell South. I did it online, which, in 1995, was also a pioneering effort.

Since I was testing it out, I decided that I should be the first executive to be assessed. At the time, I had built a high-performing team and had recently won an award for leadership excellence. I expected to get positive feedback. In fact—if I'm honest—I thought I would get *really* positive feedback.

When I saw the scores, I was dismayed. The numbers were especially low around listening. After I looked through the assessments, I reached out to my team and acknowledged my disappointment but told them that I appreciated their feedback. Thankfully, our team had established good rapport and trust, which meant I could further explore the issue. I asked them, "What does this really look like to you when you and I are engaged in dialogue?"

"Greg, we love the passion you bring to everything you do," one of them told me. "It's just that, sometimes, your passion makes it hard for anyone else to get a word in edgewise."

Even though I was trying to create an environment where there was active and welcome engagement, my struggle to listen well was working *against* that goal. My employees often felt inhibited from speaking up because I tended to be dogmatic. I realized that if I wanted to be a better leader, I needed to listen more and talk less. On a deeper level, I needed to develop an attitude that really valued what other people had to say.

After administering thousands of 360-Assessments, I've realized that it's the rare person who can name with tremendous insight what their flaws are—even if they've been given feedback about those flaws before. For instance, my need to improve as a listener was glaring; I'd gotten feedback about that my entire life. Even my Catholic school teachers complained about my poor listening on my report cards. I saw lots of Mother Superior time!

I'd had a life of feedback telling me, "You're not listening, Gregory." Yet, even as an adult, I pushed back on the feedback. It hurt. I didn't want to believe it. It wasn't until I saw those words written down in black and white on my own assessment tool that I finally came to grips with the truth. Then I had to choose to take action.

Twenty years into my career as an executive coach, I'm thankful to report that one of my traits that my clients affirm the most is my (much improved) ability to listen. Although the moment of truth stung, the feedback set me on a course to help myself improve as a listener in all parts of my life—as a husband, as a teacher, as a father, as a friend, and certainly as a coach and consultant. Inviting honest feedback and diligently seeking to develop my weaknesses has made me a better leader and, ultimately, a better human being. It enabled me to change altitude.

AN ENHANCED PERSPECTIVE

We've administered thousands of 360-Assessments throughout our leadership consulting, and we've discovered that Greg's experience is not uncommon. Leaders almost always discover a gap between *their* perspectives on how they're doing as a leader and *others'* perspectives of how they're doing as a leader.

Why would this be? Humans function with unconscious bias. We see what we want to see—or what we're *able* to see. The truth is, all of us have blind spots. The 360-Assessment is a recognition that most of us are delusional about our strengths and our weaknesses. We all have a narrative that we tell ourselves about our identity, which may or may not be a complete view of reality. To pursue leadership growth, we have to identify our blind spots; we must *complete* the narrative. We do that by increasing our self-awareness. Highly self-aware people have a more accurate view of their strengths and weaknesses.

Not that this accuracy feels good, particularly. When highly self-aware people recognize a gap between how *they* see themselves and how *others* see them, that can feel troubling—as Greg experienced. For example, if you think you're a great athlete and then learn that your teammates and coach believe you are uncoordinated, that's a cold dose of self-awareness. You've discovered a disconnect between how you perceive yourself and how others perceive you. However, that moment of disconnect can create growth opportunities.

When discovering this discrepancy, you have two choices: first, you can get defensive and dismiss other people's criticism as incorrect. Many leaders—especially those who have just changed altitude—already experience insecurities. If you're in that position, *inviting* critical feedback is the last thing you would want to do. What if it confirms the psychological wound that says you're not good enough? It becomes easier (and may even feel necessary to survive and endure in your current role) to reject the feedback altogether. But if you refuse to acknowledge the need for growth, you won't grow.

Alternately, you can change your view about how you see yourself and work to improve. That attitude *does* lead to growth. Sometimes, we see people decide they want to improve *after* first getting defensive and dismissive! That's okay, so long as you eventually find the motivation to work towards personal development. We've found that accurate self-awareness can be a great motivator; it becomes a mirror that gives you a reflection of your true self. If you're not satisfied with the picture in the mirror, you're motivated to improve.

So how do you increase your self-awareness? You can see further and pursue greater elevation by inviting feedback and soliciting mentorship. In this chapter, we're going to discuss three valuable tools for feedback:

1. **360-Assessment**: We've already introduced this first tool. The 360-Assessment tool provides a thorough, 360-degree view of your strengths and weaknesses, gathered from the people who work on all sides of you. This tool will help you spotlight areas for growth and understand the places where you most consistently excel.
2. **The After-Action Review**: This feedback tool should be done after a project or major action is completed to consider what went well, what should be improved next time, and how best to pursue that growth.
3. **Coaching and Mentorship**: A coach and/or mentor who can help you consider angles you wouldn't otherwise and enable you to increase your altitude and grow.

THE 360-ASSESSMENT TOOL

So how does it work? The 360-Assessment tool provides a list of questions related to the Seven Critical Characteristics of Leadership. You can access the 360 we've perfected over the last twenty years at www.3ELeadershipGroup.com. We recommend that you first take the time to complete it as a self-assessment. In addition, you should give these assessments to your subordinates, your colleagues, and your boss(es) to complete their evaluation of you. Consider allowing people to contribute their assessments confidentially. (More on that in a moment.)

We believe that our 360-Assessment tool is excellent, but it's not the only assessment tool out there. There are plenty of assessment tools available online that you can administer. We do, however, recommend the 360 model of gathering feedback from people on all sides of you so that you can effectively "complete the narrative" of your leadership style.

Once all assessments have been completed, go through the feedback alone or with a mentor. A mentor or a removed third party can be helpful; however, if you genuinely desire to consider this feedback and take it to heart, you can lead this assessment effort on your own. (Make sure you consider the dos and don'ts in the following section.) Then, take thoughtful action to learn more about your needed areas of growth.

When the two of us are called to conduct these assessments, we'll often do the 360 for an entire team, but we always give the debriefings one-on-one. Our focus is on helping each individual gain greater self-knowledge, and we don't broadcast the feedback they received; it's their own assessment. However, we do encourage them to discuss that feedback with their boss so that it can be incorporated into their professional development plan.

We love the power of the 360 because it not only provides insight into how you might be perceived by others versus yourself—it also clarifies how different groups might perceive your leadership style. For instance, take the simple question: "Does this person lead innovation?" On your self-assessment, you might answer yes; of course, I lead innovation. One assessment might come back from your boss, "Yes, this person innovates." But your subordinates might turn in reviews that say no. They don't see you taking needed risks. You won't allow them to take risks. And your colleagues at your same level affirm the assessment of your subordinates; they also don't see you encouraging innovation.

Once again, this disconnect allows for a major "ah-ha" moment.

The gaps in the assessments should be revealing: you're presenting yourself differently to your boss than you are to your subordinates and colleagues. There's a gap there. At this point, you should ask the question, *why?* Why is there a disconnect between how you see yourself and how other people see you? Why are you showing one thing to your boss and something else to your employees and colleagues?

The most accurate view of you will come from many different vantage points. Use the 360-Assessment, or another tool like it, to gather a full-circle picture of your leadership.

360-ASSESSMENT: DOS AND DON'TS

The 360-Assessment is a loaded document. It can stir up strong emotions and spotlight needed change. Especially if you intend to lead an assessment effort on your own, we recommend considering these "dos and don'ts" to ensure you maximize the growth potential and minimize the potential for harm.

Don't Assume You Know All

The author Malcolm Gladwell once wrote about the danger of "cockpit culture."[13] He pointed out that many plane crashes have resulted because a hesitant co-pilot neglected to give needed feedback to a domineering pilot. Either for cultural reasons or because the pilot berated the abilities of the co-pilot, the pilot did not welcome any corrections. The pilot assumed they had all the information they needed to fly the plane successfully. Time and again, this attitude had the potential to result in catastrophe.

You might be an exemplary and accomplished leader. You still do not know all. Go into the 360-Assessment with the assumption that there *will* be blind spots revealed and that you have something to learn.

---

13 Malcolm Gladwell, *Outliers: The Story of Success* (New York: Back Bay Books, 2013).

Don't Dismiss Your Subordinates

Dennis O'Neil narrates

For your subordinates to give you honest feedback, they need to know that you will genuinely try to listen. If employees sense that any disagreement with the boss is unsafe, you won't ever benefit from their honest feedback.

I once worked for a CEO of an industrial manufacturing company who would frequently tell his employees, "I could agree with you, but then we'd both be wrong." Even though he had agreed to abide by the company's value of open dialogue, he had a pattern of shutting down his audience. If anyone publicly challenged him, they were usually gone within thirty to sixty days. The firings were always justified for some other reason, but most of us understood the terminations were a result of the leader's personal offense.

When leaders dismiss their subordinates, their employees can't be honest. To get a truly accurate picture of your leadership style, you need your employees' honesty. Make sure they know you are genuinely interested in what they have to say.

Don't Attach Rewards or Consequences to Feedback

Building on the previous point, there should not be any rewards or consequences attached to the 360-Assessment feedback. No one should get fired or demoted as a result of what they shared. No one should get promoted or be given extra privileges as a result of their feedback.

We've seen 360s be used by some organizations for merit-based promotions, but this undermines the whole point of gaining an accurate picture. When the results of a 360 are tied to rewards or consequences, the system becomes gamed. One of two outcomes often occurs, both of them deeply flawed. One, people inflate each other's scores: "You rate me high, and I'll rate you high, so then we'll both walk out good." Obviously, that behavior doesn't lend itself to honest, candid feedback, which is what you actually need for growth. Alternatively, people might overinflate the negative: if you're rating your boss and want their job, you might exaggerate their weaknesses to undermine them. That's a recipe for disaster as well.

Don't Get Fixed on a Single Data Point

We always tell people when we debrief 360s not to get stuck on any single number. People can get overly fixated on an individual data point: "Why did this person rate me a three instead of a four on this question?" Or, "What do they mean by this particular word?" Don't tie your whole sense of efficacy and wellbeing to what one other person thinks of you or what one answer says about you. The most accurate picture of your leadership will come from *many* different vantage points. That's the advantage of the 360-Assessment.

Look instead for the holistic story that is portrayed. When taken all together, what are the themes in what you do well? Recognize that people are proud of you in those areas, and you should be too. Look also for the themes related to your best opportunities for growth. Remember that this is a tool meant to help your development as a leader—not to give you a complex over a single detail.

Do Make it a Development Tool

Try to conduct these assessments to maximize their effectiveness as a tool for leadership development. Set up contexts that will make people feel secure in giving you honest, candid feedback.

Do your best to give some measure of credence to all opinions. It's always a curious thing when people ask others to fill out the assessment but then dismiss much of the feedback that comes in. They'll say something like, "Well, I know who said that. I really don't care what they think." That's ignoring an opportunity to gain altitude. Understand that this is a developmental tool used to help you identify blind spots in your own behaviors. Individual data points should be taken with a grain of salt, true—but do your best to value and respect the feedback you receive. It has the potential to provide you with grounded, concrete information on areas where you can improve.

One of the best outcomes of going through a 360-Assessment is that the person receiving the feedback be required to create an Individual Development Plan (IDP). The IDP should highlight what they gained from the 360 feedback to include clearly defined goals of what they most want to improve.

Do Create a Culture of Trust and Respect

The most accurate feedback will come out of a culture with safety and trust. As a leader, promote this safe atmosphere by modeling to your team a genuine desire to grow. Accept it as a given that no one is perfect. Acknowledge the reality that everyone has blinders to needed areas of growth—and may even need to understand the places where they especially excel more fully.

When everyone accepts the premise that each person can improve by doing more of this or less of that, then the 360 can become a handy tool to identify those areas.

Do Consider Keeping Feedback Confidential

Your employees may feel more willing to give their honest assessments if they contribute those answers anonymously. Likewise, if people know that they will receive their feedback in a confidential, one-on-one session, they might be more willing to engage with the 360-Assessment. Again, receiving honest feedback can be an emotionally loaded experience. Confidentiality can often provide a measure of safety which employees need to feel free to speak honestly.

Do Model Growth

One of the most powerful things you can do for your team is to model your own genuine desire for growth. I once worked with an exceptional leader named Claude Harbarger, the CEO of a large organization. He embodied civility and thoughtfulness. Often after our coaching sessions, we'd go grab dinner together, and then Claude would drop me off at my hotel. He always waited to leave until he saw me go into the hotel lobby. Claude was the consummate gentleman.

Still, Claude had some room for improvement as a leader. He was a deep thinker by personality, which sometimes prevented him from taking decisive action when needed. He was enormously detail-focused; for example, when I would submit proposals to him, he would even redline them for inconsistent font sizes.

When Claude engaged leadership**Forward** to consult with his organization, his team was struggling. He embraced the 360-Assessment. In fact, he went above and beyond the normal scope of it. Before administering the assessment, Claude went to each person who directly reported to him. He sat them down and told them, "Look, I believe in servant leadership. I believe that I have an opportunity to be the best leader for you and the organization that I possibly can be, but I can't improve if I don't know what I need to improve upon. I want to give you what you need to be wildly successful—so please be honest with me in your feedback."

Because of Claude's humility, grace, and earnest desire for significant improvement, his team opened up. They gave him some compelling, clear, practical things to work on while also reinforcing and affirming his strengths. Then—I love this—Claude took all the feedback he got from his direct reports, synthesized the main points, and put them on a 3x5 notecard. He kept that card in the pocket of his white starched shirt at all times. Frequently, he would pull it out and use it in his one-on-ones with his leaders to check in with them. "How am I doing?" he would ask. "I want to reinforce what I'm committed to."

Claude's courageous attitude set the tone for the entire organization. People were inspired by his genuine desire for growth and sought out their own development. His humility created a positive atmosphere of trust and set an example of integrity for everyone to follow. He demonstrated that he genuinely wanted to walk the talk. Claude is successfully retired now, and I consider him one of the best leaders I've ever worked with.

When you demonstrate your wholehearted commitment to growth as a leader, you'll not only maximize your growth through these assessments—you will also encourage everyone else to be just as earnest in their pursuit of improvement.

WHAT DO YOU HAVE TO LOSE?

Maybe after reading through this section about the 360-Assessment, you feel unconvinced. Administering the 360-Assessments sounds hard and potentially awkward. You don't relish the idea of learning more about your weaknesses. Would it be so bad just to keep operating at the status quo? Couldn't people just learn to adjust to your leadership style?

Here's something to think about: Whether or not you undertake the 360, people will still have opinions about your leadership. Wouldn't you rather know what they are? You can either operate in an environment of silent dysfunction or transparent growth. We're going to recommend you choose the latter, every time.

WHAT IF YOUR BOSS ISN'T INTERESTED IN FEEDBACK?

You want feedback. You want to provide your *team* feedback. But your *boss* isn't interested in feedback, which is unfortunate—because you really wish your boss knew how significantly their behavior undermines your and your team's efforts. So where do you go from there?

- Take a deep breath. This is admittedly a very challenging situation for any leader to be in—and unfortunately, not an uncommon one for leaders below the C-suite.
- Consider your boss's interests and goals. Anything you pitch to them should speak to those interests.
- With your boss's goals in mind, respectfully communicate to them what you need from their management in order to successfully fulfill those goals. For instance, you might say, "It helps me when we agree upfront specifically what you need me to achieve. I work best when I have autonomy to figure out how I will achieve success. Ultimately, I expect to be held completely accountable at the end of the day for achieving what we have agreed to." Tying your needs to your boss's goals is a subtle way to communicate feedback which is still likely to be received well.

AFTER-ACTION REVIEW: ANOTHER VALUABLE FEEDBACK TOOL

During our consulting throughout the coronavirus pandemic, many of our corporate clients had to implement new procedures quickly to respond to the rapidly changing circumstances. A few months in, we asked our clients to pause and reflect on how things were going: "You've got a couple of months under your belt. Let's think about where you're at as a team. What have you done really well? What do you want to make sure that you implement in the future? What have you done that didn't work as well as you hoped?"

Our clients gave a number of responses, sometimes related to finances, sometimes associated with resourcing, sometimes related to logistics, and so on. During the pandemic, many of these clients realized that there were system-wide procedures that needed to be questioned and improved. Light bulbs went on. Procedures were rewritten. Logistics were tightened up.

This, essentially, is an After-Action Review (AAR). Research shows that conducting meaningful After-Action Reviews is a consistent practice of high-performing teams. How does it work? After doing any noteworthy action—be it a sales call, an event, implementing a new piece of technology or system—you consider what went well and what you can do better next time. This can be a formalized process in a boardroom with computer templates, but it can just as easily be informal—over lunch, with a sandwich. What matters is that the review happens.

We break it down to three fundamental questions:

1. What did we expect to happen?
2. What actually happened?
3. How do we understand the difference?

You can use these three questions to apply to just about anything. For example:

- A team gives a briefing to their boss on picking an area for future investment of capital expenditures. After the meeting with the boss, the group goes back and considers the outcome. They ask: Was that what we expected? Can we present the information in a better way next time?
- A team makes a sales pitch. After the meeting with a potential client, they discuss: Did we get the account? If not, *why* not? How are we going to pitch it better next time?
- There is a significant conflict between a department and another regarding an agreement on how certain customers will be served. The two department leaders hold a summit to find a middle ground and common agreement. The meeting is a disaster. The two department leaders agree to conduct an AAR to fully appreciate what went wrong and to create a path to getting it right.

We engaged in reviews like these often in our military days. In fact, the Harvard professor and bestselling author David Garvin wrote that the US Army was one of the finest learning organizations in the world because it regularly employs this simple practice. I learned it back in 1985 as a young company commander in the 82nd Airborne division. One of the most effective things I was taught was to make sure I made it safe for soldiers to critique their leaders—especially me.

Often, I would find the one soldier who reliably held nothing back. Before the review meeting, I would tell him, "If you really believe that this thing didn't go well, then I want *you* to start off the meeting. Give your honest feedback." I wanted my soldiers to see that raising the hard stuff is how we would get better. We would dive into these review questions about how to improve, and the soldiers spoke candidly.

Similar to the 360, these After-Action Reviews help promote a mindset of continual, reflective learning. Increasing your awareness is the essence of reflective learning. The 360 is about doing that for yourself; these After-Action Reviews are more about building awareness from a specific event or scenario. If organizations could embrace this practice wholesale and live it out, After-Action Reviews would significantly impact the openness, transparency, and improvement of the organization and its leaders.

COACHING AND MENTORSHIP

If you want to raise your altitude effectively, it's going to make sense to seek out guidance from someone *above* you. A good mentor—

someone you aspire to emulate, someone with aligned values, someone who, ideally, thinks differently than you—will provide you with invaluable feedback for growth. They're going to help you learn the skills you need to rise up to their level.

Not everyone intentionally seeks out a mentor, but people constantly take lessons and clues, both positive and negative, from their higher-ups. I have found that people who are actively searching for a new job at another company will often point to a person two levels up at their present company whom they don't hold in high esteem and think, *I don't want to be that person someday*. The opposite is also true: When I meet people who see their boss and their boss's boss as admirable leaders they would like to emulate, those employees want to rise to a higher position in the company where they work. In other words, leaders two levels up can serve as either warning signs or aspirational standards.

One of the best mentors I've ever encountered made intentional use of his position to mentor leaders two levels below him. Robert Cone was a brigade commander when I was a young Captain. He oversaw nearly five thousand people. He put great focus on developing the leaders two levels below him to grow his leaders of the future. The next level below Cone were the battalion commanders, who each ran one thousand-person organizations. Below them were the company commanders—those people who ran the one hundred-person organizations. I was lucky enough to be serving as a company commander at the time and benefited enormously from Cone's leadership. He knew that if he put his emphasis, focus, and talent at mentoring that specific level of leader, it would pay the highest return.

Finding someone with a bit more experience—someone who has some altitude on you, in terms of the richness of their experience and understanding—can lead to profound gains in your altitude with relatively minimal investment. You have the potential to grow enormously by simply spending time with someone who has taken the journey you aspire to take. Cone later chose to conduct research in this area of mentorship alongside our good friend, Joseph Kopser. Kopser emphasized the value of observing a more experienced practitioner, saying "You can only be what you can see."

Some organizations try to formally set up a mentoring relationship through a structured assigned protocol. However, the best mentors are those you choose for yourself. Cone and Kopser found that the most successful mentoring relationships are initiated by the junior colleague.[14] You'll be the most invested and the most inclined to learn if you have taken ownership over seeking a mentor from the beginning.

Here are a few qualities we would identify in great mentors:

- **They think differently than you.** Although you might "click" with someone who is incredibly like-minded, you'll learn more from somebody who doesn't think like you, look like you, or operate like you—someone like that can give you the feedback you would not have arrived at on your own.
- **Someone whose values and actions are aligned.** You want to learn from someone who walks the talk. A leader like this will speak fully to the complexities, nuances, and challenges of leading in their position. They've done the hard work to make their choices align with their values, and there's a good chance they're highly self-aware. That means they'll help *you* learn to be more self-aware.
- **Someone with positive relationships with their teams.** A leader worth emulating is someone who has proven to be a positive presence for their employees. You want to study the kind of person capable of moving people using a wide range of influence strategies—not just threats and intimidation. Look for leaders who have established trust and earned their teams' respect.

---

14 Joseph Kopser and Allen M. Trujillo, "People Will Be What They Can See: A Case Study in Leadership," *ARMOR* CXXII, no. 4 (October–December 2013): 65–71, https://mcoe.azurewebsites.us/Armor/eARMOR/content/issues/2013/OCT_DEC/Articles/4Kopser_Trujillo13.pdf.

Greg Hiebert narrates

When I was a young leader, I had such anxiety underneath my veneer of confidence that it didn't even cross my mind to seek out mentorship. I can remember a lot of people from the first organization I served in that went on to extraordinary heights of success. I still wonder why I did not have the good sense to go up to a couple of those leaders and say, "I want to be as fine a leader as I can possibly be. I'm impressed with how you lead, and I'd like to learn from you."

That simple statement would have been profound in opening up a deep connection with some of these outstanding leaders. I could have benefited richly from seeking out mentors early on, asking them for their insights on what I could do to be a better leader.

What held me back? I think it might be the same thing that holds many of us back from asking for help: I felt insecure that the leaders I admired would think less of me if I came to them asking for help.

Dennis and I have found that asking for help is a learned skill. There are several factors that can work against us in seeking help. First and foremost concerns our own biology. We do things instinctively to make ourselves look more impressive and to avoid showing weakness. If I met a bear in the woods, I would retreat a safe distance and then try to expand myself to make myself look more intimidating. We are subconsciously programmed to employ those survival techniques so that we don't appear weak and get taken advantage of.

Nurture plays a role too. Many young men, in particular, grow up hearing messages like, "Be a man and get over it." When you combine that with the "nature" aspect of not wanting to appear weak, it's a wonder anyone asks for help at all. Sometimes, we might assume that our would-be mentor is simply too busy. That may be a legitimate obstacle, but in our experience, we've found that leaders often feel an innate desire to pass on their wisdom as they shape their legacy, particularly leaders in the second half of their careers. Sure, they might be busy—but they might also be inclined to make time to offer their mentorship. (After all, it's good for the ego!)

Still: other inhibitions may exist. Cultural factors can also make asking for help hard. Many women in the workplace are fighting long-held assumptions that they may not be as capable as their male peers. They might worry that asking for help would confirm that wrong assumption. We worked with one brilliant doctor of Nigerian descent who explained the preconceived notions she was constantly up against. When we were helping her prepare for a speech, we encouraged her to lighten things up by employing some self-deprecating humor. She gave us a skeptical look. Later, in private, she told me, "I think that advice fails to recognize that when I get in front of an audience, I already have three strikes against me: I'm Black, I'm a woman, and I speak with a Nigerian accent." In her mind, self-deprecating humor was something that only a white male could afford to get away with.

Undoubtedly, there are cultural dynamics at play concerning biases about race and gender that can make it hard to seek out help from a mentor. Some of these dynamics are stories that we tell ourselves, based on our own personal blinders—but some may be based in reality. That's a real factor we have to consider.

Still, consider the argument for courageously overcoming those inhibitions. A well-known Harvard study, which has led to several bestselling books and TED Talks, has determined that the "key to happiness" at the heart of a fulfilling and remarkable life is the capacity to build meaningful relationships.[15] How do you build deep,

---

15   Liz Mineo, "Good Genes Are Nice, but Joy Is Better," *The Harvard Gazette*, April 11, 2017, https://news.harvard.edu/gazette/story/2017/04/over-nearly-80-years-harvard-study-has-been-showing-how-to-live-a-healthy-and-happy-life/.

rich, intimate relationships? They must be rooted in vulnerability, empathy, acceptance, and trust. When I tell Dennis, "I need your help. I can't do this by myself," I'm demonstrating my trust in him. And that's not a sign of my weakness; that's a sign of my rich, trusted friendship with Dennis.

Even though we might be biologically programmed to resist showing weakness, we're also wired for community. The Harvard Study on Adult Development attests to that. We are programmed to nurture, to cooperate, to collaborate. And when you do lower your defenses and get real, other people will recognize your authenticity and feel connected to you.[16]

Here's another point of encouragement: I can't ever remember someone turning me down when I asked them for mentorship. There are few things more flattering than hearing someone else say, "I want to be like you." It's good for the ego! If and when you ask someone to serve as a mentor, most people will be inclined to say yes.

You don't have to stop at a single mentor, either. Over the years I've spent working to develop C-suites and corporate leadership, I have often thought that everyone should seek to build their own board of directors. In fact, I've set up my own group of wise friends whom I consider my personal board of directors; we meet regularly to listen to one another, share our experiences, and offer counsel. How would this work? Get a set of advisors and friends who will speak the truth, support you, and challenge your thinking. Think about gathering with those five to six people once a quarter to gather insight. Consider how your life could benefit from being able to honestly reflect on what's going on in your life, what's going well, what you're struggling with—and get their feedback. If it benefits the most successful corporations in the world, it's likely to help you too.

As a young man starting in my career, I couldn't imagine approach-

---

16   Brené Brown, *Daring Greatly: How the Courage to Be Vulnerable Transforms the Way We Live, Love, Parent, and Lead* (New York: Avery, 2015).

ing a respected leader and asking for mentorship. That was my loss. Now, after a career full of trials, tribulations, and learning, I know the value of asking others for help. Mentorship is an incredibly powerful way to gather valuable feedback and increase your altitude.

THE PATH OF ENLIGHTENMENT

There's a wonderful story from ancient Asian folklore that reminds us of the importance of gathering feedback from people on all sides of you.

In the story, the enlightened sage, Hwan, dwells in a temple on a mountain top, along with his disciple Lao-li. Although Lao-li is bright and determined, after twenty years, he has still not reached enlightenment. The wisdom of life is apparently not his to have. For years he struggles with this dilemma until one morning, the sight of a falling cherry blossom speaks to his heart. "I can no longer fight my destiny," he reflects. "Like the cherry blossom, I must gracefully resign myself to my fate."

So Lao-li determines to retreat down the mountain, giving up his hope of enlightenment. He goes to tell Hwan of his decision. The master is sitting deep in meditation. Reverently, Lao-li approaches him, but before he begins, the master says, "Tomorrow I will join you on your journey down the mountain." The master, in his wisdom, already knows.

The next morning before their descent, master Hwan looks out into the vastness surrounding the mountain peak. "Tell me, Lao-li," he says, "what do you see?"

"Master, I see the sun beginning to wake just below the horizon. Meandering hills and mountains that go on for miles. Couched in the valley below, I see a lake and an old town."

The master smiles as they take the first steps of their long descent.

As they approach the foot of the mountain, Hwan again asks his disciple to tell him what he sees.

"Great wise one, in the distance I see roosters as they run around barns, cows asleep in sprouting meadows, old ones basking in the late afternoon sun, and children romping by a brook."

They continue their walk until they reach the gate to the town, where they rest in the shade of an old banyan tree.

After a long silence, master Hwan says, "The road to enlightenment is like the journey up and down the mountain. It comes only to those who realize that what one sees at the top is not what one sees at the bottom. Without this wisdom, we close our minds to all that we cannot see in one place with just one set of eyes, for we need to see from many places and many points of view. Otherwise, we limit our vision and our capacity to grow. This is the wisdom that opens our minds to improvement, knocks down prejudices, and teaches us to respect what at first we cannot see.

With this insight comes an awakening for the disciple Lao-li. He returns to the mountaintop and becomes a great enlightened one.

We all can learn as we move up and down the mountain of life experience. It's valuable to consider the view at many different levels, for we can't be everywhere on the mountain at the same time. We, too, need to see from different points of view. And sometimes, we need to see through the eyes of others.

The tremendous value of feedback means you see with the eyes of many. The people above you can see further into the distance. The people below you can speak to a level of detail you can't see. The people beside you can identify your methods and help you better understand your own context. Alone, you see a piece of reality, but you don't see *all* of reality. Complete the narrative of your leadership by gathering perspectives from all sides—so you, too, can walk the path of enlightenment.

ACTION STEPS

1. Complete a 360-Assessment on your own if you haven't already evaluated yourself using the questions provided in Chapter Two.
2. Ask your boss, your colleagues, your team, and possibly some of your clients to complete a 360-Assessment for you. Remember to practice the "dos" and "don'ts."
3. Review the feedback from your 360-Assessments and formulate an Individual Development Plan.
4. After completing a project, do the After-Action Review with your team; see what you learn.
5. Identify several people whom you could learn from as mentors. Reach out to one or several of them, and ask if they would be willing to meet with you on a semi-regular basis. Consider forming your own "board of directors" to provide additional feedback and support.

CHAPTER FOUR

FLYING AT OPTIMAL ALTITUDE

EFFECTIVELY MANAGE YOUR ENERGY FOR PEAK PERFORMANCE

"Life is not about waiting for the storm to pass. It's about learning to dance in the rain."

—VIVIAN GREENE

ON THE VERGE OF BURNOUT

Greg Hiebert narrates

2020 was not an easy year to be an organizational leader—especially if you happen to be the governmental leader overseeing an entire state's pandemic response. I bore witness to the stress of that role firsthand while coaching one client who found himself in that position. This man is a marvelous human being, a well-respected physician, and a confident, capable leader. Even so, overseeing his state's COVID-19 pandemic response presented him with the challenge of his life.

The work was constant. He gave the governor daily briefings, which were often high stress. He felt unrelenting, enormous pressure. The leader regularly worked sixteen- to eighteen-hour days. And it took a toll.

One night, he called me. "Greg," he admitted, "I'm not sure I can keep doing this. I'm ready to submit my resignation to the governor. My back is absolutely killing me, and it is so painful that I don't work out anymore. I've worked fifty-four days straight. I feel like I'm doing a terrible job. Honestly, I'm in a really dark space. Emotionally, physically, mentally—I'm just completely exhausted."

"You can do this," I assured him. "But you know better than anyone that you're close to burnout. You have got to take care of yourself."

My client had the courage to go to the Governor's Chief of Staff and told him that he needed to take some time off. "I can't keep going and going," he said. "I wish I could, but I physically can't." His admission ended up creating a sea change. Both the governor and several other senior executives admitted that the schedule was unsustainable—they were nearly burned out as well. "Thank you," the Chief of Staff said, "for the courage to name what's been going on inside of us, too."

They took a couple of days' recess to rest, regain their sense of well-being, and build up their stamina. They couldn't afford to take much more time off than that, but even that short recess helped them build up a renewed sense of determination to get back in the fight.

I'm happy to say that the Governor's team did an exemplary job in their coordinated response to the pandemic, and that's in large part because of the leadership of my client. However, simply because of his exhaustion, he was ready at one point to call it quits entirely. Instead, my client had the courage to voice his need for rest. He was able to take care of himself and continue to serve the people of his state.

When you proactively take care of yourself, you give yourself the sharpness of mind needed to discern optimal altitude. You know when to go high to clarify your vision and direction. You know when to go low to get on the same level as your subordinates so that you can extend empathy and understanding. You have the mental acuity you need to maneuver, adjust your controls, achieve clarity, and so on.

Leadership requires immense *versatility*. Think of all the different reasons a pilot might need to take their plane either higher or lower in altitude. At all times, they need to consider a huge variety of variables to determine the plane's optimal altitude—and the skill to take it there. Likewise, the more scope and responsibility you have, the more versatility you need. In order to achieve that versatility, you need to be at your best. And how do you ensure you're operating at peak performance? You take care of yourself. By managing your energy effectively, you can devote time to the most important priorities, working effectively and efficiently.

But the opposite is also true: when you are physically, mentally, and emotionally exhausted, you can't see accurately. You can't think clearly about how to get out of the clouds; you can't focus on your instrument panel. You lose your grip on what's true, questioning everything—even your own ability to do the job.

We could coach you in any number of ways to change altitude effectively, but if you're exhausted, none of that coaching will sink in. If you hope to take care of your organization and your people, *you must take care of yourself.* This is a discipline. It's going to require thoughtfulness about your priorities, intentional scheduling, and self-awareness. We're going to take this chapter to give you the tools you need to intentionally manage your time so that you can operate at peak performance.

> *If you hope to take care of your organization and your people, you must take care of yourself.*

Before we do that, though, it's important to understand what's at stake if you don't. The consequences of letting yourself burn out can be dire. It's going to take deliberate action on your part to fight the momentum of a downward spiral.

THE DANGER OF THE DOWNWARD SPIRAL

Human beings have a negativity bias. Thousands of years ago, this bias helped us survive; we learned to be suspicious of anything that could pose a threat. The negativity bias, arguably, is less helpful to us today. That self-protective instinct can make us unconsciously insecure—especially if you've just gotten promoted.

Let's say you've been working in a role where you feel like an expert and then transition to a position of leadership that poses many new challenges and tests your abilities. This is going to put you in a situation that may feel precarious—even unsafe. If you start to feel vulnerable, your primal brain—the "fight or flight" brain—starts to call the shots. Unfortunately, this "reptilian brain" doesn't have the most evolved instincts.

If you find yourself in a role that's much broader in its scope than what you're used to doing, that negativity bias can easily fill your mind with perceived dangers. Your head might be filled with doubt: "Can I really do this? What have I gotten myself into? I don't feel prepared for this. Am I enough?"

In that place of vulnerability, you look for the negative. You might get feedback from your boss about five things you're doing well and one area where you could improve. It's easy to fixate and dwell on that one piece of critical feedback instead of the five pieces of good feedback. Maybe you take it personally. You struggle to elevate your thinking beyond the perceived personal slight. You focus on what is *not* going well instead of looking for the bright spots you can replicate. You might ignore the real growth opportunities.

Maybe you micromanage the areas of the organization you're most familiar with, causing the staff to bristle at your management style. They become uncommunicative; they seem unmotivated. As a result, there's a lack of progress in this area of your business. That leads to more critical feedback, which means more taking it personally, and more myopic micromanagement, and more frustrated employees, and the cycle keeps plummeting downwards. You constantly grapple with the fear of failure.

Alternately, you might *refuse* to take it personally: you put up protective walls which won't allow any feedback to penetrate. Maybe you're not able to produce the results that others expect of you—but you're not about to admit it's your fault. You don't allow yourself to recognize the gap between what you're supposed to be doing and what you're actually doing. The wider that gap, the more internal stress you experience, and the more intent you become on shutting it down. Instead, anything that goes wrong is made out to be someone else's issue. You're not the problem. They're the problem!

When you're held accountable for your internalized and personalized struggle—perhaps via a tough conversation with your superiors—it's going to be incredibly hard to *not* take that home. Your work life stampedes into your home life, impacting your ability to maintain self-care and personal health. When you lose the ability to take care of yourself physically, mentally, emotionally, and spiritually, the culminating stress can become overwhelming.

THE TRAGIC RESULT

Dennis O'Neil narrates

When I was a cadet, I became close friends with a young woman who was a few years ahead of me. She was always smiling—a bright shining star.

She remained friends with both Greg and me into her career. Our professional paths sometimes crossed, and she worked for Greg several times. Although she had struggled at times, she was also successful; she was often selected for promotion. She got married and had two children. Then she started working for a new company, one famous for making ruthless demands of its employees.

The job was high stress, and she faced near-impossible expectations. To enable her to do the job, her husband went down to part-time to operate as the primary parent to their kids. She felt pressure to succeed in her new role in the company and added pressure as the family's primary breadwinner. She constantly worked overtime. Perhaps because of her insecurity, she didn't communicate with her higher-ups about how to alleviate the demands of her job.

She had some health issues, and they got worse. Her mental health declined as well, and she was pulled into a darker and darker place. It felt impossible to balance her personal needs and the needs of her family with the requirements of the job. She couldn't see a way out. Ultimately, our friend's life ended far earlier than it should have.

I grieve every time I think of my friend's story. I wish I could have helped her find the way out that she couldn't see.

Know this: The points we share in this chapter are personal. They're for ourselves, they're for the ones we love, and they're for you. Flying at "optimal altitude" is about leadership, yes—but it's bigger than that. It's also about your family. It's about your health. It's about your humanity. As much as somebody might say they can keep their personal and professional lives separate, I don't believe that's fundamentally how we work as human beings. It's challenging to have a bad day at work and walk in the door with a smile.

I've spent thousands of hours studying the psychology of the human brain, and I know how hard it can be to break the downward spiral my friend found herself in. When a person gets cognitively off balance, a negative spiral can create feelings of gloom, paranoia, pessimism, and negativity. That's why we would encourage you—beg you, even—to heed the recommendations in this chapter *before* you get pulled into that spiral. In a downward spiral, your brain's chemistry can work against you. But with some prompting, its neurological patterns can be just as powerful in pulling you upwards.[17]

THE UPWARD SPIRAL

Depression can feel like an out-of-control downward spiral, pulling us into sadness, disengagement, and even exhaustion. When human beings are at their best, we're able to create an upward spiral of positive neurotransmitters of dopamine and serotonin.[18] We are inclined to be open, curious, gracious, creative, hopeful, and optimistic within this upward spiral. That's the space of optimal altitude. *That's* the mental state where you're going to be capable of your best work. Neuroscience research helps us better understand how to rewire our brain from a downward spiral to an upward trajectory for a better, happier life.[19]

To get there, though, you need to take care of your brain, body, and emotional and spiritual needs. How do you juggle it all? Start with reconsidering your available resources. The first key to building an upward spiral is less about managing time—it's about managing energy.[20]

---

17 A disclaimer: The recommendations presented in this chapter are not an attempt to provide medical advice, including, without limitation, advice concerning the topic of mental health. The information contained in this book is for the sole purpose of being informative. It is not to be considered complete and does not cover all issues related to mental health. Moreover, this information should not replace consultation with your doctor or other qualified mental health providers and/or specialists. If you believe you or another individual is suffering a mental health crisis or other medical emergency, contact your doctor immediately, seek medical attention immediately in an emergency room or call 911. If you or someone you know is struggling with suicidal thoughts, please reach out for help by calling 911 or the Suicide Prevention hotline, 800-273-8255.

18 Alex Korb, *The Upward Spiral: Using Neuroscience to Reverse the Course of Depression, One Small Change at a Time* (Oakland, CA: New Harbinger Publications, Inc., 2019).

19 Korb, *Upward Spiral.*

20 We learned a great deal about managing energy from James E. Loehr and Tony Schwartz's book, *The Power of Full Engagement: Managing Energy, Not Time, Is the Key to High Performance and Personal Renewal* (New York: Free Press, 2005).

MANAGE YOUR ENERGY

Dennis O'Neil narrates

"Better time management—that's the key." There's plenty of written material about time management that supports this widely held assumption. However, we think it's even more important to effectively manage your *energy*. Sure, you can manage your time effectively and complete the project before your meeting, or ensure you get home by six in the evening. But if your energy is shot, you won't show up as a whole person. You'll be exhausted, irritable, impatient, unfocused—you name it. Perhaps you've lived it.

When you manage your energy well, you can approach each situation as *your best self*—whether that's walking into a meeting, ready to engage, or walking through your front door at home, ready to be a loving spouse and attentive parent. Energy is the essence of high performance. If you manage your energy effectively, you can fly at optimal altitude, whatever your context. As James E. Loehr and Tony Schwartz write in *The Power of Full Engagement*, "Energy, not time, is the fundamental currency of high performance."[21]

I remember witnessing brilliant energy management by General George Casey Jr., the former Chief of Staff who oversaw the Iraq war. I used to watch General Casey get on stage in front of five thousand people, and he would be the most outgoing, gregarious, funny, engaging speaker that he could possibly be. Most people assumed he must be an extreme extrovert because that's what he appeared to be on stage. But those of us who worked closely on his personal staff knew that he was actually an extreme introvert—even a painful one.

General Casey had learned how to manage his energy to be his best self when he needed to be. If he had an important speech to give

---

21   James E. Loehr and Tony Schwartz, *The Power of Full Engagement: Managing Energy, Not Time, Is the Key to High Performance and Personal Renewal* (New York: Free Press, 2005).

to a big crowd, he planned his entire day around preparing for that huge output of energy. There were no major meetings right before a big speech; instead, he spent the hours before the speech doing solo work. He'd read or sign the paperwork or do something else that required quiet, personal time. When he got on stage, he had conserved himself in such a way that he could afford an enormous outflow of energy. After that big speech, it was back to quiet time. He didn't go out and do big meet-and-greets for hours. He didn't go out for a meal with a crowd; he didn't linger on stage. He went home and recharged his batteries.

General George Casey had a healthy self-awareness about what was energy-draining for him. Because he knew that about himself, he was able to manage his schedule, his requirements, and his time so that he could manage his energy. In doing so, he was able to be his best self in almost every context he walked into.

You can think of this in terms of athletics. Experienced athletes know that if they go into their event cold, they're not going to perform at their optimal level. They need to warm up. When I go golfing, I always try to warm up before my round starts. If I don't manage to hit a few balls on the driving range and practice putting, then I know my first two holes aren't likely to go well! If it's true that athletes need to warm up their bodies to achieve peak performance, doesn't it make sense that some level of preparation would be wise for leaders as well? We need to be thoughtful about managing our energy so that our minds and bodies are ready to perform at their best when it counts.

Take care of yourself by learning to manage your energy. What is the energy *drain* for you, and what is the energy *gain* for you? How can you be strategic in planning your days so that you can perform as your best self when it really counts?

What is the energy drain for you, and what is the energy gain for you?

ESTABLISH PROTECTIVE BOUNDARIES

If you want to change altitude successfully, we recommend you become incredibly protective of your time and energy. You will exert an enormous amount of energy every day, and that energy is a limited commodity. You should devote it towards the activities that will have the greatest impact for success—and *only* on those things.

Usually, that's not easy to do. People are going to make demands of you all day long—after all, they can't see if your energy gauge is on "empty" or "full." Only you have the ability to maintain that self-awareness. Unfortunately, even if you're nearing "E," you still might feel pressure to meet other people's demands, regardless if people are asking you to do something that you know is a lesser priority. You must find ways to fiercely protect your time and energy so that it doesn't get wasted on the lesser things.

But what if it's your boss asking you to do something? What if your organization is high-pressure and high stakes, and you are expected to work twelve-hour days? What if your subordinates can't move forward without your help? What if your advancement in the company rides on your willingness to jump whenever they say jump, regardless of how personally taxing it is?

It's not easy to say no. The stakes might legitimately be high. But remember the story of our friend. Remember what is at stake if you sacrifice your own health and personal needs. Those stakes are even higher.

Take a word of advice from one of the most successful and widely respected men in current times, Warren Buffett: "The difference between successful people and very successful people is that very successful people say 'no' to almost everything."[22]

---

22 Amy Blaschka, "This Is Why Saying 'No' Is the Best Way to Grow Your Career—And How to Do It," *Forbes*, November 26, 2019, https://www.forbes.com/sites/amyblaschka/2019/11/26/this-is-why-saying-no-is-the-best-way-to-grow-your-career-and-how-to-do-it/?sh=8604fb9479da.

Somehow, you must strengthen your ability to say no. One helpful way to do this is to think about who's got the monkey. One of the top two most-read articles ever published by *Harvard Business Review* is called "Management Time: Who's Got the Monkey?"[23] The article uses the analogy of a monkey on the back to describe any obligation you take on. Sometimes, you must accept that monkey on your back, like if your boss gives you specifically a project. But often, we accept other monkeys—monkeys from our subordinates, or monkeys from our colleagues, or even monkeys of our own invention. We don't have to take on those monkeys. We could—and should—say no.

How do you determine when to say yes and when to say no to those monkeys? Consider these questions:

- What of my tasks, if any, are tasks that I work on just because I'm comfortable working on them? Which of those tasks could be delegated to someone else? How am I being prevented from focusing on those tasks that only I can do, because I'm spending time on these other tasks?
- Which tasks require my unique talent or skill set? Could anyone else on my team get training in that area and help take on some of those tasks?
- What are the tasks on my plate that are appropriate for *me* to fix and/or solve? Are any of the tasks on my plate better suited to one of my subordinates or someone in a different role?
- Are any of the tasks currently filling up my day due to microman-agement? How many of my tasks could be taken off my plate if I empowered my employees? (If you know this is a big area for growth for you, feel free to skip ahead to Chapter Nine, where we discuss how to empower your employees.)

Ideally, you should spend your workday doing the things that *only you can do*. This is about focusing on your key priorities. Successful lead-ers, whether you're a first-line supervisor or a CEO, do two things

---

23 William Oncken and Donald L. Wass, "Management Time: Who's Got the Monkey?" *Harvard Business Review* (November–December 1999), https://hbr.org/1999/11/management-time-whos-got-the-monkey.

well: they set priorities, and they allocate appropriate resources. If you get into a cycle of not being able to manage energy effectively, there's a good chance that one of those two things is not being done properly. In order to fly at optimal altitude, you need to identify those top priorities for yourself and then boundary your time and energy to work on those. Delegate the other tasks that other people can do and get them the resources they need to do it. We'll discuss more about how to identify your top workplace priorities in Chapter Nine, "Understanding the Environment."

Spend your workday doing the things that only you can do.

However, managing your energy successfully at work is only half the battle. Most of us can think of workplace leaders who demonstrate enormous efficiency in their jobs, but still seem exhausted and reactive. Given that stress, high demands, high expectations, and unexpected changes are a given, leaders must somehow prepare themselves to absorb and respond to them—not be undone by them. As our opening quote affirms, "Life is not about waiting for the storm to pass. It's about learning to dance in the rain." In order to have the energy to view a storm not as a crisis but as an opportunity to dance, you need to take care of yourself in practical, consistent ways.

FUNCTIONING AS YOUR BEST SELF

It can be easy to let self-care fall to the bottom of the list of priorities, but actually, it needs to remain near the top. Self-care, to some, may feel indulgent—as though you are neglecting other priorities for selfish reasons. However, in caring for your body, mind, heart, and spirit, you actually enable yourself to do *more* for others. Habits of self-care are one of the most practical, important elements of leading at your best.

Think about this in finite terms. Say that you can measure your energy in terms of buckets. If you start your day on four hours of sleep, no exercise, a hurried breakfast, and no time for mental preparation, you might have three buckets of energy to get you through the day. That's going to be problematic if you're heading into a day that will require eight buckets from you, even if you do manage that limited allotment of energy effectively, as we just discussed. But what if you could start your day with *eight* buckets at the ready? Wouldn't it make more sense to invest the time required to increase your store of energy from the get-go? That's the payoff of self-care. You have more to give to others.

We think the easiest way to do this is to make sure your rituals of self-care are woven into your daily habits. Greg's first book, *You Can't Give What You Don't Have*, discusses this idea at length. We're going to explain much more briefly here how you can bolster your energy.

As a general rule, we recommend that you try to work in about sixty minutes of self-care, spread throughout your day. That does not need to come in a single block of time; that self-care can be meted out incrementally in smaller chunks to form your "umbrella of me time."

In *The Power of Full Engagement*, authors Tony Schwartz and Jim Loehr identify four key areas which are crucial for optimal performance:[24]

- **Physical Wellbeing**: Exercise: run, walk, bike, take a class like yoga or Pilates, take the stairs, play pick-up basketball, golf, park your car far from your workplace entrance and walk the extra steps. Consider finding some opportunity to naturally move and activate your body every sixty to ninety minutes. Physical wellbeing also means getting sufficient sleep. Much has been written in the last several years about not only the critical importance of getting sufficient sleep but also the detrimental impact when you don't get enough.[25]

---

24 James E. Loehr and Tony Schwartz, *The Power of Full Engagement: Managing Energy, Not Time, Is the Key to High Performance and Personal Renewal* (New York: Free Press, 2005).

25 Matt Walker, "Sleep Is Your Superpower," TED2019, April 2019, https://www.ted.com/talks/matt_walker_sleep_is_your_superpower?language=en%29.

- **Mental Wellbeing**: Reflection or quiet time: meditate, practice deep breathing, read, journal, and some other mindfulness exercise where you take some time for your mind to be in a place of peace, calm, and stillness.
- **Emotional Wellbeing**: Strengthen relationships: spend quality time with your family members, take time to talk to your employees about their personal lives, call your best friend, get coffee with a mentor, reach out to an old friend to catch up.
- **Spiritual Wellbeing**: This is about "feeding one's spirit": it does not necessarily require you to be a religious person but recognizes the importance of connecting with something bigger than yourself. Reflect on the meaning and purpose of your life, attend church or meditative services, engage in prayer, connect with nature, volunteer at a food bank or a blood drive, catch inspiration from some uplifting story or quote.

When you make meaningful investments in these key areas, you're creating a positive, upward spiral that fuels positive energy, enabling you to do all the things that great leaders must do.

To give you a vivid picture of what these habits of self-care can look like practically, we'll give you our own versions. These are the ways we make sure we're functioning as our best selves.

OPTIMAL PERFORMANCE REQUIRES YOU TO BE

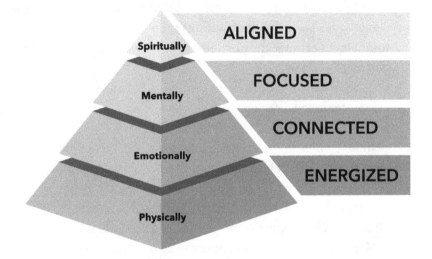

Greg Hiebert narrates

About three to four times a week, when I wake up in the morning, I get on my Peloton exercise bike and do a class. After my workout, I sit on my porch and listen to a daily meditation for about ten minutes. I check in with my gratitude app and spend some time thinking about what I'm thankful for.

I also use a very simple focusing tool after my gratitude reflection; I call it my "6Ps for Profound and Positive Living," a tool that I describe in depth in my first book. (You can find more about the 6Ps at: https://www.greghiebert.com/the-6ps). In its simplest form, I write down my thoughts about:

- P1: my *purpose* for the day
- P2: the *principles* and values I want to live out as I pursue my purpose
- P3: my *priorities* for the day that, if accomplished, will make it a great day

- P4: the *people* in my life that I have an opportunity to connect with; those could be clients, colleagues, friends, and family
- P5: *perspective,* when I reflect on those who are facing much more challenging and difficult conditions than I am. I find when I do this, it helps reframe my problems into much more manageable pieces.
- P6: *presence,* a reminder to be as present as I can to all those I will encounter in my day.

I conclude my morning ritual with a simple prayer: that I may be a blessing to all, and be blessed by all those I encounter.

Throughout the day, I try to find a few "pockets" of time to practice mindfulness. One of my favorite ways to do this is to go sit under a big Magnolia tree that's right outside my window. Even just two minutes of quiet under the tree can be grounding for me. Something like that doesn't require much except intention.

I love to play piano, and it can be restorative. I pull up my favorites playlist and play just one song. Sometimes I do "box breathing," which is a Navy SEALs technique: you inhale on a count of four, hold it for a count of four, exhale for a count of four, and hold that for a count of four. I do that breathing exercise for at least two minutes, and during that time, I'm not trying to do anything other than be still and pay attention to my breathing. I stop the incessant "monkey mind" and give myself some upward spiral momentum. As I write this, I also realize that I could make myself even healthier by having an evening ritual where I reflect on the good that happened in the day.

Dennis O'Neil narrates

My favorite form of self-care is a round of golf, which I try to do about once a week. Greg does a beautiful job incorporating habits into his daily life, but I find that I do better with structured events that I can book on my calendar. I used to feel like playing golf was indulgent, but I've recognized that it genuinely makes me a better human being. I absolutely love getting those two to four hours of exercise. Golf forces me to get outside and be with people whose company I enjoy. It gives me opportunities to clear my mind and prompts me to focus on just one thing. The game requires that I devote my complete attention to my body, my weight shifts, my club selection, identifying the right distances, and so on. The exercise focuses my mind and wakes me up physically.

On the days when I don't golf, I look for other opportunities to refresh my body and my mind. Sometimes that's taking ten minutes to go for a walk or even pacing while I'm on a phone call. In the evenings, I like to cook a good meal and devote time to connecting with my wife and family. We reflect on the day and check in with one another.

Consider how you could incorporate habits of self-care into your day. As you think about how to fuel your own upward spiral, consider what works for you. What activities in your life elicit positive emotion? What are some ways you can get creative about finding opportunities for movement or mindfulness? What two-minute activities could you do throughout the day that would help feed your positive energy?

There's one last key element of self-care that warrants attention: the importance of rest. If you want to operate at peak performance, getting decent sleep is equally as important as exercise, reflection time, and making relational connections.

Michael Phelps, the most decorated Olympian of all time with twenty-eight swimming medals, understands that rest and recovery are a key component of his ability to perform at his best. During Phelps' most intense training periods, he would swim seven days a week, three to five hours a day. What would he do for the rest of the afternoon? He took a two to three-hour nap—every day. He also got eight hours of sleep every night.[26]

There is this notion that, unlike athletes, executives somehow don't have to follow the same disciplines for performing at their best. But that's simply not true. Sports psychologists Loehr and Schwartz write:

> At a practical level, [elite athletes] build very precise routines for managing energy in all spheres of their lives—eating and sleeping; working out and resting; summoning the appropriate emotions; mentally preparing and staying focused; regularly connecting to the mission they have set for themselves. Although most of us spend little or no time systematically training in any of these dimensions, we are expected to perform at our best for eight, ten, and even twelve hours a day.[27]

To work at your best—to work in a place of curiosity, openness, discernment, and positive energy—you must have the discipline to take care of yourself. This is particularly true after you've experienced an expansion in your role and responsibilities when you must also expand your capacity for engagement. If you're exhausted and burned out, your perspective is limited; your energy is tapped. But effective energy management can help you maintain a strong sense of purpose and engagement. That's how you're going to show up as your best self and learn the skills that you need in a new role.

When you learn to manage your energy effectively and plug into the upward spiral through habits of self-care, you will inspire your team to implement some of these practices, leading to their flourishing as well. When challenges come, you will have the energy to

---

26 Catherine Clifford, "Olympic Hero Michael Phelps Says the Secret to His Success Is One Most People Overlook," *CNBC*, February 14, 2017, https://www.cnbc.com/2017/02/14/olympic-hero-michael-phelps-says-this-is-the-secret-to-his-success.html.

27 James E. Loehr and Tony Schwartz, *The Power of Full Engagement: Managing Energy, Not Time, Is the Key to High Performance and Personal Renewal* (New York: Free Press, 2005).

take them on like an elite athlete entering the arena. You'll be able to engage with focus, thoughtfulness, and determination. And as you navigate trials with agility, you will come to possess one of the defining hallmarks of the greatest leaders: resilience.

BUILDING RESILIENCY

Greg Hiebert narrates

During the months of the pandemic, I've done a number of coaching calls with different hospital leaders. I started one day with a health-care leader in the Northeast whose hospital was getting hit with a major wave of COVID-19 patients for the first time. This person expressed enormous apprehension about whether or not they were going to make it through this wave. Even over the phone, their fear was palpable.

One of my very next calls was with the Regional Medical Director for a hospital network in Louisiana, Ochsner Health. They, too, were dealing with a major wave of COVID-19 patients, but this leader's voice was calm—even enthusiastic. This was not their first time getting hammered by COVID-19; they had already seen a surge in the early months of the pandemic. They'd learned a thing or two during that first surge and displayed remarkable resilience as a result.

While talking to this leader, he expressed his confidence that they would be able to get through this new wave, even though their numbers were just as critical as the case numbers in the Northeast. He was excited about how many people were stepping up to serve in needed roles. He felt assurance that they knew what to do and that they could even improve on how they had already successfully responded in March. In a nutshell, he demonstrated the resilience that characterized his entire health care system: they'd been through hell already, and they were ready to do it again.

This wasn't the first crisis that the people of Louisiana at Ochsner had responded to, though. This community has a long history of resilience. In fact, this hospital system had grown by eight hospitals after their agile response to Hurricane Katrina, in 2005. Many hospitals at the time were overwhelmed by the needs and simply gave up, but Ochsner had many of their nurses and physicians sleeping on air mattresses for nearly sixty days, caring for patients even while the building remained surrounded by floodwaters.

The leaders of this hospital system weren't just *comfortable* operating in this new pandemic crisis; they saw it as an opportunity to get better, to grow, and to hone their patient care in an atmosphere they'd never had to take on before. Unlike the leader in the Northeast who'd felt overwhelmed by fear, the attitude among leaders at Ochsner was, "Hey—we've been through tougher times than this. If we can handle a hurricane and deal with a pandemic before there's any data about it—then we can face this adversity too. We're going to thrive. In fact, we're going to come out stronger."

That's resilience—and it's a crucial quality for any leader looking to navigate stormy skies with success. It's the ability to absorb the challenges and demands of the current environment in such a way that it does not diminish your ability to act with effectiveness. The term "resilience" actually comes from chemistry: it describes a substance that goes through tremendous pressure and change, and yet is able to revert back to its original shape and size. Essentially, it's the capacity to "bounce back," and not only that, to essentially be inoculated against struggle so that it's possible to thrive even in the midst of the challenge.

> *Resilience means you can bounce back from adversity and thrive in the midst of a challenge.*

In that way, resilience enables agility. It keeps you grounded in your prefrontal cortex, the thinking brain, so that you can make thoughtful, wise decisions, rather than reactive ones. You're able to consider the current and future needs of your organization and its people so that you can respond in the best way possible. With resilience, you know you can recover; in that confidence, you can respond; after responding, you can replenish and renew—meaning that, once again, you're ready for an agile response that will optimize the current and future needs of your organization.

Resilience also is characterized by a "stick-to-it-ness" which is often called grit—a tough determination to see something through, even when it's hard. Thomas Edison famously possessed this quality. Before he finally invented a lightbulb that worked the way he intended, he created hundreds of different versions that didn't work. When he was asked by a reporter, "How many more times are you going to fail?" Edison was said to have quipped, "I have not failed. I've successfully found seven hundred ways that won't work." That's resilience. Edison possessed the courage and grit to stick with it. To him, failures weren't a setback, but an opportunity to improve on what he'd already done.

This is just one story illustrating the kind of resilient mentality that can enable you to overcome setbacks and thrive as a leader. How do you maintain focus in the midst of chaos? How do you persevere during lengthy, draining projects? How do you endure the challenges and the hard work? You embrace this resilient attitude of "failing better." The ability to passionately pursue goals with hardiness and grit is all about resilience.

So—how do you get it?

Building resiliency requires taking on a mindset that is determined to *grow* through setbacks. There's a growing body of research in the area of post-traumatic growth (PTG), which I discuss in my first book, *You Can't Give What You Don't Have*. The research on PTG has been heavily informed by studying former POWs who not only managed to elude getting PTSD after their traumatic experiences, but even managed to thrive. I had the privilege of speaking with many former POWs during my college years and was amazed by not only their stories of torture, but even more incredibly, the wisdom they possessed in spite of that torture. I wondered, *Is torture necessary to achieve the kind of enlightenment these men possess?*

Amazingly, there was nothing about their circumstances that helped them achieve this enlightenment; their wisdom was completely due to the *mindset* these men had—the mental resolutions which propelled them to such wisdom. That mindset, which characterizes post-traumatic growth, can guide anyone through struggle towards growth and resiliency.

So, what defines a resilient mindset?

First, people primed for resilience **expect struggle.** Part of building resilience requires that you accept the truth that bad things happen to good people. Even so, it's possible to find meaning out of those tragedies. The stoic philosophers staked their worldview on the notion that struggle is inevitable; it is the nature of the human experience. The task before us then is how we *respond* to the difficulty. Focus your effort on what you can control, and let go of what you can't control.

Secondly, a resilient mindset **accepts that grief and hope can coexist.** When a soldier dies in combat, his or her fellow soldiers stick that soldier's rifle upside down in the ground with their helmet on top. The other soldiers gather around this memorial and process the death. That, along with the flag-draped casket, loaded with honor and dignity, are rituals which allow the fellow soldiers to explore their grief and get to a place where they can make meaning of the loss. This illustrates that people can experience both trauma *and* growth simultaneously—both grief *and* hope. These states are not binary—you can have both at the same time, and might gradually be transitioning from one predominant state to the other. If you can allow yourself the freedom to experience seemingly paradoxical emotions, you allow yourself to fully acknowledge pain while still maintaining your capacity to move towards resilience.

Lastly, resilient people **acknowledge the challenges of the current reality while still promoting hope and optimism.** One of the most important things that a leader can do for those they serve is to make sure people know that the future is going to be better and brighter, and you're all in this together. You acknowledge that, yes, things are hard now—but they won't be this hard forever. In doing so, you're not only strengthening your own resilience, you're also strengthening the resilience of the people around you. Find things to celebrate; find reasons to get excited. There's goodness all around us. We just have to see it, and promote it, and hope for it.

There are five positive outcomes which characterize people who have achieved post-traumatic growth, like the POW instructors I listened to. These are the "gifts" that can come from trauma, if we embrace a resilient mindset. Although these outcomes have been identified through studying trauma-survivors, the outcomes are possible for anyone who has endured a trial, whether you're a POW or a mid-level director of a company:

1. You allow tragedy and trauma to redefine your purpose in life. In other words, you conclude that you want to do something important as a way to bring meaning and purpose out of traumatic or adverse events.

2. You conclude that relationships indeed matter more than anything, and you emerge from trauma with a deeper sense of compassion and empathy than you had before the trauma occurred.

3. You are strengthened by increased resilience. You've gone through hell and come out of it; therefore, you can endure anything.

4. You feel a greater appreciation for life itself, and you don't "sweat the small stuff."

5. You come out of your experience with a deeper sense of faith and belief.

When allowing these positive outcomes to flow out of even the most challenging times, you can ultimately watch crises give way to creation; tragedy leads to transformation; failure leads to flourishing. The worst of circumstances can ultimately lead to a sharpened sense of purpose, calling, priorities, and heighten a person's sense of gratitude and faith. If you can choose a *growth* mindset, even in the midst of severe trials, you will have greater strength to weather the storm. After the storm passes, you will be more resilient because of it.

If you come to a crisis feeling exhausted and burned out, that crisis has the potential to break you. In fact—at that point—even a bad night's sleep could break you. However, when you do the hard work to manage your energy effectively and fuel your upward spiral with self-care, then you equip yourself to build the resilience that allows for such tremendous gifts. When you fuel your health, trials have the potential to transform you into a more capable, resilient leader. Resilience gives you the ability to bounce back from hardship and stay the course with grit. It's a crucial quality for any leader who hopes to maintain enough agility to flex when needed, respond to new variables, and lead with confidence.

ADMIT, ADJUST, ACQUAINT

Before wrapping up this chapter, we want to ask you to do three additional things.

First, *admit* if you are struggling. In the opening of this chapter, we discussed the government leader who oversaw his state's COVID-19 pandemic response; he had the courage to admit to us that he was in a difficult place. Essentially, he verbalized the fact that he was flying in the midst of the clouds. Unfortunately, his courageous admission is a rarity. We wish there were more instances of courageous honesty and vulnerability like his so that more people could take the steps they need to take some proactive changes.

You don't need to reach your breaking point before admitting that these changes are needed. It's far more common for leaders to operate at a constant place of mental and emotional deficiency than it is for them to quit outright from burnout. But operating from a place of exhaustion is just as damaging. When you get used to operating from a place of constant deficiency, you may not even *realize* that you could be giving so much more. If you can't even recognize when your capacity to fully engage has been severely compromised, that's when the storm gets dangerous.

Take a good look at your current energy level. On the continuum between full engagement and total burnout—where are you? Are you functioning at full capacity? Are you showing up as your best? Or do you more often feel exhausted? If you recognize that you need to make some fundamental changes for the good of your organization and your own humanity, have the courage to admit that.

Secondly, *adjust* your outlook. The nature of your outlook on work can be a telltale sign of impending burnout. When you describe your workday, do you use negative language like, "Here's what I *have* to get done today"? If your outlook is colored with a sense of obligation, fatigue, and reluctance, that negativity may be a sign that you need to implement some healthy changes. Unfortunately, that negativity can also drive you deeper into a downward spiral.

So consider: What do you want to strive *for*? One immediate step you can take to increase your engagement is to adjust your outlook to reflect real purpose. You might use language like, "Here's what I *get* to do today. Look at what I have the opportunity to do." This outlook adjustment is a deliberate attempt to put yourself in a positive mindset, one that will give you momentum towards an upward spiral.

Finally, *acquaint* yourself with the people around you. When you enable yourself to function at your best, you have the capacity to recognize the skills of the people around you and put them to good use. In this way, they are empowered to do more, and you have more space and time to do the things only you can do. You also have more capacity to see those around you who may be struggling and need support, reassurance, or empathy from you.

Good leadership requires your full engagement. It is critical that you take care of yourself so that you have the capacity to fully engage with your people and your mission. You do that by managing your energy, establishing protective boundaries, creating a hierarchy of priorities, and making investments in your mental, emotional, and physical health.

In our next chapter, we will discuss the importance of leading with integrity and building collective values of trust and respect among your people. If you are to do that, you need to show up ready to see them, ready to lead them, ready to engage. That requires a nuanced sense of your optimal altitude. It requires that you show up as your best.

ACTION STEPS

1. **Manage your energy**: What is the energy drain and what is the energy gain for you? How can you be strategic in planning your days so that you can perform as your best self when it really counts?

2. **Establish protective boundaries**: What are the tasks that *only you can do*? What steps can you take to delegate some of the tasks that could be done by other people? What "monkeys" are on your back, and which ones could you take off?

3. **Function as your best self**: What are ways you can make investments in your mental, emotional, and physical health? How can you find ways to move and experience reflective mindfulness throughout the day? What are ways you can make relational connections with your co-workers and family? What steps do you need to take to allow for greater time for rest and recovery?

4. **Build a resilient mindset**: What are some of the mindset components and daily practices for resilience that could help you learn to thrive even in the midst of difficulty?

5. **Admit, adjust, and acquaint**: On the continuum between burnout and full engagement, where are you? What are ways you can adjust your outlook to embrace an attitude of purpose rather than obligation? How can you better acquaint yourself with your people's capabilities and your available resources?

PART TWO

YOUR PEOPLE

CHAPTER FIVE

FORM AND LIVE COLLECTIVE VALUES

LEAD BY EXAMPLE AND FORM A TEAM COVENANT TO HELP YOUR PEOPLE SOAR

"[Great leaders] recognize that each person is motivated differently, that each person has his own way of thinking and his own style of relating to others...But they don't bemoan those differences and try to grind them down. Instead, they capitalize on them. They try to help each person become more and more of who he already is."

—MARCUS BUCKINGHAM AND CURT COFFMAN,
FIRST BREAK ALL THE RULES[28]

BREAKDOWN IN TRUST

Dennis O'Neil narrates

"The road to hell is paved with good intentions," as the saying goes, and Jaclyn's best intentions had created something of a hellish atmo-

---

28 Marcus Buckingham and Curt Coffman, *First, Break All the Rules* (New York: Simon & Schuster, 2005).

sphere for her team. I got to know Jaclyn as the Director of Marketing when I was working as a leadership coach for her company. From the start, Jaclyn struck me as someone with strong integrity. But after several months of working with her company, it became clear that Jaclyn's team was operating with a toxic level of bitterness and distrust.

Jaclyn had developed a close friendship with the single father, Hussein, of one of her children's schoolmates and ended up hiring him as part of her team. Shortly after he began working for her, the two developed a romantic relationship.

Jaclyn and Hussein commuted to work together every day and frequently displayed their affection openly at work. Hussein often visited Jaclyn in her office, even though other staff members struggled to get face time with their boss. Eventually, Hussein began using work hours to help Jaclyn in areas related to her personal life, like dropping her kids off at school.

None of this went over well with the rest of Jaclyn's staff, who perceived that Hussein was being treated with favoritism. The issue became a huge conflict. Later on, Jaclyn readily admitted that her favored treatment of Hussein was a lapse in judgment, explaining that initially, she was too close to the situation to see it clearly. She was unwilling to end her relationship with Hussein, but arranged for him to be transferred to a different department.

Still, the damage had been done. Jaclyn's team had lost respect for Jaclyn and distrusted her as their boss. That distrust permeated the team as a whole; the culture was cynical, distrustful, and co-workers often cast blame on one another. Jaclyn reached out to me for help to rebuild her team.

The first thing we did was establish a team covenant. We laid out ground rules for the kind of behavior that the team members could expect from one another, things like listening well, fostering more open dialogue, assuming one another's positive intent. The process of formalizing a team covenant—almost like a contract—provided a "reset" point from which we could begin rebuilding the team's trust. It specifically gave Jaclyn the opportunity to speak thoughtfully with her direct reports about the kind of leadership they needed from her.

It took the better part of six months for Jaclyn to work through the leadership challenges that the conflict had brought up, but within a year, much of the trust in Jaclyn's team was restored. She'd grown as a leader, and the culture of the team improved dramatically.

SOAR TOGETHER WITH SHARED VALUES

In 1976, anthropologist Edward T. Hall developed what is called the Culture Iceberg Model. He argued that organizational culture, like the iceberg, has the characteristic of being highly disproportionate in its actual visibility. There's a little that you can see above the surface, but there's much more underneath that is usually unseen—and also, more significant. The visible parts of the culture iceberg are the components you can see: things like quotes or pictures that hang on the wall, posters that indicate what the organization values, or fixtures in the schedule like Friday happy hour. These might include vision statements, strategic plans, policies, procedures, and the like. Those are all visible signs of what an organization *claims* to value.

But what values *actually* inform organizational behavior? That's determined by the unseen mass of ice underneath the surface. It's the "unwritten rules": the implicit values, norms, beliefs, and assumptions. It's the informal, agreed-upon cultural practices that dictate how and why people do things. This unseen part of the iceberg will usually be a much bigger influence on behavior than the visible cultural indicators. For any leader, it is essential to understand that the power of organizational culture can influence as well as impede performance and success. If you want to assess the current state of your culture, you need to look beyond the tip of the iceberg. Instead, you need to take a deeper look at what's below the surface: what are the factors truly driving organizational behavior?

Culture always exists—it is never optional. It's going to be there in some form or another. In this chapter, we want to give you the tools you need to intentionally shape a culture that will enable your organization to excel and your people to thrive. Forming these collective values starts with your own consistent modeling of them. It continues with crafting a formalized agreement of positive behavioral norms.

LEAD BY EXAMPLE: MODEL KEY VALUES

Make no mistake: any cultural change will start with the leader—and for that matter, any attempted cultural change can be undermined by a leader's inconsistency. If you want to lead a thriving organization that works efficiently, quickly addresses mistakes, cultivates innovation, and produces happy, engaged employees, then you need to help build a culture of trust, humility, and respect. That means *you* need to be worthy of trust, model humility, and demonstrate respect.

You can think of trust as a currency that you earn over time. As your organization's leader, it's important to build up this credit of trust so that your people and your superiors give you the benefit of the doubt. This credit will matter on those days when you need to make a decision that others don't completely understand, or when someone has made a mistake, when conflict arises on your team, or when circumstances go sideways. In those moments when you raise eyebrows, you want your people and your superiors to trust that you know what you're doing—not question your every move.

> *Trust in you will grow exponentially the longer you can prove you are worthy of it.*

For all these reasons, trust is the *anchor* of your leadership; it's what offers protection and reassurance to your team. But it's also the wind that will drive your organization forward with greater speed as your people feel the confidence to act boldly and take risks.

The two biggest factors in your behavior that will inform the culture of your organization are what you *emulate* and what you *tolerate*. These two factors will show your team whether or not you can be trusted to live up to the ideals you promote.

What do you *emulate*? In other words, what do you portray as being important? This gets back to the Say/Do Ratio, which we introduced in Chapter Two. Consistent leaders have a close alignment between what they say and what they do; there's an absence of hypocrisy. They demonstrate congruency between their espoused values and the values that are reflected in their behavior.

When there's an obvious disconnect between the values you espouse and the values that you actually demonstrate, you're creating an environment that is simply inhospitable to trust. The first step towards being a trustworthy leader is to be consistent in the values which you emulate. That will set the tone for all others to follow your example.

Secondly, what you *tolerate* has a huge impact on whether trust either flourishes or dies in your organization. If you tolerate people who break the values, norms, beliefs, and assumptions that your group has agreed upon, you are not protecting your team. You also undermine your own credibility as a trustworthy leader. Ultimately, trust will have a greater impact on your organization's bottom line than the revenue that one talented-yet-toxic employee can bring in. It's worth prioritizing.

A leader can also cause cultural damage by *refusing* to tolerate certain behaviors—such as anyone voicing an opinion that differs from their own. If an employee raises an idea in a meeting and is immediately shut down by the leader, that culture will eventually narrow to reflect the leader's ideas—and those only. When the leader puts forth a suggestion and "asks" for the opinions of their team, that leader will likely receive a lot of head nods from people who silently disagree but don't show it all the way around the table. Either through tolerating bad behavior or by *not* tolerating healthy behavior, a leader can promote a culture of fear rather than trust.

We're about to discuss how to create a formalized team covenant that can help codify shared cultural norms. However, if those team norms are going to stick, you as your team's leader must show consistency in what *you* emulate and in what you tolerate. How do you do that?

- Establish standards of accountability in keeping those norms and then apply them equally to all members of your team—including yourself.
- Model the way by being the first to point out when you perhaps didn't live up to the team's stated behavioral norms. When team members point out your failings or shortcomings, be overly appreciative and gracious in accepting the feedback.
- Don't give preferential treatment to the employees you like best, or those who bring in the most revenue, or even those who hold special clout because of their position.

Holding yourself accountable to these standards will require humility—and that's not always an easy trait to demonstrate when you're trying to impress others with your leadership skills. However, we have seen that the greatest leaders are those who demonstrate humility.

Showing up with an attitude of humility means you're thinking of the needs of the people around you—not just your own. Think about this in terms of a marriage. If a husband only ever responded to his wife out of *his* need, *his* instincts, and never checked in with his wife about how *she* would like to be loved, it wouldn't make for a great marriage. Similarly, your staff are people who deserve your commitment to their welfare. Have the humility to treat others the way that they would like to be treated, even if that means setting aside your own preferences.

> *An attitude of humility means you're thinking of the needs of the people around you—not just your own.*

We believe in the power of servant-leadership. You may technically be the person on your team with the most power, but your team will operate most effectively if you serve them. That doesn't mean forgoing your role as a leader in setting vision and goals; it simply means considering the needs, motivating factors, and stories of your team. Do not underestimate the powerful way your humility will shape respectful norms for the rest of your team. By having the humility to serve the needs of your people, you give them the wind to soar.

OTHER WAYS TO LEAD IN FORMING POSITIVE CULTURE

There are several other specific ways you can help build organizational trust and inspire your people's confidence in your leadership: invest in your people, embrace an attitude of lifelong learning, and get your work done.

Invest in your people to inspire their engagement, increase their motivation, and help them build trust in your leadership. Here are some ways to do that:

- Focus on building relationships through the important and valuable interactions—not simply just going along with the day-to-day activities of work, but doing your best to engage your people regularly. Get to know them, familiarize yourself with their values, and build an understanding of what matters to them. It is important to spend time with your team members focused on the current state of work; however, it is equally essential to spend time engaging them on their career and professional aspirations. Finally, help them develop the essential skills and mindsets required to accomplish those aspirations.

- Express sincere and specific gratitude and appreciation for the work your people do. Consider: Who is somebody that you need to thank today before you shut off the light and leave your office? Whom could you write a two-minute email to affirm? Take the time to reflect on someone that you're grateful for, the act or activity that they accomplished well, and take the time to recognize their efforts. Learn your people's stories to include their backgrounds. When you truly *see* other people by learning what they've been through, they will feel appreciated and understood. That will lead to increased trust, creativity, and engagement.

By investing in your team in these ways, you not only build a culture of trust in your organization, but you'll also show them that you're a leader worth following.

Secondly, **embrace an attitude of lifelong learning** and continually educate yourself. This means challenging yourself to constantly learn more and admit what you don't know, be curious, ask questions, and keep your judgment in check. Maintain a humble attitude, acknowledging that no one—including you—is perfect but that you're all going to work to get as close as possible to perfection. This attitude acknowledges that you don't know everything—and neither does anyone else on your team, so you're going to learn together. With a focus on lifelong learning, you permit yourself to be in a place of constant growth, and you also give your team permission to seek out new tools as they realize that they need them. This attitude will encourage your increased competency and set the tone for your people to pursue constant learning as well.

Finally, **get things done.** As a leader in your company, you are expected to produce results, and your team won't fully trust you if they question your competence. One of our favorite former bosses once said, "At the end of the day, I want people to say about me, 'You know, I never saw him work that hard, but damn, he gets everything done well!'" We think that's a pretty apt definition of success.

As you demonstrate integrity, competence, humility, and respect, you will become the kind of leader that inspires the best work out of your team. You will help establish a culture of trust, and you will show yourself to be a leader worthy of trust. As you set about formalizing collective values for the rest of your team, your people will be willing to follow your lead.

FORMALIZING COLLECTIVE VALUES

Call it a covenant or a contract, or call it "guiding principles," "shared values," "team norms," or the "rules of engagement." Whatever catchy name best fits your organization, the goal of forming a team covenant is always the same: to codify how you're going to operate as a group, identifying guiding principles and key behaviors that everyone agrees to adhere to. These principles will serve as your compass. When your organization strays from those principles, the covenant helps your team navigate back to where you want to be.

> The goal of forming a team covenant is always the same: to codify how you're going to operate as a group, identifying guiding principles and key behaviors that everyone agrees to adhere to.

An agreement on shared values can provide a shelter of protection for your team. By operating within those guidelines consistently, you can establish a culture that fosters trust, collaboration, and connection. According to Gallup, cultures of this kind produce organizations that excel.[29] Why would that be? Cultures that foster trust, collaboration, and connection lead to highly engaged employees. In

---

29 "What Is Employee Engagement and How Do You Improve It?" Gallup.com., December 11, 2020, https://www.gallup.com/workplace/285674/improve-employee-engagement-workplace.aspx#ite-285707.

turn, highly engaged employees consistently produce better business outcomes. Ultimately, businesses that consistently produce top outcomes are those which excel and grow.[30]

If you want to help your team soar, they must have the resources they need to fly. The tangible resources matter—the physical tools and systems and funding to get work done are important. But even more important are the *intangible* resources that your people rely on you to provide, in the way of psychological safety, honesty, respectful dialogue, encouragement of creativity, empowerment, development, training, trust, and so on. Forming collective values as a team is a major step in providing your people with those crucial intangible resources.

By creating a team covenant, you are leading cultural transformation in your workplace so that every person on your team is able to work at their peak performance. Just as Jaclyn's team experienced, the process of sitting down together to codify the norms of your team's interactions can serve as a catalyst for cultural change.

THE POWER OF A FORMALIZED COVENANT

Many families might be familiar with an "informal" covenant. When the extended family gets together around the Thanksgiving table, Uncle Bob knows that he'd better not bring up the free market with his socialist firebrand niece. Grandma Alice has learned that her son-in-law is sensitive about his weight, and she'd better not offer him a second piece of the pie. And forget about political candidates—*everyone* knows that topic is off-limits. For the family to truly enjoy the turkey and trimmings, there is an unspoken agreement that certain topics must be avoided.

These unwritten rules come to exist in any organization, whether the "team" at present is familial or corporate. So why bother actually

---

30 "What Is Employee Engagement."

codifying them? You might be part of an organization that's fortunate enough to have "fallen into" a strong, healthy company culture. But we would argue that even strong organizations still have room to grow. Additionally, without getting a team covenant codified in some form, you're vulnerable to dysfunction creeping in. A toxic new hire, an expansion, a merger, a crisis—any one of those events could disrupt an otherwise peaceful environment. However, if your team has a documented shared agreement about the values you commit to adhering to, these events won't knock you off balance.

Great leaders recognize that people's treatment of each other in good times and bad is not built on luck or personality. Instead, it comes from an *intentional* effort to build an effective and productive community around a core set of observable behavioral standards. Leaders must have the courage to confront and address when those standards are not lived out. A formalized covenant gives you the clarity to know when to address those behavioral breaches.

We helped coach an organization that started off as a small startup. They've grown into a midsize company, and from the beginning, they've made kindness a cornerstone of their culture. However, as the organization grew, that value morphed into "kindness *over* clarity." It became more important in this company to avoid rocking the boat than to speak candidly about measures that could drive performance. They wanted to like each other and keep the good feelings going; as a result, inconsistent performance and lack of accountability became accepted.

A company like this had a good thing going in its embrace of kindness, but they had developed a blind spot. The process of codifying their values helped provide a needed opportunity to take a critical look at both the pros and cons of their company culture. When we began to help them formulate a team covenant, we suggested that they include "the obligation to dissent" as a guiding principle.[31]

---

31   The "obligation to dissent" was a principle that Greg learned to embrace during his time at McKinsey & Co.

"What is that?" they asked.

We explained, "If you don't agree about a certain decision, then you are obligated to voice your dissent. It's not just your right or freedom to speak up, but it's your *obligation* to voice your disagreement. If you don't speak out with your concern—respectfully, of course—you are not upholding the covenant." For this friendship-focused organization, the notion was initially shocking. As we talked through the idea, though, you could see light bulbs going on. They began to probe their blind spot and were able to draft a set of company values that allowed for greater honesty and set them on a more productive course.

Previously in this chapter we discussed how the image of an iceberg can symbolize an organization's culture. There are *some* visible artifacts of culture that you can see "above the surface." Still, far more significant is the mass underneath the water—the unseen norms, values, behaviors, traditions, and so on that dictate "how things get done around here." When you gather your team together to formalize a set of codified values, you begin to probe what's underneath the surface.

We're going to devote the rest of this chapter to providing guidance on building a team covenant that goes the distance. We'll discuss how to enable your team to safely voice their observations about what's going on underneath the waterline and provide tips for how to best formulate shared team values. Going through this covenant-building process will give your team the opportunity to discuss the values you *want* to have and call out the values you need to reject. Essentially, you're looking to answer this question: What values do we agree to commit to in our treatment of each other so that we can do the important work we need to do and get the best out of our team?

HOW TO DEFINE COLLECTIVE VALUES

When we sit down with a team to draft a team covenant, we start by brainstorming the values that would help everyone do their best work and engage with one another in a healthy way. We typically come up with between eight and twelve values, emphasizing that these are the values that the team will not only espouse but *actually live out* in their behavior.

These covenants should be formed with a few key criteria:

- **They should be highly relevant and practical.** The values should directly relate to the work and interactions experienced by the team every day.
- **They should provide great clarity regarding behavioral commitments**, especially regarding what kind of behavior will not be tolerated.
- **They should exist to support the team's greatest success.**

Once the team has agreed on a set of values, they affirm their commitment to the covenant. Often, this agreement takes the form of a contract; there's wording like, "As a member of _____ Team, I commit to upholding these values so that our team can function at its best. Signed: _____."

Ultimately, this team covenant will become a kind of anchor when there is a conflict or some kind of breakdown; the covenant grounds the follow-up conversations. It's the baseline to reference.

"What did we agree to? How did we get off track? How do we get back to these shared values?"

Some organizations have maintained the same company values for decades, but this covenant will be a living, breathing document for many organizations. There's no reason you can't go back and modify it as the need presents itself.

One of the teams that we work with created their team covenant about two years ago, but many of the players have changed since then. Approximately half of the team wasn't there when the original covenant was formed, so they needed to go back, reconvene, and revisit the values. By revisiting the covenant with new eyes and new discussion, they could once again secure everyone's commitment to practice the values and ensure shared understanding about how the team was expected to treat each other.

EXAMPLE OF A POSITIVE TEAM COVENANT

1. We value a balance of work and personal life. We will support each other's holistic wellbeing and fulfillment, respecting people's commitment to people and activities outside of work.
2. We value getting to know our colleagues as individuals, understanding that they are human beings with unique stories, strengths, weaknesses, and preferences—not just fellow workers.
3. We value giving people the benefit of the doubt when things don't go well.
4. We value respect. When people share ideas and opinions that we disagree with, we agree to better understand why they hold that opinion. When we share our opinion, we will do so in a way that does not disparage anyone else, either implicitly or explicitly.
5. We value open and direct communication. We affirm that this kind of communication can and should be done in a respectful way.
6. We value dissent. If we recognize dysfunction or inefficiency, we agree to uphold the obligation to dissent so that our organization can hone its best practices.
7. We value effective and reflective listening.
8. We value collaboration and teamwork. We agree to constantly work to break down silos and look for ways to achieve more cross-collaboration within our team(s).
9. We value the pursuit of excellence and driving for results.
10. We value treating people well, even if/when they are not necessarily performing at the level we want.
11. We value operating with a fundamental sense of empathy so that people feel safe to make visible what is "below the waterline."

As a team member, I commit to devoting my best efforts to adhere to the values stated in this team covenant. I understand that I will be held accountable for a blatant or consistent rejection of one or more values and recognize that my commitment to these shared values will help everyone do their best work.

Signed: _____ Date: _____

EVALUATE YOUR CURRENT ENVIRONMENT

Where do you currently stand? Where do you want to go? And most of all—where do you begin?

You may already have an idea of what would work best for your team in terms of a starting place for building a team covenant. Perhaps you've already completed a number of 360-Assessments and have clarity on the perceptions of others beyond people's perceptions of themselves. You might have another, less formal survey in mind that will help your people identify what's going well and what's holding your team back. Perhaps you sense that a facilitated dialogue is going to work best for your particular group.

There's no one-size-fits-all recipe for where to begin, but if you don't have a clear starting point already mapped out, try starting with a few of the evaluative processes we're about to explain.

THE MISSION STATEMENT

Many organizations have a well-developed mission statement and/ or vision that can provide a basic roadmap for a team covenant. Take Google, for instance, which has the mission statement: "To organize the world's information in a searchable, readily accessible format." That's a simple, clear, guiding mission that can provide its teams with direction in forming their healthy team norms. A mission like that can help teams focus on what they should pursue, how they should invest their resources, and how they should set their priorities.

Many of our clients are healthcare organizations, so inevitably the mission statement will be a simple but profound one, like "Our mission is to provide the safest and highest quality care to our patients in need." Another concise one we've encountered is "Heal. Serve. Lead. Educate. Innovate." Those five words offer an incredible jumping-off point to brainstorm team values that would support them. If the mission of the organization is to heal, then your team should consider ways to help each other heal and stay whole. If the mission is to serve, then the team should consider ways to serve one another.

A well-developed mission statement can be a helpful starting point to remind your team of the meaningful goal behind your work. Every organization exists for a reason, and the mission statement can help your team understand its goals. The team covenant should be nested underneath those goals; it should seek to provide the psychological safety necessary to thrive in your organization's environment in the pursuit of its goals.

It's also important to make sure your team norms and your covenant don't actually go against the company's aims, bringing us to our next point.

ENSURE ALIGNMENT AND PURPOSE

In forming a team covenant, you need to ensure that your group norms *align with the organization's needs*. Almost any organization has some tangible output that is required. Your team covenant needs to ultimately equip your people to produce output that is aligned with your organization's purpose and goals.

But what if the organization's goals fail to inspire, raise up, elevate, or activate? Or what if you simply can't identify any cogent organizational vision, even after talking to your higher-ups? You may have to do some legwork to give your team a reason to get up in the morning. Part of changing altitude as a leader requires that you have the courage to inspire your team with a set of purposeful aspirations. They need a *reason* to fly higher with you.

Use whatever visible artifacts you can find to give you clues as to the organization's direction—plaques on the wall, posters, any sort of written document about what the organization values and/or how it defines success. Then, use the collective brainpower of your team to take it from there. Come up with a well-defined purpose for your team, which aligns with your organization as best as you can tell. After you've done that, have the discussion about shared values.

Working so hard to develop a clear sense of purpose may seem unnecessary, but actually, it's one of the most important things you can provide to your people if you want them to soar. There is tremendous research that says that when we have a life filled with purpose and meaning, we live longer, feel more excited, and experience greater fulfillment. There will be stretches of the mundane in any person's workday, but with an identified "higher purpose," the work becomes more than just going through the motions. When your people have a purpose that they're working towards, that mundane work suddenly becomes elevated with greater meaning. They're able to remind themselves that the work they do matters—and remember, that's one of the key three factors Gallup identified, leading to high employee engagement.

Dan Buettner, the award-winning journalist for *National Geographic*, wrote the bestselling book *Blue Zones: 9 Lessons for Living Longer from the People Who've Lived the Longest.*[32] He became fascinated by the scientific research that had determined certain places in the world where people lived well past one hundred—everywhere from a peninsula in Costa Rica, to the island of Sardinia off the coast of Italy, to the island of Okinawa. He looked at the cultural aspects that all these "blue zones" had in common and found that these people groups consistently possessed a strong sense of purpose, even into their old age. When the women on Okinawa turned one hundred, they began mentoring the "younger" eighty-year-old women in wisdom circles.

---

32   Dan Buettner, *The Blue Zones: 9 Lessons for Living Longer from the People Who've Lived the Longest* (Washington, D.C.: National Geographic, 2012).

His research is only one collection of data among many others that attest to the power of meaning and purpose. It's not just useful as a way to help people focus—it's good for our lives. It's good for our health, and joy, and wellbeing. If you want to equip your team to operate at peak performance and soar, make sure that the team covenant conversation is grounded in a shared sense of purpose, one that is aligned with your organization's goals.

USE PERSONALITY ASSESSMENTS

We once worked with two executives at a large firm who butted heads at their budget meeting every single month. The CEO was a "driver" personality. He valued action and results, and he always wanted them now—no, yesterday. At the end of every month, as soon as the financial reports came in, the CEO wanted his CFO to answer one question: "How did we do?"

The CFO has a personality that we call a deep thinker. Deep thinkers tend to be more reserved. They like to study data, prefer structure, and carefully and logically form a strategy. The CFO always bristled at the CEO's demand, responding with something like, "I haven't been able to thoroughly review the data yet. I want to give you the most accurate picture of where we're at. I don't want to just give you a flippant answer." The worst thing you can do for a deep thinker is put them on the spot and demand an instantaneous answer. They want to study the information, go over the data, and make sense of it. This inherently created friction as the CEO wanted an answer as quickly as possible.

The relational tension didn't result because one man was trying to thwart the other—it was simply due to differences in personalities. Once the two men came to a better understanding of how each one operated, they could extend each other more patience. The CEO gave his CFO sufficient time to go over the data, and the CFO understood that his boss would be content with an answer that was more general than his own exacting tendencies would prefer.

As these two leaders realized, it's illuminating to discover how each person on your team ticks so that you can map out the dynamics that are occurring. Personality assessments (there's no shortage of useful ones) can be valuable in doing this.

Diversity is great in theory but difficult in practice. The word is often applied exclusively to demographics like race, religion, and socio-economic status, but equally as relevant when you're forming a team covenant is the diversity of *thought* which your people represent.

Ideally, you will have a team with a diversity of ideas, opinions, strengths, and weaknesses. In fact, you won't have a high-functioning team *without* diversity. A group full of people with "driver" personalities, for instance, will get a lot done quickly but will probably make a lot of mistakes if there's no one to say, "Let's slow down and think this through." So diversity *should* be embraced—but how do you embrace someone you disagree with? How do you use their differences as a positive catalyst?

Seek to build an understanding of those differences. Provide opportunities for your team members to share their stories. Map out the diversity of personalities and preferences in your group. Remind each other that everyone has a *reason* for holding the opinions they do—and learning their rationale might be eye-opening.

In gaining a greater understanding of the diversity of thought on your team, your people will develop the capacity to flex and adapt to each other's needs. Without that understanding, your people will simply feel frustrated at the challenge of working with others who operate in fundamentally different ways. That's especially true under stress when it can be particularly challenging to cope with personality differences. However, with a better understanding of how each person ticks, forming a team covenant can become a unifying and empathetic experience.

The two of us try to hit some key points when we're helping teams map out personalities:

- Preferences for a style of communication, e.g., analytical versus interpersonal.
- Preferences for how/when you connect with people, e.g., problem and results versus relationship oriented.
- Preferences for work structure and pace, e.g., fast pace and quick to challenge versus harmony.
- Preferences for how we challenge another person's idea, e.g., easing in versus direct and blunt.

These personality assessments have even helped the two of us relate to one another better. On a scale of one to one hundred, where "one" is a preference for total spontaneity, and "one hundred" is a preference for total structure, Dennis scores a seventy, and Greg scores a twenty-seven. We used to get frustrated with each other because of our differences in how we view something like a deadline—but having those numbers assigned to our styles suddenly made our differences feel less personal. We weren't frustrating each other to cause hurt—we just operated differently. In mapping out those differences, we're able to extend each other more understanding during moments that used to cause friction.

SECURE BUY-IN

The real test of a team covenant is not during the brainstorming session. It's not in the moment when each team member is signing their commitment to uphold the agreement. The real test comes *after* the team covenant meeting. It's at the water cooler when employees are having the chats that reflect what they really think. It's after the next big mistake. It's during crunch time with the next big deadline. *That's* when you're going to see if your team has genuinely bought into the covenant. That's the test of whether or not this team covenant will "stick," and when you see if you have genuine buy-in from your people.

How do you secure your team's wholehearted buy-in? Start by ensuring that everyone has a voice in the team covenant discussion. Lay some ground rules that will allow for safety for your employees to be honest. Encourage debate but remind people to show respect towards one another as they disagree.

By permitting and even encouraging dissent, you allow employees to say what they need to say in everyone's presence—not via private gossip. The team covenant may not ultimately go the way they want it to, but if people are given a chance to fully air their opinions, they will feel heard. When a decision gets made, they're more likely to commit to it and give it their all.

Just this experience, all by itself—just the act of brainstorming a team covenant—can strengthen your team. It may be the first opportunity your people have had in a while to honestly share their feelings about what's working well and what isn't. When people work together to form collective values, they're experiencing collaboration. They're forced to listen well and understand each other. They're getting the message that everyone's opinion matters. In that act of collaboration, people will feel that they're aligning, they're connecting, and they're in this together.

What else will secure their buy-in? The integrity with which teams live up to their promises to one another is often what separates greatness from mediocrity. Talk candidly about how the team will address instances when the team covenant gets broken. Allow them time to practice and feel comfortable in addressing one another when this happens. The more that team members believe that the team covenant is being lived by all, especially their leader, the more you'll see real magic happen.

PRACTICAL CHALLENGES

Even if you've done everything right in forming a team covenant and have provided exemplary leadership to your team, you might still have a few stubborn holdouts who don't want to adhere to the team norms. Maybe it's the high performer who consistently gets results and thinks they're above the rules. Maybe it's the person who resents you or another team member for personal reasons they can't get over. One thing seems clear—they're not going to abide by this new team covenant. So, what do you do?

Remember: Leaders form culture largely by what they *emulate* and what they *tolerate*. As hard as it may be to go head-to-head with these holdouts, do not tolerate their obstinacy. Your ability to identify those who are unwilling to live up to the expectations and standards of behavior is critical. They either need to be held accountable for their disregard of the covenant and be brought to heel, or you need to get them off the bus.

Do not underestimate the damage that a toxic person can cause to a team, day in and day out. Often, when leaders finally dare to let those people go, people will come out of the woodwork to express their relief at them being gone. We've heard employees say things like, "I feel like someone just opened up a window and let in fresh air!" But if a leader has waited too long to let that person go, that relief may never come. The culture may have gotten damaged beyond repair.

The longer a leader waits to remove that person, the more damage is done. All the work you've put in to form a team covenant will be undermined if you consistently let someone off the hook for their disregard of the behavioral standards. That tolerance communicates to your team that you're not *actually* committed to the values in the covenant. It's going to zap people's belief and confidence in the organization. The cost to the organization and its health can be profound if the average employee doesn't believe there's a real commitment to living up to these values.

Make sure everyone has clarity of what's expected of them. Get everyone's agreement to honor those commitments. Then, if someone falls short, hold them accountable: "You failed to live up to the expectations of our organization that we all agreed on and committed to. Here's what you've got to do better." Offer clarity and establish boundaries as needed.

If they cannot recommit to the covenant and live it, be courageous and help them move on so that the rest of the team can get on with its work with integrity.

ASSESS YOUR CULTURE OF TRUST

Dennis O'Neil narrates

I once coached a leader—I'll call him Shane—who had just "changed altitude" by moving from his role in one organization to a more elevated role at a different company. He had spent twenty years in his first organization and knew the culture intimately. However, he didn't realize how much of that culture he took for granted. He was *so* familiar with it that the specifics of the culture were invisible to him.

When Shane moved to his new company, he assumed that the culture would be the same since the two organizations were in the same field. That was a mistake. He proceeded to work according to the cultural assumptions that his old organization dictated; he acted and worked according to those unwritten rules. However, his new team balked at his behavior. They had their *own* culture—their own set of unwritten rules. In their minds, Shane was in clear violation of them.

As you change altitude and positions at different organizations, departments, or entities, you're likely to encounter different company cultures. Each workplace has a different set of unwritten rules, and they will thrive or suffer depending on the level of psychological safety present in its culture. Each of those companies is looking to you to lead them towards a culture of trust.

In order to provide your people with the very best leadership possible, you must seek to understand the dynamics of the culture in your workplace. You're looking to understand the assumptions about time, people, communications, urgency, results, and so on. This understanding will be critical information as you seek to create a high-performing culture and urge your people effectively towards the objectives you're responsible for. In Chapter Nine, "Understanding the Environment," we'll provide an assessment tool to help you evaluate the state of your cultural trust.

MIDDLE SCHOOL MISBEHAVIOR

Greg Hiebert narrates

Speaking of being on or off the bus, there's a story I like to share to remind people that these team covenants are not so complex. They can be embraced by people in any stage of life—even middle schoolers.

Middle schoolers aren't particularly known for their common sense. Still, even at the ages of twelve and thirteen, kids have already developed the capacity for critical thinking and insight into the importance of psychological safety. They recognize the value of allowing for a diversity of thoughts and opinions to be shared in a group setting. I witnessed that firsthand when I was forced to—excuse me, had the *opportunity*—to teach some of them.

It was my wife's idea; she volunteered me, in fact. When our daughter was a preteen, my work schedule required that I travel constantly, and my wife thought teaching my daughter's Sunday school class would be a good way for me to get more time with Molly. I agreed—but that didn't mean I wanted to teach middle school. I had taught undergraduates and graduate students at West Point—but middle schoolers? Now that was an intimidating thought.

I leaned on what I knew and started the first class in a way that I hoped would make the time meaningful for the students. I said, "Let's do some good work together. What are some of the behaviors we want to follow to make our class experience safe and meaningful for all of us?" I was honest with them that I'd never taught middle school before and that the last thing I wanted was for them to be bored and dread coming to class.

The kids gave me a fine list of behaviors:

- Only one person should speak at a time.
- We should respect each person's comments.
- No hitting.
- Have fun.
- No single person should dominate discussions.
- Everyone should be allowed to speak.
- It's okay to disagree but do it from a place of kindness.

All in all, they did a beautiful job identifying values for what ended up being a first-class team covenant. Every student signed.

Several weeks later, I took my middle school class to North Carolina for a church retreat. I was the chaperone of the boys, eight of them bunking in the same cabin. One night, they were playing cards. I was in my own little room, but only a thin wall separated us, and I could just make out what they were saying. It seemed that whenever one of the boys played a face card, they had to make up a story about one of the girls in the class. When I overheard my own daughter's name, I began to pay close attention. The story they shared about Molly discussed her body and her clothes. Some of the comments were not very respectful.

I did not shut the card game down that night, but I did decide to confront them about it the next morning at breakfast when everyone was more alert. After they finished eating, I called the boys together. I said, "I listened to some of your card game last night." Some of the boys began to nervously fidget. I asked, "Was your conversation during last night's card game consistent with our class covenant?"

The boys didn't have to think long before answering, and their responses tumbled out. "No, it wasn't." "We were just kidding around, though!" "Yeah, but it was disrespectful." "Yeah, we're sorry, Mr. Hiebert." "Very sorry."

I said, "Saying sorry to me—is that sufficient?"

Some of them looked down sheepishly at their feet. "Well, no," they said reluctantly. "We probably have to say it to the girls."

I said, "Do you think that's a good idea?"

They said, "It may not be a good idea, but we probably need to anyway."

With their permission, we gathered the class together, and in the girls' presence, the boys apologized for their card game. The girls didn't make a big deal about it, but the experience showed the class that we would take the covenant seriously. In respecting the covenant with that kind of reconciliation, the dynamic of the class changed over the next several years. Their level of thought in discussions elevated in maturity and depth; they knew they were being held to high standards. They shared important ideas, trusting in each other's respect and in their own voice. Several of the boys later asked me to be their mentors. I ended up teaching that group for the next two and a half years—and loved it. It was a profoundly meaningful experience for me.

If middle schoolers can do this and live according to the standards of a covenant, I know you and your team can as well.

ACTION STEPS

1. Assess your consistency in modeling key values. What values do you think you emulate? What values do you tolerate? If you've already completed a 360-Assessment for yourself, reference this feedback. Do you have alignment in what you say you value and what you actually do?
2. Are you proactively leading positive norms by investing in your people, demonstrating an attitude of learning, and getting your work done? Name any area in which you'd specifically like to target improvement.
3. Take any needed preliminary steps to prepare for a team covenant meeting. Review your organization's mission statement, issue surveys, conduct personality assessments, and/or assess your current culture of trust. Go over the collected data as appropriate with your team.
4. Go through the process of forming a team covenant. Have each team member sign the covenant and take additional steps as needed to ensure universal buy-in.
5. Hold people accountable to the standards by taking action as needed. If there are any people who willfully reject the team's shared values, get them off the bus.

CHAPTER SIX

COMMUNICATION

INCREASE YOUR ALTITUDE WITH ACTIVE LISTENING AND REFLECTION

"The most important thing in communication is hearing what isn't said."

—PETER DRUCKER

EMPOWERING THROUGH COMMUNICATION

Dennis O'Neil narrates

When I was living and working in DC, my family was given a number of unique opportunities. One of the best of them was extended to two of my daughters, Nora and Kate. When the Obamas were serving in the White House, both the First Lady and the president established mentorship programs for young people. We were honored when Michelle Obama selected Nora to participate. We were twice as honored when, two years later, Mrs. Obama chose my second daughter, Kate, to be part of her program as well.

On the first day, Mrs. Obama addressed the parents of the young women she'd gathered, telling us that our daughters had all been chosen because they had a great deal to offer. "I want to provide these young women with experiences they could not otherwise get. I want them to be as comfortable walking into the White House as they would be into their own home, and I'm going to do everything I can to establish that."

After two years in the program, the young women in my daughter's cohort had a graduation ceremony, but our family was out of town and unable to attend. Michelle Obama reached out to us and said that she still wanted to do something special for my daughter. She set up a separate program, just for my wife and Kate and me, where she gave Kate a diploma and thanked her for being part of the program.

What strikes me most about this memory was Michelle Obama's presence. This was one of the most powerful women in the world—intellectually brilliant, enormously eloquent, physically striking. I'm sure she had a packed schedule. And yet, this First Lady of the United States could make us feel like we were the most important part of her day.

She conveyed that she wanted to hear us, understand us, get to know us on an individual level. She demonstrated that she had gotten to know Kate well—she knew her hopes and dreams and unique traits. Over the past two years, Michelle Obama had practiced an incredible ability to *listen* to each of the young women she'd mentored—and we bore witness to her ability to listen closely when we attended Kate's ceremony.

TWO EARS, ONE MOUTH

We're going to make a bold statement here: The foundation of high performance is how you treat the people around you. And conversely, the epitome of dysfunction will be grounded in your treatment of the people around you.

How do you show respect to others? How do you demonstrate that you trust the people around you? It starts with communication: the way in which human beings relate. It would be great if we could all be mind-readers but, since we can't, the only way we can connect and relate to one another is via communication. That's the *vehicle* by which we treat each other poorly or well.

The foundation of high performance is how you treat the people around you.

Here's the challenge: communication can be slippery. You might think you've communicated a message to your colleague with perfect clarity and sufficient respect, but their actions imply they've gotten a completely different message. That's because communication goes beyond simply the words that are exchanged between two people. Communication starts with how you think:

- Your *thinking* will form your interpretation of another person: you admire them, you loathe them, or you interpret them in some other way.
- The *interpretation* you bring to a conversation will determine your manner of how you listen to them: "This person is so fascinating" versus "This person is completely ignorant."
- Your *manner of listening* will ultimately determine the quality of your connections and conversations; you might demonstrate that you value someone's voice and want to build on their expertise, or conversely, you might imply that you think they're a waste of breath.
- The *quality* of connections and conversations you build—or dismantle—will ultimately *determine what gets accomplished*.

Did you catch that? Good communication and listening determine what gets accomplished: that's why we feel comfortable claiming that solid communication is the foundation of high performance.

Needless to say, we believe that active listening forms a huge part of that equation. When working with clients, we often share the quip that Greg's fifth grade teacher wrote on his report card: "If Gregory could use his two ears like he uses his mouth, he might learn something." In other words, effective communication is two-thirds intake versus one-third output.

And of that one-third output, an even *smaller* percentage relates to actual spoken words. Your output of communication begins as soon as you think, conveying itself before you ever open your mouth to speak—via your expressions, your demeanor, and your accessibility.

COMMUNICATION BEGINS WITH ACCESSIBILITY

Greg Hiebert narrates

I have three daughters. When they would bring home their friends during their teenage years, I tended to communicate in two distinct ways, almost instinctively. If my daughters' friends were girls, I welcomed them in. I was inviting and conversational and asked them lots of questions. But if the friends were boys, it was a different story. I was intense and scrutinizing. I did ask questions, but they were more of an interrogation than an invitation to get better acquainted.

My daughters complained about this. "Dad, all our girlfriends think you're amazing, but the boys all think you're scary!"

Although I feel very embarrassed to admit how quickly my demeanor would change when a teenage boy crossed my threshold, I share this story to make the point that our nonverbal cues speak volumes. Additionally, the judgments that we imagine are only known to ourselves also can have a significant impact on the effectiveness of our communication.

Effective communication starts with openness. In order for a boss to genuinely understand what's happening on the ground of their organization, they need to be approachable for their employees to clue them in; they also need to maximize the time spent with employees. If employees feel safe to communicate, they can speak directly, pragmatically, openly. If they're feeling massively intimidated—along the lines of a teenage boy doing his best to answer questions from the imposing father of his crush—the communication is going to be muddied, nervous, and inefficient.

Think of two bosses on either side of the spectrum of openness and intimidation: One boss sits inside an office with a closed door. When he comes out, he rarely issues any sort of greeting. He scowls; he almost never smiles. If he speaks to anyone, it's because they're in trouble. The second boss keeps her door open; she often emerges and greets her employees by name. She asks them questions about their family members or pets and remembers details about their lives. She issues affirmations when things go well.

Which boss invites communication? Which boss inhibits it? Who's going to be easier to report a mistake to? Which boss would encourage an employee's suggestion of a new idea, or a pitch to take a new risk? Hopefully, the answer is obvious. There's a common saying in the healthcare world that "the safest hospitals have the noisiest nurses." In other words, wherever nurses feel the safety to voice their concerns and feedback, those hospitals will also operate most effectively and therefore be safest for patients. Organizational leaders make a huge impact on the success of their organizations by inviting—or stifling—open communication from their people.

I know an extraordinarily wise man, John Bonviaggio, who was a sanitation worker in Manhattan, and he readily admits he never made it past the fifth grade. However, through his immense service to others, he came to be deeply respected as a revered and wise spiritual leader. John often gave talks on spirituality on West Point religious retreats, and I had the privilege to work in prison ministry with him. John used to say, "If you're happy, notify your face." It was his subtle reminder that how we show up for others strongly influences how we are perceived, well before we say a word.

Remember: Your employees, just like you, all operate with an instinctive negativity bias. Particularly because you, as the boss, have some degree of power and control over their lives, your employees will instinctively feel a sense of vulnerability around you and look for threats. They are more likely to assume that you are displeased with them than to believe you are pleased—which means it's important to send intentional, deliberate cues that invite communication. If you're happy, notify your face. If you want good communication, start by opening your office door and intentionally be welcoming. Take the time to look in their eyes and, with sincerity, ask, "How are you really doing today?"

Here are some intentional steps you can take to make yourself accessible and improve the flow of communication among your team:

- Check your body language. If you're not already familiar with body language that sends hostile versus welcoming cues, do a quick Google search. What category would your preferred body movements fall into? Are there some subtle changes you could make in how you move your body that would make you a more accessible boss?
- Transmit warmth and openness by smiling and asking your team members sincere questions about their lives. Later, take the time to follow up with your colleagues about what they have shared with you. Most people will appreciate this, although some people are very private. If a person is not forthcoming, don't force it by asking more questions.
- Send environmental signals of accessibility: leave your office door open for stretches each day; keep yourself available for phone calls; send acknowledgment emails letting people know you received their thoughts; do surveys to invite your people's opinions; meet with team members one-on-one to dialogue and get feedback.

I coached one leader who made a point to go to all the offices of his direct reports to chat with them. That blew them away; their organization's culture dictated that if you were promoted, the subordinates should come to *you*. This leader's efforts communicated tremendous accessibility. The implication was that he was so genuinely interested in spending time with them and giving credence to each of their voices that he would go to *their* offices.

This story is an excellent example of a characteristic that we often like to come back to: humility. If you truly want to make yourself accessible and open to communication—you're going to have to decrease your altitude at times and get on the level of your team to see what they see and know what they know. The more deeply connected you are to those you lead, the more they will identify with your leadership and the purpose your leadership serves.

THE HUMILITY FACTOR

Dennis O'Neil narrates

Knowing what's happening on the ground of your organization is critical. One of the biggest challenges for leaders who have recently changed altitude is a feeling of disconnection from the work they used to directly supervise. In order to keep tabs on the smoothness of your operations, you now need to rely on *communication* from the people who work underneath you. Leaders often have a top-down perspective, but they also need to shift, at times, to look at things from their employees' perspectives. That requires "getting down off the balcony" to learn and listen to what your employees are actually experiencing; in other words, that requires humility.

When I worked with General Dempsey during his time as the Chief of Staff of the Army, he used to tell us a story from when he was in the field. His soldiers were marching through the Middle East, carrying over eighty pounds of weight in their combat loads. The incredible weight on their backs challenged people's maneuverability in a combat situation.

One day, General Dempsey made them all unpack their bags and scrutinize the contents. One particularly heavy item was the entrenching tool—basically, a collapsible shovel that had probably become a standard-issue during World War I. "I don't know when the military engineers last took a look at the design of this tool," Dempsey said, "but I'm guessing it hasn't fundamentally changed in about a hundred years." He looked at his soldiers. "Do you think there's a way we could dig a hole without carrying around this extra five pounds of steel?"

Dempsey would conclude that story by making the point that senior leaders need to take a break from looking down all the time. Instead, they need to lie on the floor and look *up* so they can understand and resolve their people's needs. We could all use this simple lesson: look from our subordinates' perspective to see where we could remove five pounds of load off their backs.

Many of us are often on autopilot. And frankly, the more intelligent someone is, the more likely they will assume that the way they perceive reality is the objective truth. But truly great leaders are constantly challenging their view of reality. They engage from a place of curiosity, looking to discover what's really going on in their organization and with their employees. Granted, it would be too mentally exhausting to stay in that place of constant curiosity all the time, but it counts the most when things get hard. When the issues get highly complex, and wicked, and thorny—*that's* when it's most important to adopt an attitude of humility and seek to learn the things we don't know. When we don't bother to check our blind spots by getting honest feedback from our people, we're likely to get into trouble.

When I coach organizations on their communication, we talk about how to improve the energy, engagement, and exploration of their communication. Most people have experienced the drain of attending a meeting where a single person drones on and on, or where they're never invited to speak up. Communication experiences like that tend to wear people out and shut them down. But there are certain communication norms that leaders can instigate which will help increase the energy, engagement, and exploration of their teams:

- Make sure everyone gets to talk (but not too much).
- Ensure mutual respect and regard across team members.
- Frequent encouragement from the leader for all to contribute and when they do, provide positive affirmation for their ideas.
- Encourage social time together in a work setting.
- Team leadership should encourage democracy in action, making sure everyone has access and opportunity to contribute; the leaders should listen as much as they talk (and the listening should be energized and focused).
- Make sure relationships across all team members are healthy.
- Communication should be appropriately exploratory—seeking ideas and input from outside the group but not at the expense of group engagement.

Communication norms like this require that you lead with humility. It means inviting others to speak up, closing your mouth, and listening well. For many leaders, that would require a fundamental shift. However, it's this kind of shift that will get the best out of your employees, enhance your organizational communication, reveal your own blind spots, and lead to higher performance.

The single most important thing you can do as a leader towards achieving this end is listening—and listening well. We're going to devote the rest of our chapter to discussing just that.

ACTIVE LISTENING AND EMPLOYEE ENGAGEMENT

"Dennis, I don't do culture. Culture is just a bunch of feelings. I don't do feelings."

The Chief Technology Officer, Russell, was not initially open to my suggestion that we work on his organization's culture. A former college hockey player, Russell looked like a tank. If a moment in a meeting rubbed him the wrong way or if he got angry, all it took was him getting up out of his chair for people to feel physically threatened. His intimidating presence and aggressive style caused a natural reaction among his employees to shut down. Whether or not Russell wanted to "do feelings," his communication style was *causing* a whole lot of feelings—and they were undermining his efforts to lead a thriving organization.

Russell had to realize that his leadership style posed real shortcomings, and those shortcomings had the potential to derail his career. Although his long-term goal was to eventually take over as CEO, he was not going to be offered that position unless he could improve his ability to develop a high-performing team grounded in a positive culture.

I worked to show Russell that his unintended intimidation style of leadership had a negative impact on the organization. I said, "It's not just *your* feelings that we're dealing with here, Russell. We're talking about the feelings of others and the climate of the organization. The way that your employees feel is critical to their engagement and therefore the organization's success."

When Russell began to understand that culture was more than "just" feelings and that his employees' level of engagement had a comprehensive effect on his organization's success, he started to get on board. He realized that his communication style was critically linked to employee retention, turnover, and even connected to customer satisfaction. In not allowing his employees to have a voice, that disregard for listening extended to their clients, who didn't feel heard either.

Russell, I'm happy to say, now "does" both culture and feelings. His employees are much happier as a result and much more engaged. Their profits have matched.

Remember the secret sauce for employee engagement that we discussed in previous chapters: For full engagement, your people need to feel like their work is meaningful; they need to have connected relationships at work; and *they need to feel like they have a voice.*[33]

Your active listening gives your employees that voice. If you work on your listening skills, you can enhance your employees' engagement and improve your team's performance.

But all kinds of listening are not created equal. Whereas *active* listening can help teams fly higher and work with greater efficacy, ineffective listening can compound dysfunction. We're going to identify two forms of ineffective listening and then explain what truly active listening looks like.

INEFFECTIVE LISTENING

There are several ways to be a bad listener. Frankly, it's much easier to be an ineffective listener than an effective one—it takes far more energy to listen well. However, poor listening will create far more headaches than it will solve.

The first type of ineffective listening is **passive listening**. In this ineffective mode of communication, you might *appear* to be listening to the person speaking to you, but your mind is elsewhere:

How long is it until lunch?

I need to check the notifications on my phone.

Did I put a coat on my kid before he left for school?

This kind of listening is not fully engaged. It's passive in that you're not putting in any real effort to understand the person communicat-

33 "What Is Employee Engagement and How Do You Improve It?" Gallup.com., December 11, 2020, https://www.gallup.com/workplace/285674/improve-employee-engagement-workplace.aspx#ite-285707.

ing to you. The head nods, or the "hmms" you utter are nothing more than patterned instinctive responses. You're just letting the words wash over you without trying to engage. In passive listening, you're "hearing," but your mind is wandering somewhere else.

Automatic listening is another form of ineffective listening. This type of listening is narrowly focused on a few key details—whatever will help you fix the problem and move on—but it ignores the whole picture of what's being said. Think of a doctor half-listening to a patient, only interested in what symptomatic clues will help determine a prescription. Automatic listening is often informed by how you may have been primed by training. It surrounds the question: "What in this conversation is *for* me, or what is needed *from* me?" When doing automatic listening, you're not seeking to fully understand or empathize; you just want a few key pieces of information so that you can move on.

The third type of ineffective listening is **reactive listening**. This form of listening is not only ineffective; it can actually be damaging. Reactive listening, aka "rebuttal listening," comes from a place of judgment. In this mode, you're not focused on understanding the person speaking; you're mentally tearing apart the other person's argument and waiting to issue your rebuttal. In this mode of listening, you're hearing but not understanding. In fact, you're not even *trying* to understand; you're too busy thinking of all the reasons you don't respect what's being said or the person saying it. Instead of trying to thoughtfully process their rationale, you're in fight mode; you're reacting from your gut. People listening reactively have a "Yeah, *but*—" mindset. They're just waiting to prove the other person wrong.

Reactive listening is a zero-sum game. There's no interest in pursuing shared understanding—someone is the winner, and someone is the loser; you're right, and they're wrong. Instead of listening to the other person, you're listening to your *own* thinking, which in your opinion is objective truth. You don't allow any flexibility that a different point might have merit. Rather than encountering each person with respect, you judge them on their status and alignment with you: Are they important enough to deserve your attention? Do they agree with you? If so, then they pass. If not, then the conversation is written off as a waste of time.

Unfortunately, you're not going to make any progress with anyone if you're sending clear signals that you believe they're an idiot. You're also not helping your employees engage. Reactive listening doesn't encourage people to offer up ideas or bring their best work—it shuts them down. It's discouraging and demoralizing.

But *good* listening is a game-changer. Teams will fly higher if they communicate effectively—not listening passively, automatically, or reactively, but using generative listening and reflection to enhance their efficacy.

EFFECTIVE LISTENING

So how do you begin to listen actively? There are two ways to demonstrate active listening—and take note: "active" is an accurate description for these forms of listening. They require energy and focus on the part of the listener.

Reflective listening happens when the person listening "reflects" back to the speaker the same words and sentiments which were just said. This requires that the listener pay close attention to the person speaking. It functions as a two-step process: first, you listen to understand what someone is telling you; then, you demonstrate your understanding by repeating the ideas and words the speaker just said back to them.

For example, a speaker might say: "I have major concerns about the specific words we're using in this marketing copy."

Someone doing reflective listening will reflect those same words and feelings back with a response like: "I hear you saying that you have real concerns about the words we've chosen for this copy. Is that right? Can you help me better understand your concerns?"

Reflective listening could also begin with words like, "What I hear you telling me is..." or "It sounds like you want..." or "I heard you say..." After repeating the speaker's thoughts to clarify that you've fully understood them, strengthen the effectiveness of your listening by asking a follow-up question for further understanding. You might ask something like, "Can you help me understand why?" Or, "Can we further explore that?" Or even simply, "Tell me more."

This might seem laughably simple to some—you just *repeat* the same words they just said? In spite of its simplicity, reflective listening is enormously powerful. It accomplishes several things: you clarify your proper understanding of what the speaker just said, which helps avoid miscommunications. But you're also doing something more than that: simply by showing someone that you've truly heard what they said, you affirm and validate them. Even if you don't necessarily agree with what a person is saying, reflective listening opens the door to productive dialogue and shared understanding. In that way, it can strengthen relationships and help ease hurt feelings.

Another tremendously powerful form of active listening is **generative listening.** As the name suggests, generative listening wants to learn something new—it seeks to *generate* a new idea that reflects the impact of what you've just heard. You're also generating questions in this type of active listening because you're pursuing deeper understanding.

When you practice generative listening, you begin each conversation by telling yourself: "This person is interesting. I'm going to learn something from them." That attitude will cause you to actually pay attention to what the other person is saying. You're not trying to form a rebuttal; you're not letting your mind wander. Rather than telling yourself, "This person is an idiot," you're tuned in to what they're saying, seeking to better understand why they hold the view that they do.

The thoughts going through a generative listener's mind are characterized by a desire to learn, empathize, and understand:

- *I appreciate this person.*
- *Something good is going to come out of this conversation.*
- *How is this person contributing to me? How can I contribute to them?*
- *What is going on in this person's world?*
- *What am I missing? What can I learn?*
- *What can we create together?*

Remember: In any communication experience, your *thinking* forms your *interpretation*. These sorts of generative listening thoughts lead to an interpretation that invites learning and possibility. Rather than reactive listening, which filters everything through a negatively biased lens, generative listening helps open you up to collaboration and deeper understanding. It *invites* engagement. When people sense your interest and respect in their ideas, they bloom.

It's imperative to practice generative listening in difficult conversations. When emotions ride high, it's easy to slip into reactive listening and seek to force your own agenda, regardless of what others think. It's also easy to move into automatic listening when you're stressed or tired from juggling too many things. Both reflective and generative listening take more effort than any form of ineffective listening. However, through learning and practice, active listening will transform your ability to listen and connect *well*.

We want to encourage you to embrace the platinum rule in your interactions with others on your team. Not the golden rule, mind you—the rule which says to "treat others the way you would like to be treated." Most of us were taught the golden rule from a very young age, but there's a problem with the golden rule: it doesn't encourage you to consider the needs of others. It only asks that you consider your own needs, and then treat people however *you*, in particular, would like to be treated.

Consider, instead, the "platinum rule": As a leader, it is powerful to "do unto others as *they would have done unto them*." Regarding communications, the platinum rule requires that you try to understand the *other* person's needs and address those to be most effective. A key way to do that is through using generative listening to explore better ideas and strengthen your understanding of your employees' experiences. You'll make assumptions—quite possibly, unfair assumptions—if you fail to fill in the knowledge gaps with accurate, effective communication.

> The platinum rule: Do unto others as they would have you do unto them.

In challenging or difficult conversations, you can deliberately take steps to put yourself in a generative listening frame of mind:

1. *Recognize* if you are coming into the conversation with a passive, automatic, or reactive filter.
2. *Choose* to listen with appreciation and respect.
3. *Ask* open-ended questions that will help you learn and better understand; stay curious.
4. *Acknowledge* both your and the other person's feelings and contributions.
5. *Create* a plan for the next steps that create progress.

You can't listen actively all the time—it would be too exhausting.

There are plenty of times when you have to downshift into automatic listening just to save your mental capacity. However, in the conversations where you and colleagues are working through difficult issues, strained relationships, or challenging problems, making a conscious effort to step into a reflective and/or generative listening frame of mind can create the possibilities of breakthroughs in understanding and in your relationships. Begin with intention; get your thoughts in a respectful, open, curious place. Manage whatever distractions have the potential to create barriers between you and the other person. Show the person that you intend to give them your full, undivided attention. If you have baggage with that person, do your best to set that aside in the interest of deeper understanding.

Prepare yourself to ask questions—lots of them. Those questions will start in your own thoughts: *How can I gain insight from this person that I wouldn't otherwise learn? How can their insight help me analyze problems in new ways? How can this dialogue help me tackle ambitious situations, shape strategy, and form vision?* The inward questions should inform the outward questions that you ask the other person, in pursuit of that insight. These sorts of generative questions are necessary in order to have a strong understanding of your organization's identity, culture, climate, and most certainly, your people.

Here's the good news: By putting in the effort to listen generatively, you will lead better. Why? You'll get better information, which means improved planning and fewer mistakes. Your employees will be more motivated and empowered, which means increased engagement. You're far more likely to command the respect of your team, which will help you improve your efficacy across the board. You'll learn more than you ever realized you would, which means you'll make decisions with greater wisdom. The psychological safety and cultural trust of your organization will be strengthened, leading to more effective communication. Ultimately, this can translate to improved performance and results from those you lead.

COMMUNICATION CHALLENGES

Even with trust, respect, and positive regard in place, communication is still a task that can pose plenty of challenges. Just ask any married couple! When the turbulence hits, here are a few strategies to help manage the ride.

THE HARD CONVERSATIONS

When difficult conversations need to happen, the most important thing you can do is get clarity about your desired outcome ahead of time. In other words: determine what you really want to get out of that conversation. What is your goal? What do you want to happen after the conversation ends? What do you want in the quality of your relationships? What does the other party desire? If you don't have clarity on your desired outcomes, you can easily wander down the wrong path as emotions escalate. With that clarity, however, you can manage the conversation towards that end.

We'll say much more about conflict management in Chapter Eleven.

THE BAD IDEAS

Thomas Edison was famous for coming up with world-changing inventions that began as great ideas. One of his less-great ideas? Inventing a ghost catching machine.[34] That one never quite took off.

Particularly if you've achieved the ideal of running an organization with solid trust, there will be plenty of ideas floating around your office. Some of them will probably be great. Some of them will probably be less than great. So how do you support someone's idea even if you don't like it?

Understand that no idea ever became great without dialogue, debate, and rigor. An idea might strike you as overly simplistic or "bad" ini-

---

34   Cole Gamble, "6 Spectacularly Bad Ideas from History's Greatest Geniuses," Cracked.com, March 26, 2010,
      https://www.cracked.com/article_18465_6-spectacularly-bad-ideas-from-historys-greatest-geniuses.html.

tially, but try to look for something to build upon. Just because it strikes you as the wrong answer doesn't mean there aren't elements that are still thoughtful and meaningful. Your voiced affirmation of those qualities will help encourage the open communication you want to foster: "I can see that you have a different point of view than I do. Let's find a way to take your idea and build on it. If we couple it with my idea, how can we make them both better?"

The best thing a leader can do for their teams is to create safety. One of the team norms of high-performing organizations is the capacity to bring new ideas forward without the risk of being condemned or negated. The *safety* of those teams invites new ideas. They may not all be the ones that eventually go forward, but without that kind of creative encouragement, there's never going to be any brilliant ones. If someone voices an idea that you're tempted to write off as worthless, force yourself to search for the small nuggets of worth. "What I like about that idea is..."

Putting down other's ideas will shut people down. Affirming some worth will *open* them up. And who knows? That idea may not make sense at first blush, but if it were to be enhanced or modified, perhaps it could provide the seeds for greatness.

TRULY LISTEN, TRULY SEE, TRULY UNDERSTAND

When you listen well—listen deeply—listen generatively—you have the ability to create something new. Hearing on this level has the capacity to change the nature of your relationship with other human beings. It can even change what you see, and know, and understand.

That's the kind of increased perspective that can come from changing altitude when you devote the energy to truly see.

ACTION STEPS

1. Evaluate your accessibility. What steps could you take to make yourself safer to communicate with as a boss?

2. What communication "norms" (if any) are in place at your organization? If there aren't any, consider gathering your team to establish some, to work in conjunction with the team covenant we discussed in the previous chapter. If you already have some, revisit them and ensure they offer sufficient protection for open, safe communication.

3. Consider the three types of listening we discussed in this chapter. When is it most important to listen generatively? What are some takeaway points that can help you improve your skills as a listener?

4. Do you think your organizational culture promotes the worth and dignity of each person? If not, what steps could you take to change that?

CHAPTER SEVEN

LEADING CHANGE AND EXERTING INFLUENCE

HOW TO EFFECTIVELY MOVE YOUR PEOPLE

"Keep the end in mind."
—STEPHEN COVEY, *THE 7 HABITS OF HIGHLY EFFECTIVE PEOPLE*

WHY DON'T THEY JUST DO WHAT I SAY?

He'd had enough. Paul Johnson marched into the CEO's office and pointed to his badge. "What does this say?" he asked.

The CEO looked at the badge. "It says Vice President of Finance."

"That's right!" Paul said angrily. "That means my team should listen to me."

Unfortunately for Paul Johnson, they weren't listening. Up to that point, he had enjoyed a successful career. He'd been promoted upwards as an accountant until he owned his own firm. He'd gotten used to being in charge, functioning as both the CEO and CFO. However, when he sold his private firm and merged with a larger corporate organization, he started to lose his footing.

His new organization gave him a full-time finance role while also making him the Vice President of Finance. That put him in the unique position of functioning as both a practicing accountant and an administrator. He was chosen for that position because he had a history of building relationships among his team, but he lost sight of the big picture in this new role. Instead of investing in his staff, he got distracted by administrative work—writing contracts, making schedules, and so on—tasks that he could have delegated to someone else. As a result, he claimed to never have time to do the more important aspects of his job—including building relationships among his colleagues and staff.

Rather than utilizing a variety of influence strategies, Paul tried to rely solely on the power attached to his title. It didn't work. His team didn't feel appreciated and didn't respect his method of leadership. As a result, Paul's impressive badge didn't hold much weight with them.

On the day that Paul stormed into his CEO's office, he let loose a diatribe that had accumulated over months of stress. He announced that he was done. He complained that no one respected him or listened to him. Then he went further: he claimed he didn't believe in the direction of the organization and didn't think it was right; he complained about the lack of transparency—and on, and on. Finally, he announced he was quitting.

The speech was a bridge burner. It alienated him from his boss and the entire organization. When he changed his mind a week later and asked for his job back, he was politely declined. The organization informed him they were going to process his severance, and left him with a parting thought: they informed him that he still had thirty-three months remaining on his contract and they could hand him the bill owed for the financial detriment caused by breaking his contract.

Paul Johnson struggled in several ways—and his struggle is not uncommon. Besides failing to build trust and respect, he critically underestimated the importance of building influence.

THE DEFINITION OF LEADERSHIP

Leading requires more than wielding a job title. Leadership is the process of influencing human behavior to accomplish the goals and outcomes of the organization.

Essentially, effective leaders get people to *go with them* to achieve outcomes. This is true for any size organization—a team, a department, an entire company, and so on. As you change altitude and move from direct leadership to indirect leadership, the challenges become more complex. The scope, the breadth, the depth, and the ambiguity of your purview all expand exponentially. You're no longer asking people to take a simple path from point A to point B; now, you're juggling points from A to Z. The paths may need to move in a variety of directions, the times may need to be staggered, and the priorities may need to shift. You need your people to completely trust your leadership when directing their next move. Because of this, the ability to influence others becomes even more critical.

> Leadership is the process of influencing human behavior to accomplish the goals and outcomes of the organization.

The fact that you've changed altitude into this new role means your responsibilities have likely gotten infinitely more complex. It works well to function like a hammer when everything you're facing is a nail. But when the projects get more complicated, you need to start accessing a greater variety of tools; you need a fundamentally different skill set. You can't simply repeat what made you successful before. You need to produce more complex conceptual skills—a clearly communicated vision, setting the climate and culture, leading change with agility, ensuring organizational alignment. If you want to do that, you need people to *want* to align with you. You need people to *willingly* follow you.

So how do you effectively lead change and influence others? In this chapter, we're going to outline a process to help you effectively lead change and then identify a number of influence strategies to ensure your people *want* to pursue that change with you. Having more influence strategies at your disposal provides you with the essential tools to engage the complexity of the world you're in now.

LEADING CHANGE

Winston Churchill was faced with many near-impossible tasks in his leadership as prime minister of England during World War II. Not only did he need to figure out how to quadruple his country's aircraft production to counter Hitler's air forces, but he also had to convince the US President Franklin Roosevelt to throw America's military might behind the allied forces, in spite of the US's strong preference to not get involved. He had to ask the people of his own country to make countless sacrifices and convince them that those sacrifices were worth it. He even decided to act as his country's war minister so that he could exert even greater personal influence in the areas most critical to the war.

Churchill first identified the changes that had to be made. Then he had to exert influence in countless ways in complex contexts to bring that change about. He did that by using an incredible repertoire of influence strategies. At times, he inspired. At times, he cajoled. At times, he threatened. And in every communication, Churchill maintained a clear purpose, direction, and motivation. Their purpose: Beat the Nazis. Their direction: Quadruple production, join the Allied Forces, and make every necessary sacrifice. Their motivation: If we don't, our world will be overcome by the "axis of evil."

Purpose, direction, and motivation are the three lynchpins of effectively leading change and exerting influence. Those three points are key if you want your staff to follow you anywhere because they identify the *target* of where you want to collectively aim. Leaders need to ensure that their staff is clear on their top priorities and that they have the resources they need to accomplish their goals. That's the first requirement in leading change.

If you want your staff to follow you anywhere, you need to provide them with three key prerequisites: purpose, direction, and motivation.

As you lead in your new role, you're likely to identify compelling needs for change—in fact, that's a key responsibility for any leader. Perhaps you can see that the current interface your company uses is cumbersome and a time suck. You can see a need for change there, but that will require time, training, an investment in a new system, and everyone's commitment to making the change. Or, perhaps you can see that a particular department has a bloated staff, while other departments are stretched too thin. You need to make a change, but people probably aren't going to like it.

You've done one great thing as a leader: you've identified a compelling need for change. Your second goal is to figure out *how* to make that change. You can do that by taking your cues from Churchill: provide your people with *purpose, direction, and motivation.*

And how do you do that? We've developed a Comprehensive Change Model, which spells out precisely what you need to do to provide those three key prerequisites. Once you've thought through these steps, then you'll be ready to employ strategies for influence to get your people to follow you towards the change you want.

THE COMPREHENSIVE CHANGE MODEL

Effective leadership requires a Comprehensive Change Model that can proactively manage organizational change. Your goal is to create the greatest amount of buy-in so that your people embrace the change rather than fight it. The following five steps will help ensure that you provide your people with a clear plan for the change you want so that they have the confidence to move towards it.

1. **Destination**: Ensure that people know where they're going. If you want people to feel secure leaving a familiar system to transition to a new one, they need clarity about the destination and reassurance that there's a plan in place to get there. Explain clearly what that destination will be, so they feel confident about where you want to take them.

2. **Motivation**: Give your people a clear reason to get from Point A to Point B; help your people understand why the status quo is no longer sustainable. In doing so, you're providing them with "the big why" to take action. You're creating dissatisfaction with the current state so that they feel a desire to go somewhere else. Any effective change management starts with helping people understand the compelling need for change. Point out why the current system is not working—the pain that the staff, the organization, or both are experiencing because of it. In doing so, you're helping people identify the need for change, which will give them the needed motivation to move away from the old system.

3. **Inspiration**: Once people have the motivation to depart from the status quo, inspire them with a dream of where to go. Motivation is a push; inspiration is a pull. Paint the picture of how much better life could be with the new change in place—and then keep that inspirational messaging throughout the journey towards that successful end state. Inspiration will require sustained effort on your part to constantly inject enthusiasm and positive emotion into your team during the hard work of change. Remind them often of the vision for a better tomorrow.

4. **Navigation**: Create a map of how to get there. Identify where you're currently at, where you want to go, and the gaps between the two points. Assess those gaps and provide a plan for getting from here to there. How will you shift your priorities, if necessary? What tangible steps will be taken to fill each gap? This is the "how."

5. **Activation:** Provide your team with a clear plan of action. If at all possible, get them involved in developing the clear plan of action so that they increase their buy-in to the plans. Assign each step a date for completion to clarify timing. Identify the resources required to achieve the next step, and provide those resources. Make sure each team member understands their priorities and how to achieve them. This is the "what."

LEADING UP: HELPING YOUR BOSS EMBRACE CHANGE

Greg Hiebert narrates

Change is inevitable. It's even written in our DNA and the laws of physics—the second law of thermodynamics notes that everything is in some state of change. Still, change is hard! People often prefer the status quo, even if it's not working well because it provides for certainty which most of us crave. Great leaders know that if you don't intentionally manage and lead change, it will lead and manage you.

One way to successfully lead change is to enroll as many of those affected by the change to buy into the change. Although you'll implement the Comprehensive Change Model most thoroughly with your subordinates, you'll also need to ensure that other managers, your boss(es), and even your clients understand that there's a reason for everyone to buy into the change and that the status quo is no longer sustainable.

This is important. The most effective leaders create confidence not only in those they lead, but also in those they follow. If you can prove your reliability and competence with your boss, they'll give you greater autonomy to do your job. You're also more likely to continue to advance. It's a strange fact in organizations that people usually aren't promoted for their leadership, but for their "followership"— how well they follow their boss and help them achieve success.

> *If you don't intentionally manage and lead*
> *change, it will lead and manage you.*

Early in my career, I remember being in a position where I recognized a compelling need for change but needed to get my boss on board—not only for his vocal support but, more critically, to get funding. One of my additional duty assignments as a young infantry officer was to run a large dining facility at an installation level in northern Italy. I was a company executive officer and was additionally responsible for overseeing eighty workers in the dining facility and the feeding of over three thousand military personnel three meals a day.

I had my work cut out for me. The facility was losing money. There were all sorts of disciplinary problems. Morale was critically low. My boss felt pressure from senior leadership to make the place perform better, but he had his own extensive challenges to focus on. Somehow, I had to figure out a way to turn things around.

I noticed that the dining facility staff had periods of time in midmorning and mid-afternoon when they were off. The time was supposed to be used for growth and development, but no resources were being offered for that development, nor were subordinate leaders thoughtful enough to focus on it. I decided to build relational capital with my people by showing them the organization wanted to invest in them. I reached out to a central Michigan college that had a history of offering courses at military posts around the world. Offering undergraduate courses to everyone at the facility would require our organization to invest a considerable amount of money. Fortunately, I persuaded my boss that the program would increase morale, engagement, and ultimately performance. In the end, I pointed out, the investment could help us stop losing money.

My boss was convinced and made the appeal to the higher-ups. We received the funding we needed, and it was unbelievably success-ful. The moral of the story: "Lead up" by showing your boss that your goals align with their own, that you understand where they're coming from, and that you have a solid plan to achieve a successful outcome. By going through the Comprehensive Change Model with your boss in mind, you'll effectively communicate the information that your boss will need to embrace change.

But that's not all you can do to help your boss get on board. The Comprehensive Change Model will help you *begin* the process of leading change. However, if you really want to hit a home run in this area, you need to also secure buy-in from everyone, using the power of influence.

INFLUENCING OTHERS

Paul Johnson was frustrated at his lack of influence. He had power, didn't he? He had an executive title—so why wouldn't people respond to his power and listen to him? Something critical for any leader to understand is that there's a difference between power and influence.

Power can be overt—like in the case of a job title—or covert, like the power wielded by a bully. Power can be seen or unseen, real or imagined. Power is also restricted to context. A person may be powerful in one venue, but may become completely powerless in another. For that reason, power—even great power—is limited. It only goes as far as the greater "powers that be" allow.

Influence, on the other hand, is reflected in what gets done or doesn't get done. A person can have comparatively little power but enor-mous influence. Consider figures like Mother Theresa, for instance, Dr. Martin Luther King, Jr., or even Nelson Mandela, writing from his prison cell. None of those people were in positions of great power initially, but they wielded enormous influence in shaping people's behavior.

On the other hand, a person can wield substantial power within an organization but enjoy very little respect or influence. An order from that leader may be followed, but likely with skepticism, reluctance, and even resentment.

What does this mean for you? It means that, even as your job title increases in distinction, you need to improve your ability to influence others. You need to get them to *want* to go with you.

EIGHT STRATEGIES FOR INFLUENCE

As you seek to influence your subordinates so that they accomplish the goals and priorities you've set forth, we recommend you call upon a variety of strategies to maximize your influence. There are many strategies that can be used as positive effect by themselves, or in combination. However, there's one strategy worth mentioning that would be best to avoid.

Ironically, one of the most common strategies that frustrated leaders reach for first is the *coercive strategy*. When attempting to influence others using coercion, you're using your power in combination with a threat: "Do this because I'm telling you to do it, and if you don't do it, you're going to lose your job." It's often characterized by pressure or demands: figuratively, you've got your thumb on the person's chest. Leaders solely relying on the coercive strategy don't attempt to give their subordinates any reason to do something different, other than the threat of negative consequences if they don't comply.

Here's why this doesn't often work well: Coercive influence may get short-term results but could cause long-term damage to your organization. Your staff might give you an immediate response, but they won't feel any ownership over the task. There's no enhanced motivation to serve the goals of the organization—there's only the desire to avoid pain. Your staff might do what you want when somebody is looking, but they won't be aligned with you when your back is turned.

Leadership is about enabling people to make effective decisions in the absence of your guidance. Coercive influence doesn't offer any guidance—only threats.

Coercive influence may be appropriate to use in the rare instances when you need quick results, and there's no other way to get them. However, this kind of influence comes at the cost of providing your staff with an understanding of the purpose and motivation behind what you're trying to accomplish. Coercion can easily erode trust, demoralize your team, lead to high turnover rates, and create a toxic environment that impedes productivity.

> Coercive influence doesn't offer any guidance—only threats.

Although times of high stress can prompt leaders to lean on coercion as their chief tool for influence, we don't recommend it. There are better ways to lead your organization forward. Here are eight common strategies for influence that can be effective in a wide range of scenarios.

1. INSPIRATIONAL APPEAL

Greg Hiebert narrates

The strategy of inspirational appeal is one of the least used because it requires the capacity to tap into the emotions of the people you're trying to influence. That takes work, a willingness to listen, and empathy. However, when done well, inspirational appeal can secure some of the highest levels of commitment and buy-in.

Why is an inspirational appeal so powerful? The book *Switch*, by

Chip and Dan Heath, explains why, using an amusing analogy that illustrates how our brain works.[35] Imagine that there are two essential parts of our brain: there's the powerful, emotional brain which is akin to an elephant. Then, there's the thinking brain, which is limited in its power but cognitively important—you can think of it as the small driver sitting on top of the elephant. Inspiration accesses the emotional part of our brain, which carries the greatest sway over our actions. The inspirational appeal is a way to get that powerful emotional brain charging forward in the direction you want—and if the driver can get the emotional elephant moving down the right path, it can be unstoppable. When using the inspirational appeal, you are seeking to align your people's emotional energy with a cognitive focus that you supply.

Here's an example. I have a memory from my time at Harvard Business School when I was put in charge of directing an original musical called "Les Biz"—a spoof on *Les Mis*. It was brilliantly written but was incredibly ambitious as we had a cast and crew of approximately sixty-five, along with twelve original musical numbers to perform and perfect. Initially, the participants did not show the level of commitment required to produce a successful show. People were coming late, they weren't learning their lines, and getting the musical numbers prepared seemed like an impossibility. We called a meeting of all to address the issues. My other leaders and I could have used coercive power, but it didn't seem like the right tool—these were our classmates. My other leaders and I decided the best influence strategy would be the inspirational appeal.

I told the cast, "Picture opening night. Picture when the curtain comes down after the last scene in the show, and picture the audience jumping to their feet and giving us a two-and-a-half-minute standing ovation." Up until that point, most of the students had serious doubts that Harvard Business School students could—in their spare time— put together anything that was genuinely moving and entertaining

---

35 Chip Heath and Dan Heath, *Switch: How to Change Things When Change Is Hard* (New York: Penguin Random House, 2010).

and funny. Because we had extraordinary writers, we all knew that we could do something spectacular, but only if we were willing to truly commit the time, energy, and as much discretionary effort as possible.

The vision caught on, and it changed everyone's motivation. The cognitive goal of putting on this performance was suddenly fueled by everyone's wholehearted emotional energies, and the work transformed. It was probably one of the most powerful influence tools I've ever observed and been part of.

In order to do the inspirational appeal well, you need to practice enough empathy to consider what matters to the people you're trying to influence. You're trying to identify the unmet needs of those you're leading and figure out a way to tap into that. If you *can* tap into those needs—people will go with you a long way.

Consider: What would these people feel passionate about, beyond just more money or a new title? What energizes them? How can you put together both *intrinsic* and *extrinsic* motivators to give people a strong desire to achieve? Or, to put it differently: What message will appeal to both the driver and the elephant so that you get powerful forward momentum in the direction you want?

2. PERSONAL APPEAL

"It would mean the world to me if you could support this initiative."

"Would you be willing to step up into this new role? I'm asking as a personal favor."

"Can I ask you a question? I could really use your help."

These are the sorts of phrases that would characterize a personal appeal. You're seeking to influence another person by explaining that this matters to you, personally. If you want to influence others through a personal appeal, you need relational capital.

We used to work with a gentleman on one of our client teams named Hector. While Hector was working with a large retail chain, one of his colleagues gave him a great compliment. She said, "Hector, it's like you see each of us as a piggy bank. You're constantly making deposits of affirmation, deposits of support, and deposits of goodwill. Then, when you have to make a personal appeal, you've got so much credit in there that it's easy for you to take a deposit out." Through all of Hector's relational "deposits" in his staff, he had the capital he needed to make any personal appeal extremely compelling.

That relational capital is required for the personal appeal tool to have substance and power underneath. You've got to genuinely invest in people's lives so that when you do ask a staff member to take on a new challenge, that person is ready to go ahead. You've got to be there for them so they will be there for you; that's how the personal appeal works.

But can a personal appeal translate more broadly across an organization and not just between individuals? You can leverage the relational capital needed for a personal appeal by establishing a respected reputation. If your employees respect you—if they know that you are a person of integrity and that you are effective in pursuing the vision of the organization—they will be ready to take you at your word when you make a personal appeal for the good of an organization.

Dennis O'Neil narrates

One of the doctors I consult with at a hospital made this kind of personal appeal at the start of the COVID-19 pandemic. The urgency and resources required by the COVID-19 pandemic had obviously upended business-as-usual for the hospital. Dr. Ketil went around to each one of the hospital department heads and made her appeal. She said, "Okay, here's what you have traditionally done within the organization. However, here are our *immediate* needs. Would you be willing to help out in some new ways to help serve the pressing needs of our community right now?" Anesthesiologists who had been doing routine surgeries agreed to help out in critical care units. Orthopedic surgeons stepped away from dealing with knees and stepped into other areas badly in need of support.

Dr. Ketil appealed to her department heads' values, exhorting them to do something greater on behalf of the community. She knew them well enough to understand that they were all there to do something greater—to fundamentally improve the lives of their patients and, in this case, to keep them alive. Her staff respected her and trusted her. As a leader, she had the reputation of living consistently according to her values. As a result, when she made a personal appeal to them to use their skill sets in a different way, they were willing to follow.

3. AUTHORITATIVE INFLUENCE

When Paul Johnson pointed to the title on his name tag, he was trying to use the strategy of authoritative influence. This strategy is fairly cut and dry: you try to influence your subordinates by referencing your authority, i.e., "I am your superior, and I'm giving you an order, so get it done." This strategy wields its influence by appealing to the authority of rank and the capacity you have to yield power through that rank.

In certain contexts, like the military, rank is a compelling influence, and the authoritative influence strategy can often stand alone. However, you won't get people's genuine buy-in with this strategy alone—as Paul Johnson painfully experienced. You'll get the most lasting results and the best performance out of your employees if the authoritative influence is used in conjunction with several other strategies.

4. MAKING LEGITIMATE

The "making legitimate" strategy bases its authority on any source that is widely agreed to be legitimate. This might be a written policy, law, or procedure—such as an operating manual or a company culture code. You could recognize this strategy at play if your legal counsel were to say something like, "These are the standard operating procedures, so I want you to do it according to the written standards." Or, perhaps, "The law dictates we do it this way, so that's how I need you to do it."

A person can also be a source of legitimacy. For instance, if you've brought in an expert consultant to work with your organization, you might ask your employees to act on the consultant's recommendations, simply because the consultant has legitimate expertise. When people responded to Dr. Anthony Fauci's advice during the COVID-19 pandemic, they were accepting him as the source for legitimate information. This source of legitimacy could also be a book written by experts, a newly issued law, HR procedures, a highly respected coach, and so on.

Rather than appealing to someone's value system or using your own relational capital to secure people's buy-in, the "making legitimate" strategy appeals to a set precedent of requirements. It's rational persuasion, based on logical arguments, factual evidence, historical traditions, cultural practices, a person's accepted expertise, and/or written norms—in essence, the practices which everyone in the organization agrees are legitimate.

The "making legitimate" strategy works well for getting minimal compliance—but not wholehearted buy-in. People are not generally inspired by contractual formalities or the "letter of the law." Even if the source of legitimacy is a compelling person, their recommendations may not be taken wholesale if a person feels skeptical of their advice. As a result, you might find that people "toe the line" officially, but take advantage of loopholes where they can.

There can also be confusion about the specifics in how written standards are interpreted. I can remember when I was in Mosul, Iraq, in 2009 and the coalition forces had just signed the State of Forces Agreement with Iraq. Unfortunately, although the agreement had been clearly written up, our two sides interpreted some of the standards quite differently. One standard, for instance, said that the American forces would not operate unilaterally in cities. That seemed straightforward. We agreed that—in cities—we would operate with Iraqi support. However, then we realized that the Iraqi government had a narrower definition of "unilateral" and "cities" than we did. They didn't want to see an American vehicle on the streets in *any* place where there were Iraqi people, unless the Iraqi army was also involved. The US forces pushed back, saying that the wording was open to interpretation. Running a logistics convoy, for instance, or moving through a city to get to our military bases should not, in our opinion, fall under the standard. The process of working out the details was a challenge and often created logistical headaches.

And so it goes in the workplace. The "making legitimate" strategy will get you some traction and can provide helpful standards for accountability. However, its reach is limited. If you want full employee engagement and buy-in to your organization's vision, the "making legitimate" strategy would be best combined with several others.

5. TRANSACTIONAL EXCHANGE

This influence strategy is one of the oldest in the book. It's based on reward power: if an employee performs at the level you want them to perform or higher, they're rewarded for it. A boss might say, "If you pull off this presentation at our international conference, you'll get a promotion." Essentially, it's a quid pro quo—and it's an entirely appropriate strategy for influence.

Some form of this strategy is almost ubiquitous in the workplace, and it happens all the time. For instance, employees are given a salary but told that they need to do extra if they want to earn a bonus. The transactional exchange strategy is a practical way to increase desired behaviors in your employees: "Do more of this desired behavior, and receive a reward."

This strategy can be a powerful motivator for your employees. However, when used by itself, it won't likely secure their loyalty. If a competitor offers them a more significant reward—a higher paycheck, better benefits, a work environment that's more conducive to their lifestyle—they may take their work elsewhere.

6. INGRATIATION

Greg Hiebert narrates

The ingratiation strategy involves ego. You try to stroke someone else's ego before asking them to do something so that they feel inclined to say yes. Essentially, you butter someone up. This can be used disingenuously to manipulate, but it can also be used in a meaningful and positive way.

I'll share a "proud dad" story to illustrate. My daughter, Molly, works at a company that used to have a Wednesday happy hour gathering. Starting around 4:30 p.m., they'd serve drinks and hors d'oeuvres and collectively "pool" their learnings, insight, and wisdom with each other. They called it the Pool Party, but there was no swimming involved—just the sharing of ideas and new learning.

One week, Molly shared a reflection she'd had about a quote I often shared with her by Victor Frankl, author of *Man's Search for Meaning*: "Between stimulus and response, there is a space. In that space is our power to choose our response. In our response lies our growth and our freedom."[36] She told her teammates about an equation I'd come up with to illustrate that concept: where "E" is an event (the stimulus that affects you), and "R" is the reaction you respond with, and "O" is the outcome you get based upon your reaction: E + R = O. The "O," outcome, may be good or bad, depending on whether someone reacts to the event in an effective or ineffective way.

Molly also shared, "After the event happens, we should think about the most optimal outcome we want for our organization. Then, based on the outcome we want, we form a response. So the more strategic equation is E + O = R."

Later, her boss sent her an email with the subject line: "A + O = Molly." In the email, he wrote:

A = awesome

O = outstanding

Molly, you are extraordinary. I am going to borrow that equation from you, if you don't mind.

This email was a beautiful example of how a superior can use the ingratiation strategy in a wholly positive way. The fact that her boss took the time to acknowledge, affirm, and promote her ideas was incredibly meaningful to Molly. She felt that much more inclined to perform at her best, offer up her creative ideas, and seek to problem solve. Her boss's genuine appreciation also made her want to support his goals for the organization and work towards his vision. Molly was so proud of that note that she even sent it on to me, which I'm sure she regrets now because I'm constantly telling other people about it.

---

36 Viktor Emil Frankl, *Man's Search for Meaning: An Introduction to Logotherapy* (New York: Houghton Mifflin Harcourt, 2000).

Similar to the personal appeal, the ingratiation strategy can be a way to build up powerful relational capital. That capital, in turn, can help you influence your employees to align their efforts with your goals and priorities.

7. COALITION

Imagine a teacher standing at the front of a classroom, holding up a test key. He says, "I know that some of you were looking at these answers when you took the test. I'm asking those students to please see me privately after class and turn themselves in." He pauses, and then turns up the heat. "Otherwise, *the whole class* will fail the test."

This, essentially, is the coalition influence strategy. You're using the power of an entire coalition to influence a person's behavior: the *whole class* will fail the test if the guilty students don't fess up. When you express a desire for a certain behavior, you're bringing the whole weight of the coalition into your ability to influence.

Often, within a coalition, you have different stakeholders with varying degrees of power and influence. Those various degrees of power can amplify the influential weight of the alliance. For instance, when Israel was trying to build its clout by getting other nations to recognize it as a state, they appealed to those nations using the coalition strategy. When they went to Sudan, they pointed to the United States, which had just recognized their statehood. With such an influential stakeholder as the United States in Israel's coalition, Sudan was quickly persuaded to follow suit and issue their own recognition of Israel's statehood.

As with many of the other strategies, the coalition strategy has the potential to be used in a negative way. Any teenager who has fallen victim to the peer pressure line "Everyone's doing it" has experienced the negative power of the coalition strategy. However, when used well, it can help create a sense of shared ownership among employees. It can build unity, trust, and accountability. When a boss helps their teams recognize that everyone's work impacts the organization as a whole, they not only influence their employees towards a common goal, but they also help their employees recognize that their work is meaningful. That's powerful.

8. CONSULTATION

In the consultation strategy, you're *consulting* with your subordinates to secure their buy-in. This collaborative process helps build their commitment. Keep in mind: you're doing this strategically to still promote your agenda. When approaching the consultation, you are bringing to bear your proven experience, expertise, appropriate thoughtfulness, and thoroughness of your recommendations. You'll present your strategy in a compelling and meaningful way but in a forum that still allows other people to share their ideas and feedback. You give people the capacity to say no, but by putting your argument persuasively, you're moving them in a direction where they're more likely to nod their heads and say, "Yes, that makes sense. I can get behind that."

This strategy poses an obvious risk—your people might actually say no, if you give them the opportunity. However, when people are *denied* a chance to say yes or no, such as with the coercion strategy, they may fake compliance. The consultation strategy, on the other hand, allows people the opportunity to *choose* to comply, which heightens their genuine commitment. Remember that, in using the consultation strategy, you have expertise that others may not have. If you put your arguments persuasively, listen well, and thoughtfully dialogue with others, you're very likely to elicit their positive response. If they do, their buy-in will be genuine.

This strategy can also help promote trust in your own organization. When you seek your employees' assistance and input, your employees will feel like they have ownership over an idea. You also get the benefit of other minds helping to refine your idea. You'll have a better understanding of what your idea looks like from the "ground, up," not just the "top, down."

This strategy is a favorite of ours. On calls with senior leaders, we often begin by consulting with them. We ask, "Okay, what's going on? What's important to you? What would be most helpful?" This gets the leader engaged in the process and gives them the opportunity to feel heard and respected. Inevitably, our dialogue will lead us to render recommendations for that leader: "Here are three things we recommend we work on with you in our first session together." We may have come to the meeting with those recommendations already formed if we've been supplied with data ahead of time. However, if we were to have *started* with those recommendations, the leader may not have felt like we'd really heard or valued their needs. But in mutually developing a plan, through a consultative way, we now all feel ownership towards the quality of the product. As a bonus, that leader now wants us to succeed in our consulting work because they feel their needs have been understood. If and when we need to push on that leader to make some difficult changes, we have the benefit of their trust and buy-in.

HOW DO YOU KNOW WHICH STRATEGY TO USE?

Inspire or transactional exchange? Coalition or personal appeal? How do you know which strategy to use?

When trying to determine which strategy (or strategies) to use, remember Molly's equation: keep your desired *outcome* in mind, and let it determine your *response*. This is a time to not only gain in your altitude, but also your distance. You want to take a bird's eye view of your situation, your organization's needs and—this is critical—the needs of your people. If you want people to respond to your leadership, it's crucial to seek to align the needs of the organization with the needs of your people so that they see the importance of the work you're asking them to do.

WE CHOOSE HOW WE RESPOND

Normal Response

A More Thoughtful Response

All of this requires that you take the time necessary to thoughtfully form a strategy. Get out of the "fight or flight" reptilian brain. Urgent work circumstances can easily take you to that place of reactivity, but then you will have lost control of your targeted outcome. Instead, take a deliberate pause between the stimulus and the response. Put the brakes on your brain, so you can shift to thinking with your "upper brain," the prefrontal cortex. Think about where you want your people to go and the best way for you to motivate them to go there.

By slowing down and deliberately considering your desired outcome, you'll have the capacity to make better choices. And the better the choices you make as a leader, the more credibility and respect you'll earn from your people. Ultimately, that's the currency that will get people to follow you. As they see you make good decisions, they'll build confidence in your leadership and are far more likely to respond to your influence. This "informal" power—your interpersonal capacity—will ultimately be a much greater force of influence than the formal power reflected in your job title.

Once you've envisioned a better future with the Comprehensive Change Model and identified your desired outcome, consider what influence strategies will be best to use. Which strategies are available, given your resources and limitations? Try to stay as positive in your strategies as possible so that your employees can see the possibilities of where you want to take them. Then, form a plan based on your needs, resources, and long-term goals.

If you need basic compliance, you might want to use the "making legitimate" strategy, drawing upon some law or other legitimate authority for influence. Inform your employees of the evidence, the law, the regulation, or the dictates of the policy: "We don't have a choice about following this, so here is what we need to do." If your employees don't like the policy, invite them to be thoughtful about how your team or organization could advocate for change. For basic compliance, other strategies like authoritative influence, transactional exchange, or the coalition approach may also be appropriate.

If you want deeper commitment, you need to go further. The strategies that are most likely to secure your employees' genuine buy-in will require more effort on your part. These are the strategies like the inspirational appeal, where you get your employees excited about where you want to go; personal appeal or ingratiation, where you've invested time into building relational capital; and finally, the consultation strategy, when you take the time to listen, consult, and mutually form goals with your employees. In all these strategies, you're inviting your employees to consider the outcome in a way that will influence their choices. By ensuring people understand the intent behind your desired outcome, they're empowered to figure out the most effective way to get there—and they'll be genuinely motivated to work for that. We're going to discuss this topic of empowering your employees in much greater length in our next chapter.

Remember: The definition of leadership is to influence human behavior to accomplish the goals of the organization. There are two major players in that definition: the goals of the organization, and the *humans*. The two of us were brought up under the teaching of great military leaders who taught us the mantra: "Mission first; soldiers always." The broader interpretation of that mantra would be "mission first; people always." When leading our people, we were constantly working to accomplish our mission but also making sure we were doing everything we could to promote and safeguard their wellbeing and success.

Mission first; people always.

As a leader, you're juggling those same two priorities. The mission comes first, but your people are also *always* a priority. If you can find that sweet spot between fulfilling the needs of your people, along with accomplishing the aims of your organization, that's a win for everyone. It's a win for the organization, a win for the people you lead, and a win for you. Consider: What strategies will help you find that sweet spot?

CHANGE BY CHANGING ALTITUDE

In all the years that we've taught organizational change, there are times when clients take a brief pause from the intensity of the business to do a day of team development. We'll ask the client to give us examples of where they've seen successful and unsuccessful change. Their answers vary. For instance:

"When we switched over to that new system, everyone complained constantly. What a nightmare."

"Yes, but remember when we moved Darrell into the executive role? People were so relieved to work for him instead of Rob. The whole atmosphere changed."

We'll then ask, "Based upon what you've observed, what might be some of the key principles that are necessary to drive successful change in your organization?" Or, put differently, "What principles, if they weren't in place, would lead to an unsuccessful change process?"

Without fail, when clients rise in altitude to consider these questions from a greater height, we see them become incredibly thoughtful and intentional about how to manage effective change. They start to articulate a thoughtful, step-by-step process of the key elements that need to be paid attention to. They start to feel the urgency of that needed change and can identify the reasons why their people should be dissatisfied about where they're at. By stepping back, leaders are able to think more intentionally about the steps they need to take to lead positive, thoughtful change.

This "pause" will also give you the opportunity to identify what strategies of influence will be most compelling for your people, and most needed for your organization. Rather than using a reactive strategy for influence that could ultimately produce negative results, like coercion, you have the time to consider how to implement a more lasting strategy of influence, like the inspirational appeal or the consultation strategy.

Change by changing altitude. Then you'll have the clarity you need to lead your people forward with their commitment and buy-in.

ACTION STEPS

1. Identify an area (or areas) where you can see a compelling need for change.
2. Go through the Comprehensive Change Model and write down some notes in response to each step.
3. Consider your boss(es). What strategies for influence are most likely to secure the trust and buy-in of your leadership?
4. Consider the people on your team. What can you identify as their values, sources of passion, and chief motivating factors? You might have different answers for different people.
5. Taking into account the level of commitment you need from your people, identify several influence strategies that are most likely to secure their commitment and buy-in.

CHAPTER EIGHT

EMPOWERING OTHERS

HOW TO BRING OUT THE BEST IN YOUR EMPLOYEES

"At the end of the day it's not about what we have accomplished...it's about who you've lifted up, who you've made better."

—DENZEL WASHINGTON

THE PROBLEM WITH BEING GOOD AT EVERYTHING

Shannon was exceptionally talented. In fact, that was part of the problem. She got promoted because she was so capable in her previous role—she could do everyone's job well. Unfortunately, once promoted, she *continued* to do everyone's job. Only rarely would she attempt to delegate tasks to her subordinates. When she did, she would second-guess their work, criticize their every move, and micromanage them. Her employees got used to hearing, "You didn't do it right. That's not the way I would do it."

Shannon began to feel exhausted—mentally, physically, emotionally—by the effort of attempting to fulfill the responsibilities of her new job, while also managing employees that seemed incapable and unmotivated. Meanwhile, her employees were also suffering. Shannon's management style made them feel reigned in, distrusted, and devalued. Their lack of motivation was primarily grounded in their belief that nothing they did would ever be good enough for their boss.

When the COVID-19 crisis arrived, everything got worse. The stress and urgency of making organizational changes compounded everyone's emotional and psychological fatigue. Shannon doubled down on the management strategies that felt most comfortable and familiar to her—i.e., doing everyone else's job even *harder*—and the employees' low morale sank even lower. In one of the shakiest economies since the Great Depression, the organization struggled to survive. Shannon constantly complained to her employees that the organization's failures were their fault. "You're not moving fast enough! You're not working hard enough!"

Actually, in situations like these, it's the leader who needs to look in the mirror. The problems that plagued Shannon's organization would be resolved mainly by her effectively *empowering* her employees. By shifting her management style to one that inspired, encouraged, and guided, she would see her employees' motivation increase. By increasing relational trust, she'd see their creativity awaken. By allowing for their autonomy, she'd see an increase in their ownership and buy-in. These are the characteristics of organizations that thrive!

One of the most important qualities of an effective leader is knowing how to empower the people who work for you. This might seem like an obvious point, but leaders are often reluctant to do it—the logistics of doing so might seem challenging or even threaten their ego. But once leaders *do* learn to effectively empower their teams, they'll experience a wealth of rewards in their organization. These rewards—especially when compared to the consequences that come with a *failure* to empower—are worth every bit of effort required.

WHY IS EMPOWERING OTHERS SO CHALLENGING?

Human beings like certainty. We like predictability. In fact, our brains are wired to seek out both. In any given person's workday, the path of least resistance is to keep doing what you've always done.

Let's imagine how this tendency plays out in the scenario when you've recently been promoted. You experience a gravitational pull to go back to what gave you a sense of accomplishment in your prior role—the very tasks that got you promoted. Unfortunately, those tasks should no longer be your priority—they're the job of the people you now supervise. We love that point made in the title of the book by Marshall Goldsmith, *What Got You Here Won't Get You There*.[37] Although it's comfortable to keep completing the same tasks that got you promoted, when you continue to do so, you rob your subordinates of a chance to grow into their roles. You also prevent yourself from developing the new skills you need in *your* role.

Ego gets involved too. Throughout your career, you've likely been rewarded when you answer people's questions correctly. You've probably developed a few tried-and-true methods that brought you success in your previous roles. When a new opportunity or task arises, you might prefer to remain in whatever area makes you feel like an expert.

But, as we've discussed elsewhere in this book, when you change altitude, you need to *develop new skills*. When you assume that you're correct, simply because you're used to being correct, you're actually operating blind. You might feel a built-in resistance to shifting gears when policies change, or the requirements for your role shift, or your organization requires a different tactic. You don't want to try something new—what if you look like a fool? The desire to *look* competent, ironically, can prevent you from gaining the new skills you need to truly *be* competent.

As a leader, part of your new role now requires that you empower others. You need to step away from tasks that you're good at doing

---

37   Marshall Goldsmith and Shane Clester, *What Got You Here Won't Get You There* (London: Profile, 2012).

and empower others to do them well. You need to allow your employees to wield real ownership over their responsibilities—even when that means allowing them to use different methods than you would use. You need to empower them to do more, so that you can do less, so that you can do more of what you *need* to do, now.

THE CONSEQUENCES OF FAILING TO EMPOWER

What if you don't learn to delegate responsibility to your staff? Is it really so bad to keep doing the things you've always done?

In Chapter Four, we asked you to consider: Are you focusing your greatest efforts on those strategic and operational tasks that *only you can do*, and in turn, delegating and empowering those around you to do the things that they can do?

In spite of your good intentions ("I'm just trying to get the job done right"), you might be inadvertently preventing progress in the organization by failing to delegate. You're distracting yourself from your own needed growth in new skill areas, and you're preventing your employees from owning their areas of responsibility. In other words, you're keeping everybody stuck.

A failure to empower your subordinates may also end up driving your highest performers away. If you hold on to the tasks that you're comfortable with because they give you security and protect your ego, your highest performers will ultimately grow frustrated. They'll lose motivation when they're not given opportunities to stretch themselves or contribute in meaningful ways. They'll recognize that this is not a place where they will be able to grow, develop, and thrive. Ultimately, they'll look for a new employer who *will* empower them to thrive.

Unfortunately, it's not uncommon for leaders to conclude that they are superior to everyone who works for them: "I'm better, I'm smarter, I'm more capable—that's why I'm the leader!" But what happens as a result of this attitude is a critical lack of trust. The leader won't trust their employees to do the job well, and the employees function under a cloud of their own presumed incompetence.

When the senior leader has to be the brightest star, it leads to a diminishment of other people's stars. This kind of leader takes away people's capacity to feel a deep sense of personal efficacy. The Chinese philosopher Lao Tzu said, "A leader is best when people barely know he exists. When his work is done, his aim fulfilled, they will say, 'We did it ourselves.'"[38] Lao Tzu describes an *empowering* leader: the kind of leader who creates a sense of efficacy and destiny in those that she has left behind.

The opposite is the leader who claims he can never take a vacation because—supposedly—it would all fall apart if they left. Or maybe this leader finally gets himself to Hawaii, but he sits on the beach with his laptop. He can't trust his employees to operate effectively in his absence. That's *his* failure to develop others—not theirs.

> *When the senior leader has to be the brightest star, it leads to a diminishment of other people's stars.*

When there's no trust, leaders micromanage. They pretend to empower by delegating tasks, but they still want to maintain control. What does that look like, practically? The leader will start by giving an employee a directive: "Here's your mission; go forth." Then, as the employee goes forth, they're second-guessed, micromanaged, and undermined. They're not given the time or support to actually succeed. The leader who is pretending to empower them may create avenues where their employee is actually set up to fail.

For example, the leader might insist the employee use a certain

---

38   Laozi, *Tao Te Ching*, trans. Stephen Miller (New York: Vintage Books, 1972).

method that worked well for the leader in another time, or another place, but wouldn't work well in this context. When the person who's supposedly been empowered inevitably fails, the senior leader concludes, "See? I shouldn't have given this to you in the first place."

Micromanagers don't just define the destination for their employees; they also want control over the how, the what, the who, and the where. They define *every* step towards the destination in the way that they would do it, assuming that that's the best (even the only) way to get it done. No employee wants to be managed like this. Rather than drawing out their employees' potential, a micromanaging leader will end up discouraging them, demoralizing them, and may risk losing them altogether.

WHEN YOUR OWN BOSS IS A MICROMANAGER

What do you do when your senior leader questions your efficacy? Here are a few tips:

- Make sure your senior leader knows you're aligned with their vision and you understand their expectations. Provide them with an assurance that you're committed to this vision.
- Do this through effective communication. Share with your leader the plans that you have developed so that they can see you working through the "how" and "what" of what is required so that they can be confident of your success.
- Share your thought process, your intent, and explain the means you're using to accomplish your goals.
- You may need to step up the frequency of your interactions by checking in with your boss often: "Hey, I'm checking in to let you know that I've taken these steps and put these plans into place. Is this consistent with your guidance and intentions? Have I missed anything?"

In taking these steps, you'll help build credibility and confidence with your senior leader. Ideally, that will help increase their trust in you and show them you don't need to be micromanaged.

WHAT YOU STAND TO GAIN BY EMPOWERING YOUR EMPLOYEES

There are profound benefits that come when you empower your employees. First, you'll enjoy higher retention. Employees *like* working in an environment where they feel trusted and empowered. You'll also secure greater buy-in when you allow employees to own their vision for how to fulfill their job requirements versus if you were to micromanage their every move. And, by taking the time to train your staff well—by ensuring they understand the vision of the organization and the goals you're working towards—you'll create more thoughtful and reflective employees.

In a recent session, we worked with two leaders who have young workforces, mostly people in their mid-twenties just starting their careers. These two leaders were all about giving their employees more to do and supporting and coaching them along. Empowering their staff was part of their leadership DNA—and it was clear that their employees *loved* working for them.

The two leaders acknowledged it wasn't easy: "Leading this crew is not for the faint of heart! They're always asking for more, and they all want to move up faster." The two leaders had realized they needed to establish some guardrails for their young employees to help them slow down. They created a process to help their team members triage problems, thinking through the degree of difficulty and also the degree of unintended consequences. Rather than rushing forward with an idea, employees had to consult with the leaders to ensure they weren't walking into something that would likely blow up on them. The leaders would ask them questions like, "Tell me how you're going to work through this challenge." Then, "Okay, now what happens if it doesn't turn out like Plan A? What will you do then?" The thoughtful interplay helped their employees envision how their solutions could unfold over time.

It took effort, time, and a lot of conversation—but these two leaders were developing a team of motivated, thoughtful, reflective workers who took ownership over their tasks and had real buy-in. Can you imagine what a staff like that could accomplish for an organization?

Part of what these two leaders did well was that they demonstrated trust in their employees. An atmosphere of trust is critical for efficient communication and flourishing creativity. Why? Because empowering your employees helps foster high, psychological safety. When employees don't feel that safety, they can't perform at their best levels; they're too afraid to take risks and incur criticism. But when a leader is willing to let go and trust their employees, that leader sends a clear message that they want to help their staff become their very best selves. As a result, employees feel supported rather than threatened—which means they feel safe to perform at their best.

Communication opens up in an atmosphere that feels safe; employees feel comfortable exchanging ideas and acknowledging when they're struggling. Mistakes are inevitable as you work to empower your employees—after all, they're learning to do something new. But when there's safety, those mistakes aren't hidden; they're discussed and analyzed. Employees feel enough safety to have an authentic conversation with you: "I know you've given me full trust, and I deeply appreciate that. Can I run a few things by you? I'm concerned about this particular component, and I don't want to mess this up." With trust and safety, dialogue becomes richly productive.

Employees will experience a deeper sense of ownership and self-efficacy. We often joke that no one ever washes their rental car. Why would they? It's not their car. That's the difference between a "renter" and an owner. If employees are micromanaged, they get the message that their own ideas and efforts aren't wanted—so why bother trying so hard? But when leaders push decisions and authority further down in the organization, they allow people to feel a greater sense that this is *their* organization.

By deepening your employees' sense of ownership, you're going to see higher levels of performance and deeper levels of accountability.

You also promote people's confidence in themselves: "Wow—my leader believes I'm capable of taking on this project. That's awesome! I'm going to give this my all."

Perhaps best of all, *you* stand to directly benefit when you empower your employees. When you spend less time doing tasks that other people can do, you gain more time to think strategically and reflectively. You have the space to research the needs of your new role, to systematically consider opportunities, to think more broadly about the future. You're able to do the kind of evaluative reflection that enables you to improve things and make them better. Rather than reactively putting out fires, you can ask proactive questions to plan for the future.

You also experience the fulfillment of impacting a future generation of leaders. Younger workforces, in particular, desire the opportunity to be stretched and promoted. By empowering them, you're not only increasing their job satisfaction, but you're also helping them *grow*. Consider how fulfilling it would be to measure your legacy by the number of people you helped grow, develop, and access opportunities. When you delegate well, you can actually change lives. You help empower others to discover and achieve their fullest potential. That must be one of the most rewarding investments you can have in life!

There's no question that empowering others takes work. It takes patience to coach your employees in their development and progress. You'll likely have to mentor them through making some mistakes. It often requires creativity to seek out new resources or training. You must humble yourself enough to acknowledge that other people could do your old job well and understand that you need to grow in new areas as well.

But consider the profound rewards that come when you do. The investment is worth it!

HOW TO EMPOWER: PRACTICAL STEPS

So how do you do it? What are the practical ways a leader can move away from micromanaging and task monopolization, and move instead towards empowering their teams?

CLARITY OF EXPECTATIONS

Clearly identify, then communicate, your expectations to include your vision of success. Remember our discussion about advocating for excellence in Chapter Two: your team needs to have a definite sense of what you're working towards as an organization. Consider questions like, "What are the three to five things I want my team to do really well? What are the absolute key priorities that will be our differentiators? What are the effective milestones that we're going to establish to measure our progress toward these goals?" Get a clear vision articulated for your organization (if it's not formed already); then, identify the key priorities for your team, in support of that vision. Once you have a definite sense for yourself what your expectations are for your team, you can ensure those expectations are clearly communicated to your employees.

Clearly identify, then communicate, expectations.

We recently coached a data analytics firm and gathered all the upper, mid-level managers in a room together. These leaders made up about fifteen percent of the organization. We asked them to describe the vision of the organization. Almost everyone could articulate a general description of what their company was all about, but if you asked six people to write down the vision, you got six different answers. With no clear, cohesive understanding of vision, the employees couldn't synchronize their efforts in a coordinated direction. How are they going to lead their teams of employees to score wins for that vision if there isn't clear communication about what they're aiming for?

So map out a clear vision for your organization and communicate the priorities. Then, define your expectations clearly. To do much of anything well, your employees need the answers to three key questions:

1. **What exactly do you expect them to do?** Get your expectations for your employees written down. We recommend using a method like SMART goals (goals should be Specific, Measurable, Attainable, Relevant, and Time-stamped) or a similar goal-defining format to ensure your expectations are clearly communicated. We're going to speak more fully about goal-setting in a moment.

2. **Why are the outcomes you want them to accomplish important?** When people have a powerful enough "why" in addition to the "what" you want them to accomplish, you have set them up for amazing success.

3. **What do they know, and what do they *need* to know?** Your job as a leader is to ensure your employees have what they need to be successful and to remove any barriers that stand in their way. Many leaders opt to tell their employees things like, "Just make it happen!" But they don't provide the tools, the education, the training, or the resources that would enable them to actually *make* it happen. Consider: Do your employees already have the skills, techniques, and resources they need to successfully achieve their goals? If not, what do they need? How can you allocate resources to supply those needs?

One of the most important ways to clarify your expectations is through your method of goal-setting. Quality goals are measurable, attainable, realistic, time-stamped, and incremental. They should also be directly relevant to the priorities you've already identified. The SMART goals method that we mentioned earlier helps ensure that goals hit these benchmarks. When you're not intentional about mapping goals out in this way, it's easy to give your employees goals that are unrealistic, not time-stamped, or vague. With goals like that, employees are set up to fail. They don't know exactly what to do, or they don't know by when, or they feel like they've been given an impossible task. With well-written goals, however, employees can enjoy clarity, accountability, and—ideally—success.

> *Quality goals are measurable, attainable, realistic, time-stamped, and incremental.*

Goals also need to be formed *mutually*. If you want your employees to feel ownership over the goals, it is incredibly helpful to have them involved in developing those goals. Effective delegation doesn't mean you map out every detail of what you want the person to do. Rather, you're going to guide that person in defining their own goals, based on strong alignment with the overall vision of your organization. The more they can own them and agree to them—instead of feeling like a goal is imposed upon them—the higher their motivation will be to see those goals achieved.

Goals should also be clearly nested. People need to understand how their goals connect to everything else in the organization. In other words: what is the *point* of doing X? Ensure your team members see how their goals fit into the broader picture: when we do *this*, the other team can do *that*, and so-and-so will have what she needs to do to *get things done* on her end. This will help your employees understand that their work is meaningful and contributes to a greater whole.

REMOVE BARRIERS

Your next step as a leader requires you to take a step back and consider any other barriers that might impede your employees' success. Is everything under your influence working to support your priorities? Your team members will get frustrated if they're confounded by a barrier for too long. So, check in with them from time to time to get a sense of their progress. When they share that progress, celebrate and affirm their success. When they open up about what may be getting in the way, support their efforts to problem solve and—only if necessary—step in to remove barriers. Your role might be to remove constraints related to time, money, people, or bureaucracy.

Nothing will solidify loyalty and support for your leadership more than when your team members see you advocating and standing up for their cause and capabilities.

SECURE BUY-IN

Once you've removed all barriers, your next step is to secure buy-in from your employees. You can do this in several ways.

- **Communicate strategically.** Remember the different strategies for influence we described in Chapter Seven. Consider: What influence strategies will be most effective to get buy-in? Do your employees need an inspirational appeal to help them catch your vision? Perhaps a personal appeal or a coalition appeal could further strengthen their sense of ownership. Use tools of influence to get your employees excited about where you want to take them. Remember: You want these changes to stick. When you empower employees, you're not just looking for them to comply with your demand in the short term—you're looking for long-term, sustained change. How can you, as your team's leader, create the winds required to drive sustained change among your employees?
- **Think like your employees.** Instead of looking from the top down, try to "lie on your back" and look upward. How can you see things from the perspective of those who actually have to do the work? This will help you understand how to communicate strategically. It will also require humility on your part—you'll need to step out of your office and really dialogue with your people. What message do they need to feel inspired? What incentives do they need? How could you shift your communication to make them feel more heard, equipped, or encouraged?
- **Provide growth opportunities.** As you dialogue with your

employees and identify barriers that need removing, you might recognize skill gaps in your staff or opportunities for growth. Providing professional growth opportunities can be a way to help address those gaps. More importantly, it sends the message to your employees that you care enough about them to invest in their growth and development. You might send employees to seminars, cover tuition for an online course, or provide funding for a project.

- **Cultivate open and honest feedback.** In order to secure your employees' buy-in and effectively track their progress, they need to feel safe to dialogue with you. Netflix has a wonderful culture of radical candor; they gather constant feedback from their employees which helps them track progress and—importantly—celebrate successes.[39] They have four "rules" for feedback that promote a communication loop that's open, candid, transparent, and safe. Their feedback model is based on four A's:
  - *Assist:* The person giving feedback shares it purely from a place of *assisting* the other person to be more successful and effective. If you're the boss, you're *not* giving your employees feedback because you want to complain, or humiliate them, or make yourself look better. You're giving that person feedback because you think you can help them improve the quality of their work. Feedback should be driven by the intention to serve others: it's a service to the other person and a service to the organization.
  - *Actionable:* The feedback must lead to *action*. The person you're giving feedback to must be able to do something with it. Are you providing a clear next step when you give feedback? If there's not a clear next step, consider: Is there a better way you could have asked that question? Is there a clearer way you could have said that? If the person receiving feedback can say, "Great, I can identify something actionable I can do that will be helpful," then your employee will feel motivated to act.

---

39 Reed Hastings and Erin Meyer, *No Rules Netflix and the Culture of Reinvention* (New York: Penguin Random House, 2020).

With no clear action step, however, they might instead feel demoralized and frustrated.

- *Appreciation:* This direction is for the person receiving the feedback. Create a culture in your organization that values feedback as an important tool. Employees should *appreciate* the feedback given to them, recognizing that it's delivered in their best interests. If the feedback is truly given to *assist* and is *actionable*, employees should respond with gratitude: "Thank you for taking the time to help me; I appreciate that." This helps promote a positive feedback loop.
- *Accept:* The employee must be given the free choice to *accept* or reject the feedback. If feedback is given with the expectation (or even demand) that the employee *must* accept it, there's no genuine employee buy-in. One of the greatest needs of human beings is autonomy—and that's especially true for motivation. If you want your employees to feel genuinely empowered to change, they need to choose that change—not have it forced upon them.

PROMOTE A HEALTHY CULTURE

You can do all of the above, but if your employees hate coming to work because they don't feel seen or appreciated or connected to others in the organization, you're still not going to see their best work. Creating a healthy, supportive community is part of effectively empowering your employees. We recommend two key steps here, based on Gallup's research about how to maximize employee engagement:[40]

- **Ensure that employees feel valued.** Do you express appreciation for the work your employees are doing? When things go well, do you take the time to communicate, "Job well done!" Do employees feel that the work they do is meaningful? That is one of the most important messages you can provide to them in securing their buy-in. Employees need to be reminded why

---

40 "What Is Employee Engagement and How Do You Improve It?" Gallup.com., December 11, 2020, https://www.gallup.com/workplace/285674/improve-employee-engagement-workplace.aspx#ite-285707.

they're important to the team and organization. Their motivation and sense of buy-in will be enormously strengthened when they believe their work provides real value to the organization—especially when it's seen and appreciated.

- **Encourage meaningful relationships among staff.** It's absolutely critical to employee engagement that people feel connected with their peers, other members of their team, and other staff within the organization. When they feel connected, they're going to genuinely desire to help the larger team achieve its vision. On the other hand, if they feel like a lone island, they're going to feel less convinced their work matters. They'll feel lonelier, dissatisfied with work, and less motivated to improve. Additionally, when leaders create or tolerate dynamics where there are "in"-groups and "out"-groups, it contributes to significant dysfunction and can greatly affect team performance.

WHEN AN EMPLOYEE CAN'T HIT YOUR BENCHMARKS

Greg Hiebert narrates

Let's say you've successfully done all of the above, but your employee still just doesn't perform at the level you want. What then? We recommend taking the following steps.

Check the clarity of your standards. When I was a young officer conducting training with my unit, I often carried a stack of cards called "Task, Condition, and Standards" that laid out in great specificity what was required for that specific training. Having those cards helped me be very clear with myself and my soldiers regarding the precise tasks we were accomplishing, the standards we would measure ourselves by, and the conditions under which we had to achieve those standards.

Employees need this kind of clarity when you delegate tasks. Without that clarity, they'll resort to making up the standard themselves. If *their* standard doesn't align with yours, you're both on track for a potential collision course. Clear communication of your standard expectations is essential for employees' successful outcomes. Remember the three questions that employees need to be able to answer: What do you expect them to accomplish? Why do they need to accomplish them? What do they need to know and do to achieve success? If the problem was due to a lack of clarity, provide clarity. If the problem was *not* related to clarity, consider the next point.

Determine if the problem is due to a lack of desire or a lack of skills. Sit down with your employee and have an intentional conversation. Try to determine what's behind their lackluster performance. Specifically, you're trying to identify if you're dealing with a lack of motivation or a deficit in their skills. Great team players will feel a hunger for success in their area of work, which drives motivation. If there's no hunger—figure out why. What's behind their lack of motivation? It might be due to an interpersonal or communication issue that needs addressing.

Alternately, the problem might be due to a lack of skills. As the leader, take an honest look in the mirror and ask yourself if you've given this person the tools they need to succeed. Was this a stretch assignment for a growth opportunity? If so, provide guidance to help them see a better outcome next time. If this was a goal that they should have been able to achieve independently, then seek clarity over why they didn't make it happen.

Provide resources if the problem is due to a lack of skill. If your employee lacks a certain skill, provide them with resources to be more successful, including training, education, and/or mentorship.

DOING VERSUS BEING

One last point to make as you consider how to effectively empower your employees. Too often, leaders want to put all the focus on *doing*:

they want to discuss tools, tactics, knowledge about people, about process, about technology, about the work to be done.

Ultimately, however, leadership failures are usually not related to "knowing" and "doing." More often, leadership failures are related to their *being*. It's a lack of alignment with the values they espouse, versus the values they actually live—what we discussed earlier in this book as the "Say/Do" Ratio.

When we observe leaders with a Say/Do Ratio that is out of alignment, we see their employees struggle to respect or trust that leader. Maybe these leaders don't live in a place of integrity. Maybe they're poor communicators—not because they don't know *how* to communicate, but because they're not *willing* to understand that good leadership requires communication. The insecurities and ego issues we discussed earlier in this chapter are usually failures of the *being* of leadership.

Ask yourself: As you seek to empower your employees, how can you improve your own *being* as a leader? How can you increase the alignment between what you *say* you value and what you actually *do*?

TIGHT, LOOSE, TIGHT

When we sit down with leaders like Shannon, whom we described earlier in this chapter, we often leave them with this insight about empowering their employees: "Be tight, then loose, then tight."

Tight: Make sure there's good, strong agreement about goals and expectations. The worst thing that can happen is when you *think* you've empowered an employee, and you have a clear view of what their success looks like, but they have a completely different view of what they're aiming for. That's a recipe for disaster! Ensure you both start off with a tight agreement and alignment around expectations.

Loose: After securing tight alignment, loosen the reins. Give your employee the trust and autonomy to determine how they will accomplish their goal. Allow them space to use methods and tactics you might not have used yourself. Remember: They know exactly what your expectations are, and they're aligned with your same goals. Trust that their growth and development will largely be informed by this stage of you stepping back. They will learn how to mobilize the right people, get the right elements in place to orchestrate a path towards success, learn how to problem-solve, and optimize their solutions. Give them full autonomy, but don't abandon them. Check in periodically to provide support, encouragement, and accountability as they need it. This is often where people grow the most. One caution, however: when you have someone who is very new to their role and the learning curve is quite steep, it may be necessary to be much more directive at first. As they gain confidence in their abilities, you can give them more autonomy and latitude in how they get their work accomplished.

Tight: Finally, tighten things back up again in holding them accountable to the outcomes and expectations you initially agreed to: "Okay, Jaime. We agree that this task is going to be delivered next week at 2 p.m. Both of us are going to get this on our calendars as an important milestone, and we'll talk about how it went when we get there." On the date when success is supposed to be achieved, or shortly after, hold your employee accountable with a debrief conversation. If they didn't successfully complete the task, have the hard discussion required. Ensure expectations were clear, find out what happened, and discuss how you can get beyond the breakdown to achieve a breakthrough. If they *did* succeed, they still need a conversation with you. Show them you see and recognize their efforts—otherwise, none of their efforts will feel like it mattered. Affirm their skillful execution and discuss next steps toward continued growth.

We work with a leader who is a master at empowering his people. When his team achieves success, he is the first to loudly and publicly give others the credit. When there is insufficient progress, he is quick to take the blame and reiterate the team's commitment to recover and get it right. Recently his organization was selected for an industry award for high-quality performance and—wouldn't you know it—the first thing he said when told about the award was, "My team of leaders and staff made it all possible. I just show up!" Because of how effectively he led and empowered his people, they gave him their best—and likewise, he was freed up to work at *his* best.

When you do the hard work of empowering your employees—working tight, loose, tight—you will ultimately surround yourself with motivated, creative, excited, and capable individuals. You will be freed up to do the work and vision-casting that only you can do.

And here's some good news: Like Shannon, you are probably exceptionally talented! You would not have gotten to the position you're in without intelligence, ingenuity, and an ability to get results. As you empower your employees to grow in new ways, allow yourself the permission to struggle and grow as well. Empowering others is a skill, and it's one you can work at and acquire—just as you've worked to develop many others.

ACTION STEPS

1. Consider your current leadership style. Do you tend to micromanage your team, or do you seek to empower them? How would your employees describe your leadership style?
2. Identify some steps you can take to enhance the communication of your team members' goals, based on the recommendations we discussed.
3. What barriers, if any, should be removed? What resources, if any, would help your employees hit the goals you want them to hit?
4. Consider the steps you can take to secure buy-in from your team and promote a healthy culture. Where specifically would your organization benefit from improvement in those areas?
5. In your own leadership "*being*," what are some things you do especially well? What's something you could do to better align your "Say/Do Ratio" and enhance your leadership "being"?

PART THREE

YOUR ENVIRONMENT

CHAPTER NINE

UNDERSTANDING THE ENVIRONMENT

USING CONTEXT CUES TO STRENGTHEN YOUR STRATEGY

"Skate to where the puck is going, not to where it is."
—WALTER GRETSKY, FATHER OF "THE GREAT
ONE," HOCKEY PLAYER WAYNE GRETSKY

A COMPLEX AND VOLATILE ENVIRONMENT

Dennis O'Neil narrates

I can still picture that red and white Volkswagen Jetta. There was something wrong about it—Iraqi civilians didn't normally try to insert their cars into our military convoys. Still, this Jetta tailed us as we moved throughout the city of Mosul, trying to maneuver into our three-vehicle convoy. Unfortunately, my team had become very familiar with this kind of threat: any car trying to approach a military convoy had the potential to be a vehicle-born improvised explosive device—i.e., a car bomb.

We had one of the Iraqi battalion commanders with us—*maybe that's why they're targeting us*, I mused. But then again, we had come to expect constant threats. During our 365 days in Iraq, we conducted 255 combat operations. We were only sixteen days into January, but already, those two weeks had seen more than their fair share of violence.

Our lead vehicle commander, Jared, was able to divert our route, and our trail vehicle did great maneuvering to cut off the Jetta from our convoy. The trail gunner, Josh, finally confirmed that the Jetta had departed the convoy. It was no longer a threat. We continued driving towards our targeted destination, relieved that we once more seemed to be carrying out a routine operation.

About three minutes later, there was a huge shock and explosion. We quickly moved to the sound of the guns and saw smoke pluming up at one of our security checkpoints along the road. At the base of the destroyed buildings was the wreckage of the detonated vehicle that had caused the explosion: the same red and white Volkswagen Jetta that had been tailing us.

There were bodies in the wreckage—the Iraqi soldiers that had been manning the checkpoint were all dead, and so was the suicide bomber. We responded quickly to secure the scene. The first responders arrived in an ambulance and began looking for survivors to aid. That's when we discovered that the car bomb was only the beginning of a well-planned, organized ambush. The attackers intended to destroy the checkpoint and then wait for the first responders to arrive and kill everybody who showed up to help the wounded.

As we moved about the area to secure it, we started taking direct fire. Three hand grenades were lobbed and aimed towards me, my soldiers, and the other first responders. I was positioned on a raised street, and the grenades fell just short of where I stood, landing on the street below. They exploded in quick succession, rocking the ground underneath me. The noise created a significant concussion right below us but not enough so that I caught the shrapnel that was intended for me. More gunshots sounded, and bullets pinged off the concrete around us. Somewhere, snipers were firing.

I directed our intelligence officer and a group of Iraqi soldiers to dismount and clear the building to my left, and sent my operations officer to clear the building to the right with our Iraqi counterparts. In short order, we cleared the buildings, got security, called in reinforcements, established a larger perimeter, brought up Iraqi vehicles to return fire to the snipers, engaged multiple individuals, and eventually killed them. Then, we had to evacuate the wounded and the dead while preventing any more casualties, both military and civilian.

Unfortunately, in 2009, this was destined to be "just another day" in Mosul. We would engage in some form of combat operation approximately two out of every three days for the rest of that year. It was an environment where every vehicle, every alleyway, every doorway, and every action had potentially negative consequences. To ensure mission success and preserve my soldiers' lives, it was necessary to anticipate the unanticipated and to stay ahead as many steps as possible of the enemy. Contingency planning was essential. We had to constantly ask the "what-ifs" and try to see things from our enemy's perspective.

The volatile environment dominated our decision-making. The "what" of our *goals* never shifted; we were there to help oversee and protect Iraq's first democratic elections and to strengthen the Iraqi army. However, our strategy on "how" to pursue those goals changed constantly because of the environmental factors. They had to. You had to learn how to read the entire environment and all the complexities that come with not only conducting combat operations and developing a foreign army but with working to build a democratically elected government as well.

Leaders looking to change altitude with agility—to respond quickly to new challenges with thoughtful strategy—must take the crucial step of building a strong understanding of the environment. Only through thoughtfully evaluating your environment will you know what you need to know, understand what you need to understand, and see what you need to see. In this chapter, we're going to provide you with a systematic approach to understand your environment so that you can develop an optimal strategy to achieve your goals.

KNOW WHERE YOU ARE

The nature of the world we live in is constant change. That's been a given for all of human history. However, in recent history, advancements in technology have caused the pace of change to intensify. Then, if you throw a crisis into the mix, the magnitude and speed of change picks up even more. Agility is what enables leaders to respond quickly and effectively to that change.

What are the consequences of ignoring environmental cues? Many leaders were blindsided by the dramatic changes in their environment as the Coronavirus pandemic hit in the early months of 2020. Almost overnight, many businesses had to overhaul their strategy to continue delivering their products to their customers. Some businesses were able to quickly flex; other businesses were not, for any number of reasons. Those leaders who responded successfully did so through an agile adaptation to a rapidly changing environment.

As our world wrestles with healthcare crises, environmental, social, political, and civic unrest, organizations require agile and versatile leaders like never before. Agile leaders can respond effectively to a changing environment. They can also predict second- and third-order effects that could unfold in a rapidly changing context and update their plan constantly. They don't change *what* they're trying to accomplish, but they possess great flexibility in *how* they get it done.

One definition of agile leadership is the ability to manage continual change in anticipation of future requirements. As a leader, you're evaluating what's happening in the fast-moving game in front of you, looking to anticipate what's coming next—then, you move yourself and your team in that direction. The essence of agile leadership is to take your team, your department, your organization to a better place they wouldn't have gone without you.

> Agile leadership: the ability to manage continual
> change in anticipation of future requirements.

Another definition of agility supplied by the authors of *Leadership Agility* defines it as "the ability to take wise and effective action in the face of rapidly changing and highly volatile conditions."[41] This definition implies clear-mindedness, a thorough knowledge of the environment, and a sense of how your action will play out.

Although agile leaders might seem to possess this skill effortlessly, it's a discipline that you can learn. It starts with close attention to your environment.

FIVE QUESTIONS TO EVALUATE THE ENVIRONMENT

Before flying anywhere, you need two crucial pieces of information: You need to know where you're *going and where you are starting*. Then, within those two points, you're able to consider other variables: What are the weather patterns and air currents within those two points? What will be your passenger and supply loads? How much fuel will the plane need? What will be the appropriate cruising altitude be? What's the flight plan?

Similarly, when you're forming an analysis of your environment, you're considering: Where do you want to go, and what is your cur-

---

41 Bill Joiner and Stephen Josephs, *Leadership Agility: Five Levels of Mastery for Anticipating and Initiating Change* (San Francisco: Jossey-Bass, 2007).

rent state? Once you identify those two points, you can start dealing with the where, the how, and the what. Again, that's going to give you clarity about how best to navigate your environment.

We've identified five steps to help our clients analyze their environment and identify their clear next steps; collectively, these five steps function as an amazing tool. They work in the simplest processes but also in the most complex of environments, in everything from developing a nation, to leading a business, to helping your team engage with a broader organization.

These steps will walk you through collecting information in key areas which will help you fully understand your current situation as fully as possible. When you know where you're *starting*, and then you identify where you *want to go*, you can iterate the *where*, the *how*, and the *what*.

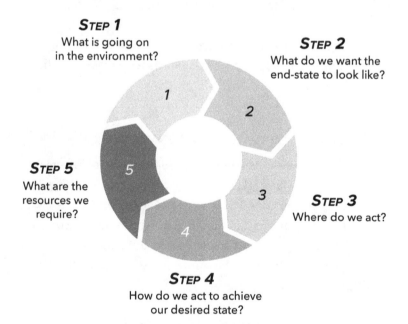

STEP 1
What is going on
in the environment?

STEP 2
What do we want the
end-state to look like?

STEP 5
What are the
resources we
require?

STEP 3
Where do we act?

STEP 4
How do we act to achieve
our desired state?

STEP 1: WHAT IS GOING ON IN THE ENVIRONMENT?

Dennis O'Neil narrates

The first step requires that you take a close look at what's going on today in your environment. You're looking to consider some of the following points:

- Who are your primary stakeholders? In other words, who will experience the greatest impact from your project's success or failure?
- What do your senior leaders and peers think of your part of the organization? In other words, what is the current "brand" or reputation you've established? Make sure you have a thorough understanding of this. Is your reputation consistent with what your senior and peer leaders think it should be?
- Who are your competitors, how are they operating, and what are their core strategies?
- Make a list of what's going well and what's not going well. What factors contributed to the areas of success? What factors seem to be related to the areas of weakness? Where are there performance gaps between where the organization is currently at, and the results it should be achieving?
- What environmental "proxies," or cues, will help alert you to a change in your environment?
- Take a look at the systems you engage with constantly and look for correlations, such as:
  - How in tune is your team with the environment it operates in? When environmental factors change, does your organization maintain agility and mastery of the environment or does it get caught off guard and unprepared? The efficiency and efficacy of the systems that are required for your organization to function today, like the personnel systems or the financial systems.
  - The smoothness of inter-departmental exchanges, like how smoothly a client transitions to customer service after work-

ing with the sales team. This is becoming even more salient regarding how data and information are moved through an organization.

· What kind of opportunities are available to you, and how could you develop them?

All of these considerations are meant to invite your close examination of your environment so that you can spot potential risks and potential opportunities. For example, when I was leading my team in Iraq, we had to operate in a chaotic, dangerous environment defined by competition over power, control, and money. There was no script to tell us what to do. Instead, we had to make sense of our environment in a way that enabled us to make informed decisions. We did so by *reading the proxies of our environment*. Let me explain what that means.

Our best indicators of environmental stability or volatility came from small indicators from the locals, what we call "environmental proxies." Environmental proxies are those unspoken signals that communicate important dimensions of a changing environment. For instance, if a market was willing to stay open past dark, that was a mostly reliable sign that the area wasn't facing threats of terrorist activity or gang warfare. However, if the markets closed well before dark—there was clearly a reason for that. The locals were giving up an opportunity to make additional revenue during those hours, and we knew they wouldn't make that sacrifice unless they understood that they would be in danger otherwise. So, that sign tipped us off to also take warning.

Another environmental proxy was the auto repair shops. If an auto repair shop showed a willingness to work on an Iraqi army truck and take the Iraqi government money for the repairs, that was a good sign. However, if they told us, "Sorry, we're just too busy. We could never fit your vehicles in," we learned that was a sign that they were receiving external threats from other groups, warning them not to do business with us.

Our movements were all about risk determination. On a normal day at 7:30 a.m., there would be kids walking to school on just about any street, in any community. On the days when we didn't see kids walking to school, that was another proxy. We took that sign as an indicator of a problem in that area that would warrant our time and focus. Often, it meant there was an attack planned for later that day, which locals had gotten word about.

These environmental proxies helped us determine what strategy to employ next and where to push our resources. First, we had to determine the local stakeholders—that might be a mother, a local tribal leader, a shop owner, and so on—and look at those stakeholders through multiple lenses. For example, we knew that parents wanted their children educated; shop owners wanted the opportunity to make money. If their behavior went against those motivations, that was a sign that something was wrong. Next, we had to build a collective understanding of the environment, the people, their motivations, and the stakes to plan our next step in this complex, volatile environment. Then, we had to bring all that information together to do more creative decision-making to manage this environment of continuous change and make some headway toward our goals.

We also had to try to think like our opponents if we wanted to anticipate their next move. The same is true in a business context. Take a look at what your competitors are doing and think about their advantage in those moves. How are they trying to differentiate themselves from you, and how should you differentiate your company from them? Consider the risk they pose and the potential opportunities they might inadvertently open up for you. As we previously discussed, most of us were under-prepared for the global pandemic. Yet many organizations were able to pick up on environmental cues and see new opportunities for growth and positive change.

Additionally, a business thrives when it has very loyal and engaged customers. Take the time to look at your organization through the lenses of your customers and see what they see and feel what they feel in their experience with you. Where are there opportunities in the midst of environmental change to actually strengthen customer loyalty and satisfaction?

When analyzing step one, it's important to be present to where the work is being done to learn what's really going on. Pay attention to the natural leaders among your workforce; hunt down the inefficiencies and problem spots; take a look at the points of resistance. Know where your people are frustrated or struggling. Then, considering all that, form an opinion about what's going on in the current environment.

Your understanding of what's going on today is point A—but you still must get to point B. Recognize that the status quo of your current state is not ideal; growth is possible and needed. For that reason, step two—consider your desired future—follows right on the heels of step one. These two steps are closely linked, just as when you're buying a plane ticket, you need to know both where you are and where you're going nearly simultaneously. Your understanding of what's happening today should lead you right into a consideration of where you hope to be tomorrow.

STEP 2: WHAT DO WE WANT THE END-STATE TO LOOK LIKE?

In his famous book, *The 7 Habits of Highly Effective People,* Stephen Covey wrote, "Begin with the end in mind."[42] He began there because he felt strongly that the essence of effective leadership always begins with the leader's desire and commitment to take those she leads to a better future. Likewise, the science of planning begins with a vision of future success. You need a clarified mission and purpose that will help guide you forward. Name your targets: Where do you want to be one year from now? How about five years from now? How about twenty years from now? What will be your definition of success as an organization? What are you seeking to

---

42   Stephen R. Covey, *The 7 Habits of Highly Effective People* (London: Simon & Schuster UK, 2020).

accomplish as a team? What culture are you building? What kind of a leader do you want to become? What do you want for those you lead to have and feel when you have taken them to a better future?

Once you determine what you want the future to look like and carefully examine and determine your current state, you can start to establish the "A to Z" plan that will enable you to get there. Break your plan into monthly, weekly, and daily activities and tactics: chart goals, metrics, and objectives. Next, share your vision of where you want to go with your team so that they can get on board and throw their effort into the journey. When you provide your people with tangible steps to take towards a meaningful end objective, your team can experience the incredible satisfaction of making progress towards that goal. They'll also have greater clarity about how they can align their efforts with that vision for success.

The restaurant chain P.F. Chang's built its reputation for upscale Chinese food with ornate dining rooms, decorative food displays, and great service. However, during the COVID-19 pandemic, they had to rapidly change tactics to remain in business. They put together a leaner "to-go" menu which helped them weather the pandemic, but then they developed a vision for the future that stretched far beyond the restraints of 2020. They realized they wanted to expand their opportunities and diversify their offerings. As a result, they started opening "to-go" only restaurants in various large cities. Their short-term goal to remain in business ultimately led them to consider new opportunities and generate an enhanced vision for future long-term success.

When defining a clear vision of where you want to take your organization, spend the time and effort required to make that vision as compelling, inviting, and inspiring as possible. Too few leaders bother putting in the effort to do this well. When they go out to mobilize organizational members around that vision, their efforts fall short. This key step, when done well, truly engages organizational members to experience a deep, almost visceral understanding of the destination they are embarking on, allowing their excitement and enthusiasm to match their leaders.

Based on what you've observed about your current environment, what does that mean for where you want to be tomorrow, and next week, and next month, and next year? What do you need to do to get there? First, define your desired future state and secure your people's commitment and buy-in. Then, move back into the concrete to determine *where* you will act.

STEP 3: WHERE DO WE ACT?

Often, leaders are so concerned about speed and results that they lose the ability to spot opportunities for tremendous growth. Instead, they're always trying to chase incremental growth, and it ends up looking a lot like chasing their tails.

The 125-year-old company Alcoa did the hard work to thoughtfully consider where to act, after evaluating their current state and their desired future. Alcoa is known as the world's aluminum producer. In 2015, one-third of the business focused on mining materials for aluminum out of the ground; the second division built engineered products out of aluminum; the third part of the company was aerospace-centric and created some of the most technologically advanced metal products in the world. Despite the excellent engineering happening at Alcoa, however, the company's stock rose and fell correlated with the price of aluminum as a commodity, which was largely out of their control. When considering their vision for a better tomorrow, they decided it made the most sense to create two companies: Arconic would focus on metal manufacturing, allowing them to experience the stock benefits of their excellent engineering; Alcoa would primarily focus on bulk aluminum production. For a 125-year-old company, this was a courageous step to take, but it was the right one to unlock value to shareholders. The division enabled the company to benefit from their engineering and metal expertise. Later, Arconic would split again into two even more specialized companies.

So, considering the gap between your current environment and your desired future end state, where do you need to act first? What steps need to be taken first? What are the fundamental problems of your current state, and how can you work to address those problems or remove obstacles? What opportunities can you pursue that will allow you to move from here to there? By careful discernment and reflection, you may find that there are key actions that you can take that can accelerate your efforts to move your organization to its future state.

This step will help you form a hierarchy of priorities. Then, just as a pilot completes a series of steps before they bring the plane up to cruising altitude, you're going to start to hammer out a task list that will need to be done in a certain order to most effectively achieve the right critical path.

STEP 4: HOW DO WE ACT TO ACHIEVE OUR DESIRED STATE?

Once you've identified the "where," you consider the "how." If you've identified that certain departments need your focus and attention first, then decide *how* to develop those departments. Set the priorities for what needs to happen first, who will take it on, and how your organization can best support them.

If you've thought through the first three questions, then by the time you get to the "how," you'll be ready to seek out a solution that acknowledges the full complexity of a situation. Sometimes, when change is coming fast, or a crisis is unfolding, it's tempting to reach for "band-aid solutions." But, as H.L. Mencken once said, "There is always a well-known solution to every human problem—neat, plausible, and wrong."[43] In other words, complex problems will require complex solutions. Therefore, agile leadership requires the ability to understand what you are trying to achieve yet be flexible enough to know that the solution will be complex.

---

43 Henry L. Mencken, *Prejudices: Second Series* (New York: Knopf, 1920).

Think about the situation that many real estate agents found themselves in, at the start of 2020. They were used to relying on open houses and in-person showings to sell houses. But with the forced shuttering of the pandemic, their "how" had to shift drastically. Suddenly, clients needed to be given enough information about a property that they could feel secure making an offer on it virtually unseen. Whereas agents' business models prior to 2020 might have relied more heavily on in-person interactions, the new restrictions required a much more robust online presence. They had to generate new tactics to remain competitive in a housing market with booming demand and limited inventory.

The "how" is often complex. Agile leadership asks that you push past the initial solutions put forward, which usually won't cut it. Instead, identify a more comprehensive strategy to accommodate the full breadth of the variables.

The "how" also will usually require flexibility. Your tactics about how to work towards your desired future may need to change frequently, depending on what's going on today. However, by keeping a clear focus on your goal and slowing down enough to take in needed information, you will have the agility needed to flex on your day-to-day "how." Your priorities may shift, even while your attention towards your end goal remains fixed.

Just ensure you bring your people along with you as you change tactics. Too often, decisions are batted about by senior leaders for days and weeks at a time. When the decisions are finally made, there is insufficient time to make sure all those who must carry out the decisions fully understand *what* they have to accomplish, *why* they have to accomplish it, and *how* their piece of the decision relates to others involved. Make sure that all those who will be involved in implementing the "how" have a very specific understanding of what they are to do, along with the responsibilities they must perform. Great leaders are constantly changing altitude to walk in the "shoes" of their team members to make sure their people understand and embrace the "how." The more well defined and tested the "how" is, the higher the probability of achieving the "where."

In sum, consider *how* you will use your people, your communications, and your relationships to move the environment towards the more desirable end state. How specifically do you need to act?

STEP 5: WHAT ARE THE RESOURCES WE REQUIRE?

At this point, you should have a sense of *what* resources will be required to complete the where and the how. Consider:

- Do we have sufficient human capital with the right skillsets and mindsets to achieve the where and accomplish the how?
- What resources do my people need to overcome some of these problem areas? What can be done to remove these obstacles?
- Do we thoroughly understand the time required and how that timeline fits the broader organizational timeframes?
- Do we fully understand and appreciate all the other priorities and efforts that are being asked of our team members? Far too often what leaders interpret as a motivation problem is often an exhaustion one of being "overwhelmed."
- What resources are needed to pursue key opportunities?
- Is training needed? What kind of training, and for whom?
- Are new tools needed? What kind of tools?
- Are staff changes needed?

This step requires that you locate resources as needed in order to carry out your goals and priorities. When you ask people to go on a journey, you need to ensure they have what they need—and that their packs aren't overloaded with things you've already asked them to carry, like other responsibilities and initiatives, etc.

When John F. Kennedy Jr. pitched the famous "moon shot," the technology didn't yet exist to put a man on the moon. However, in his speech to Congress, Kennedy was candid about the needed resources, along with his plan to obtain them:

> I believe we possess all the resources and talents necessary. But the facts of the matter are that we have never made the national decisions or marshalled the national resources required for such leadership. We have never specified long-range goals on an urgent time schedule, or managed our resources and our time, as to insure their fulfillment. ...This decision demands a major national commitment of scientific and technical manpower, material and facilities, and the possibility of their diversion from other important activities where they are already thinly spread. It means a degree of dedication, organization and discipline which have not always characterized our research and development efforts.[44]

Kennedy's clear articulation of the needed resources helped spur on the vision to put a man on the moon. The vision caught, the country came together, the resources were obtained, and in 1969, Neil Armstrong walked on the moon.

The "what" will also help clarify your ranking of priorities. If you know that your team needs an obstacle to be removed before they can open the floodgates of productivity, removing that obstacle needs to be one of your top priorities.

These five questions don't need to take multiple meetings or lengthy consulting sessions to answer—they're meant to assist you in making quick, wise decisions. That's why this framework will aid you in your agility as a leader, when change is coming at you fast. If you were to take five minutes right now to jot down notes responding to each question, what would you come up with? See what clarity might emerge.

---

44   John F. Kennedy Jr. Address Before a Joint Session of Congress, May 25, 1961.

STEP 0: REASSESS ASSUMPTIONS

In times of difficulty or crisis, a nicely organized hierarchy of priorities can easily be upended. So then—not only then, but especially then—we encourage you to think through Step 0. Step 0 asks that you look at the *assumptions* which led you to where you are today. Which of those assumptions are still valid? Which of those assumptions are now invalid?

Remember the importance of humility in leadership. You do not know all, and your read on any situation will always be less than perfect. As new information and insight come in, or as unanticipated changes unfold—be ready to bend. Be ready to shift. Be ready to listen, and listen well.

Leading with agility requires a willingness to reassess your own assumptions.

When you become fixed on any one way of doing things, you can set yourself up for danger. Think about Blockbuster when a fledgling start-up named Netflix offered them an opportunity to acquire all of Netflix and its successful DVD mailing solution for a measly $30 million. Blockbuster's leadership resoundingly rejected the offer; they assumed that this upstart Netflix couldn't possibly disrupt their business model. But that blindness to their assumptions became their demise.

As you reflect on steps one through five, look at your own assumptions. Identify which ones are still valid and which ones are no longer true. Then, with a clarified, corrected assessment of assumptions, you can go back to step one and continue through the rest.

OTHER FACTORS

In addition to the five-step analysis, there are several tools you can use to further strengthen your understanding of the environment.

UNDERSTANDING CULTURE

Greg Hiebert narrates

I recently worked with a young leader, Jeong, who unfortunately was set up to fail when he was brought into his new company as a director. Jeong took orders from his boss and set about bringing his team in line with his boss's vision. What Jeong didn't know, however, was that his boss was in the process of being moved out of the company.

Once Jeong's boss was fired, Jeong suddenly realized that all of the objectives he had been pursuing—at his boss's instruction—were deeply unpopular with the other leaders of his company. So, he had to start over from scratch, looking to acquaint himself with a vision that truly reflected the organization's goals. He also had an uphill battle to undo, and then redo, much of the work he'd embarked on with his team.

The main issue for Jeong was a lack of understanding about the culture at his company, and this forms a key element of understanding your environment. Leaders must quickly build a cultural understanding of their team and organization. They need to identify key underlying assumptions—including who has power, how it is gained, who has influence—and identify the prevailing "norms." All these dynamics impact how human beings work with each other. If there's a highly collaborative, accountable culture, leaders will function differently than if they're engaging in a dog-eat-dog environment. Organizational culture is so significant, in fact, that research has consistently shown it can make or break the success of a merger or even well-developed strategies.[45]

---

45 Oliver Engert, Becky Kaetzler, Kameron Kordestani, and Andy MacLean. "Organizational Culture in Mergers: Addressing the Unseen Forces," McKinsey & Company, March 27, 2019, https://www.mckinsey.com/business-functions/organization/our-insights/organizational-culture-in-mergers-addressing-the-unseen-forces.

One of the most prominent thought leaders on organizational culture, Edgar Schein, identified three distinct levels of organizational cultures that refer to the degree to which the different cultural distinctions are visible to an observer:[46]

1. **Artifacts**: Artifacts include any tangible, overt, or verbally identifiable elements in any organization. Architecture, furniture, behaviors, dress code, office jokes all exemplify organizational artifacts. Artifacts are the *visible* elements in culture, and they can be recognized by people who are not even part of the culture.
2. **Espoused values**: Espoused values are the organization's *stated* values and rules of behavior. It is how the members represent the organization both to themselves and to others. This is often expressed in official philosophies and public statements of identity. It can sometimes often be a projection for the future of what the members hope to become. Examples of this would be employee professionalism or a "We are family" mantra. Problems occur when espoused values are inconsistent with the deeper assumptions of the culture.
3. **Assumptions**: Shared basic assumptions are the deeply embedded, taken-for-granted behaviors which are usually unconscious but constitute the essence of culture. These assumptions are typically so well integrated into the "fabric" of the organization that they are hard to recognize from within. Examples would be: how time is managed, how much autonomy leaders give, how people should be treated and managed, how tightly managed an organization's goals and outcomes are.

Highly effective leaders understand that "culture eats strategy." In order to lead and manage positive change, they must take stock of those patterns. Take the time you need to get a firm understanding of the three levels of culture. Then, test your understanding with your key stakeholders.

---

46 Edgar H. Schein and Peter Schein, *Organizational Culture and Leadership* (Hoboken: Wiley, 2017).

Another leader I know was recruited to an organization and given a mandate by his board to increase organizational efficiency. He was quick to identify what was wrong and how it should be fixed. Unfortunately, he pushed his changes forward without trying to understand how the people would receive them. The organization he was working with had a history of being a high-performance organization, and they had a lofty opinion of the ways they did things. When this leader tried to push changes without keenly appreciating the team's opinions about themselves, his effect was equivalent to a bull in a china shop. He offended people he needed as influencers and created enormous built-in resistance to every change he wanted to make. Because he was the CEO, though, people publicly welcomed the changes while privately sharing their concerns throughout the organization. His goals were good, but he went about it in the wrong way by failing to learn and appreciate the group dynamics.

Good leaders take stock of the patterns of interpersonal dynamics, including (and especially) who has power and influence. Then, when you do act, it should be well informed by a full appreciation of your operating environment and strong efforts to lead change consistent with that appreciation.

In the shaded box below, we've provided some questions that will focus your lens on cultural and group dynamics. Use these questions as a tool to help you better understand your culture, examining both the tip of the proverbial iceberg and what's underneath. We recommend answering these questions on your own initially; then, consider distributing these questions more broadly among your team to help gather a well-rounded understanding of the culture you're dealing with.

CULTURAL ASSESSMENT QUESTIONS

- How would you describe your team's culture? Put differently, what are some of your team's defining values?
- Are the cultural values written down and communicated clearly for all to see? Is there any process of accountability in place to make sure team members uphold those cultural values?
- Consider the level of psychological safety present among your team. On a scale of one to ten, where "one" correlates to no safety and "ten" correlates to total safety, where would you put your team?
- Assess whether or not there are visible patterns that display trust within your organizational culture. Consider in particular the example set by leaders:
  - When people make a mistake, do they willingly acknowledge and own it?
  - Do team members know each other as individuals? Do leaders know something about each person's story?
  - Do leaders have a clear sense of what their team members want and need from them? Do leaders have a sense of how their employees would like to be treated?
- Assess whether or not there are visible patterns of respect within your organizational culture. Again, consider in particular the example set by leaders:
  - How are people treated when they make a mistake? Are they shown respect and dignity when the mistake is addressed? Are they given opportunities to improve?
  - Across the organization, do people demonstrate courtesy and politeness to one another? Are people given the benefit of the doubt? Is speech consistently respectful?
  - To what degree is disrespectful language and behavior tolerated? (Disrespectful language/behavior could include workplace gossip, disparaging humor, sexist or racist remarks, insults, yelling, etc.) Are there any consequences established for people who disrespect other people on their team?
- Are there broken aspects of trust that need to be repaired in your organization? Where does that trust break down, and/or who has broken that trust? Are you willing to make changes to fix this break (or these breaks) in trust?

VUCA: VOLATILITY, UNCERTAINTY, COMPLEXITY, AMBIGUITY

VUCA is an acronym often used in the military to describe highly dynamic and radically changing battle environments; it stands for volatility, uncertainty, complexity, ambiguity. **Volatility** refers to the intensity and rate of change; **uncertainty**, to the lack of clarity around what's going to happen in the future. **Complexity** is the state of having many different parts connected or related to each other in a complicated way, and **ambiguity** means there's no clear way to interpret what you're seeing. When all these conditions come together, you get VUCA—and unfortunately, the forces of VUCA hit more often than any of us would like, making the task of leadership that much more challenging.

Whether you're on a battlefield in the Middle East or in a boardroom, your operating environment may likely contain all of the above. So before plunging headlong into any decision, assuming that you've got it all figured out, make sure you take a good look at VUCA. Determine potential ways for you to anticipate what elements of VUCA could be most disruptive to your plans, strategies, and operations.

Taking VUCA into account, leaders should take a high-altitude view of their projects to understand the larger forces at play and get low to the ground to understand what the changes will mean for the people directly implementing them. But—what if you don't want to? What if it feels too time-consuming to bother gathering all that data—or unnecessary? In that case, you might well be dealing with the Dunning-Kruger effect.

The Dunning-Kruger effect describes a psychological bias that basically does not want to acknowledge VUCA-anything.[47] People with this bias overestimate their knowledge and abilities. They say, "There is no ambiguity or uncertainty—I know all. And whatever volatility and complexity come my way—I'm sure to beat it, head-on!"

---

47   Justin Kruger and David Dunning, "Unskilled and Unaware of It: How Difficulties in Recognizing One's Own Incompetence Lead to Inflated Self-Assessments," *Journal of Personality and Social Psychology* 77, no. 6 (1999): 1121–34, https://doi.org/10.1037/0022-3514.77.6.1121.

Research shows that men, in particular, are guilty of this bias.[48] The internet also has exacerbated this bias—everyone feels like an expert in anything, thanks to Google and Wikipedia.

However, this bias serves no one when VUCA actually hits. A failure to probe the areas of volatility, uncertainty, complexity, and ambiguity ahead of time means leaders will be caught by surprise. That's not going to lead to agile leadership—it will lead to reactive floundering.

Adam Grant, the organizational psychologist, and popular TED Talk speaker, recently published a book called *Think Again.*[49] In his book, he argues many problems arise when people assume that they know all. He claims that people adopt essentially four archetypal roles when they're trying to change people's minds: the preacher, the prosecutor, the politician, and the scientist. The scientist, Grant argues, is the most effective at actually changing people's minds because it begins with a hypothesis. Beginning with a *guess* of what might be, instead of *certainty* about what might be, opens the door to doubt. In that place of doubt and openness, people can admit there are possibilities they haven't thought of yet—and maybe one of those possibilities might be a good idea about how to do things differently.

So, before you conclude that you've got a comprehensive idea of what's going on, think again. Go out and survey your landscape; get high and get low. Consider the volatility, uncertainty, complexity, and ambiguity. *Then* act.

FEEDBACK MECHANISMS

The higher the volatility and uncertainty of the context you're in, the more you need feedback mechanisms to enable you to take stock of what's happening as rapidly as possible. Feedback mechanisms enable you to gather information from people above you, below you,

---

48   Kruger and Dunning, "Unskilled and Unaware of It."

49   Adam Grant, *Think Again: The Power of Knowing What You Don't Know* (New York: Viking, 2021).

and across from you, significantly broadening your understanding. Regular methods of feedback also allow you to constantly update your information.

In Chapter Three, we provided a tool called the After-Action Review. We highly recommend that you use this tool along with other feedback mechanisms to broaden your understanding of what's truly happening in your environment and ensure your information is current.

DRIVING FORCES

Finally, a strategic understanding of your environment requires that you take the driving forces into account. If we return to our plane analogy, these driving forces would be equivalent to a headwind or a tailwind: there are external forces at work that could have a significant impact on how and when you reach your target.

What are some examples of driving forces in a workplace organization? These might be factors like workplace politics, organizational frameworks, personal dynamics informed by a long history, historical precedents, and so on. It could also include strong external elements such as tight labor markets, inflation, pandemics, climate, and even civic volatility that has affected recruitment and retention issues. Driving forces describe whatever trends have helped to create the current situation.

Even when we're taking stock of today, we've got to make sure we're looking beyond the horizon of what's right in front of us. To use the familiar Wayne Gretsky metaphor, agile leaders can predict where the puck is going. That requires a sense of the momentum already at work, the forces already at play. True, the reality presented by VUCA won't allow you to get a certain sense of what will happen around the corner—but by studying the driving forces and seeking to know what you do not know—you can put together a pretty solid hypothesis.

If you've got a tailwind, you can let that propel you towards your target with speed. If you've got a headwind, you know to alert your passengers of a possible delay and do what's necessary to make the trip as successful as possible.

BOOTS ON THE GROUND

In the book *Neptune's Inferno*, there's a story told that illustrates the tremendous importance of understanding your environment.[50] The author, James Hornfischer, describes a story from July of 1942 when Navy Admiral Gormley took charge of the battle with the Japanese over the island of Guadalcanal. The admiral's headquarters were located roughly 1,500 miles away from the island battlefield. He had traveled directly from Washington, DC, and when he finally arrived at his headquarters on the island of New Caledonia, he was exhausted. Presumably, because of his fatigue, he never bothered even visiting the island of Guadalcanal. He failed to look into the eyes of the gallant Marines and sailors who were fighting the battle against the Japanese. He didn't engage well with his leaders; he did not acquaint himself with their skills; he didn't identify the key stakeholders; and he never really understood the environment where the battle was being fought.

Hornfischer writes:

> Greater cost for insomnia lay in not knowing the proficiency of one's crew. This uncertainty had hampered Admiral Gormley. He didn't know what his ships and his commanders were capable of. He hadn't spent time with them, from their intangible spirit to the physical soundness of the machinery. He was candid about this: "I did not know from actual contact the ability of my officers, nor the material condition of the ships, nor their readiness for battle, nor did I know their degree of training for warfare, such as was soon to develop in this area." ...This is a startling admission of leadership failure.

---

50   James D. Hornfischer, *Neptune's Inferno: The US Navy at Guadalcanal* (Novato, CA: Presidio, 2012).

Gormley did not get a clear understanding of his situation because he wanted to see what he preferred to see. His communications to his superiors and subordinates usually related to how close they were to failure. Naturally, Gormley's defeatist attitude did not inspire trust from most of his key stakeholders. Because of Gormley's failure to acquaint himself with the environment, resources, and people he was responsible for, he fundamentally failed to lead them.

But there's a part two to this story. Admiral Gormley ended up being replaced with Admiral "Bull" Halsey. Admiral Halsey came into the same situation, with the same enemy, under the same conditions—but he was willing to get his boots on the ground of Guadalcanal. After flying to Guadalcanal, even as enemy artillery flew over his head, the first thing he did was get face to face with the Marine Corps 1st Division Commander, General Alexander Vandegrift. Halsey asked him, "What do you need to win?" He saw the determination of the battle-hardened Marines, and he felt their unflagging courage and tenacity. Halsey knew what he needed to do: get the Navy engaged closer to the action and send the strongest signal possible to the Marines that the Navy had their backs. Together Halsey, Vandegrift, and the US Navy and Marines were undefeatable, despite the Japanese throwing everything they possibly could at Guadalcanal.

Halsey recognized the importance of understanding the environment up close. By thoroughly acquainting himself with what his team was dealing with, he was able to form a strategy tailored to his people, his mission, and his context.

In this book, we've spoken to leaders who have recently changed altitude—going from one level of leadership to another. But we've also discussed changing altitude as a necessary maneuver. To deftly form a strategy that fully accounts for your environment, you need to both get low and get high. Get low to understand, in-depth, what your people are experiencing. Get high to fully view the larger picture—where you're going, what assumptions might be in place, the driving forces at work. Effective leadership requires a clear view of where you're going but also a full understanding of where you're at. With those two points in mind, you'll have a sense of where to act, how to act, and what you need to be successful.

This requires your self-awareness to know when you need to set aside your own biases and preferences. It requires agility: that you bend and flex, anticipating future requirements. Finally, it requires resilience: that you succeed during the storm and bounce back after the hits from the storm have landed.

That's your mission—and it's one you're capable of. You can fly through the storm. You can thrive in changing altitude.

ACTION STEPS

1. Go through the five steps to analyze your current environment.
2. Form a conscious strategy that takes your analysis into account.
3. Go through the cultural assessment questions to consider how best to implement changes within your team.
4. Try to "know what you do not know" by reassessing what assumptions you might have, looking at the VUCA factors, and examining the driving forces impacting your environment.

CHAPTER TEN

CONFLICT MANAGEMENT

HOW TO MAXIMIZE GROWTH AND MINIMIZE HARM

"Change means movement. Movement means friction. Only in the frictionless vacuum of a nonexistent abstract world can movement or change occur without that abrasive friction of conflict."

—SAUL ALINSKY

SOME TOUGH MUDDERS

Imagine that you're preparing to run a Tough Mudder obstacle course with three other friends. The shot goes off, the timer starts, and everybody bolts from the starting line. Your team sails through the first few obstacles—then, you reach the wall: it's roughly ten vertical feet high, and your entire team needs to climb over it. The four of you start quickly discussing the best approach to get over the wall.

The first person to speak up has the personality of a "driver." That person barks at the rest of the team, "Just get over the wall! Get over it NOW!"

The second person wants to collaborate. "I think we need to work together as a team. What's the best way for us to all get over the wall together?"

The third person might sit back and say, "Well, let's analyze this. What's the wall made of? How far apart are the boards? How can we use this knowledge about the wall's structure to get over it?"

The fourth person says something like, "Can't we just walk around it? This looks painful."

Which of those four people do you see yourself being? In reality, most people have a combination of all four types, although one response may dominate others. But leaders, in particular, are confronted with these competing responses all the time: sometimes you must drive forward, sometimes you should choose to collaborate, sometimes you need to press into understanding your environment, and sometimes you're playing devil's advocate, suggesting that people consider other alternatives.

These competing responses are all valuable. A team full of drivers, for instance, might speedily make a great attack—but capture the wrong hill. A high-functioning team, on the other hand, will practice speed, collaboration, environmental analysis, *and* consider alternatives. That requires that people with different perspectives listen to one another. It also means that you may have to temporarily set aside your strong preference to opt for a different response, based upon the needs of the situation.

Each one of us has the ability to change and flex our strategies at any time. However, choosing to flex may require deliberate, conscious thought. As we've discussed elsewhere in this book, times of high stress can make it extremely difficult to access that thoughtful, analytical brain. If you're covered in mud, freezing cold, staring up at a wall, while your teammate yells, "Just get over the wall!" you might find yourself yelling back, "We have to work together, idiot!"

When you're leading a team, you're guaranteed to have a collection of people with different perspectives and preferences. It's also certain that you will be forced to grapple with those differences of opinion when facing your equivalent of a wall—when something must be done, and there are different ways to do it, and the outcome matters. Inevitably, stress will arise, which means everyone will be inclined to double down on their own preferences and try to force their idea forward.

This chapter acknowledges that reality: conflict is inevitable. It is certain. It is an impending fact. But there's another reality to understand about conflict: It can lead to growth and learning, provided it is *managed* effectively to minimize its potential for harm and to maximize its potential for good. As a leader, you will need to increase the clarity of your personal lens and grow in your ability to see things through other people's eyes if you are to pursue effective conflict management.

So, wipe the mud off your face, stop yelling, and take a breath so that you can listen to your clamoring teammates. Then, you're going to form a plan to get over that wall.

THE INEVITABILITY AND OPPORTUNITY OF CONFLICT

Let's take a closer look at the word "conflict." The word often brings to mind struggle and fighting, but disagreement doesn't have to lead to that, as a matter of course. A better way to think about conflict might be "managing differences of perspective." If people approach a disagreement as an exploratory dialogue where they want to learn from each other or get to the best solution, conflict can be incredibly positive.

Disagreement is inevitable. However, the result of conflict depends entirely on how it is handled. Handled badly, differing views can lead to bitterness, resentment, frustration, and ultimately rot an organization from within. On the other hand, managed well, conflict can produce incredible opportunities for learning and be the impetus for needed change.

Many of the world's most profound developments *required* conflict. The United States Constitution was assembled after many heated conversations among flawed human beings who hammered out their compromises in its text. The Constitution is an embodiment of their collective resolutions, stemming from many different perspectives on governing a country. We've also discussed the brilliant guiding principle that Greg experienced during his work at McKinsey: "Upholding the obligation to dissent." Any idea put before one of McKinsey's clients has gone through the rigor of dissent, debate, and dialogue to arrive at the best solution possible; that's one reason the organization has experienced such tremendous success.

> *Managed well, conflict can produce incredible opportunities for learning and be the impetus for needed change.*

So not only is conflict inevitable; it is *necessary*. You can't get to a better idea unless you're willing to challenge the first idea, which necessitates disagreement. The role of a leader is not to eliminate conflict but to manage it towards a productive end. This chapter aims to provide you with strategies to address conflict and resolve it in a healthy way.

THE GOAL: MINIMIZE THE HARM AND MAXIMIZE THE VALUE

Managing conflict well means you minimize the harmful effects and maximize the useful effects. Given that conflict is inevitable, your goal is to keep it both constructive and positive.

> *The role of a leader is not to eliminate conflict but to manage it towards a productive end.*

Many people simply want the conflict to disappear as quickly as possible. However, a superficial attempt to smooth things over won't lead to healthy transformation or better understanding; it may lead to greater harm if people perceive their voices aren't really being heard. The opposite approach is also damaging—there's no point in "poking the bear" and stirring up unnecessary conflict by needling issues that will cause emotional distress among your people. You'll have plenty of conflicts to deal with already, just doing your best to run a productive and healthy organization.

Instead, manage constructive conflict by seeking to better understand both sides of an issue. Don't run from it; don't stir it up; simply lean into it and try to learn and understand. Sometimes, this may require that you do some detective work to get to the root of an issue. Many conflicts evolve over time. The behavioral symptoms that manifest as conflict might actually relate to a deeper root, such as:

- A fundamental absence of trust or respect, either between a few people or across the organization
- A lack of clear understanding about direction or objectives or even a divergence in direction and objectives
- A difference of opinion related to values and beliefs

When preparing to manage a conflict, you're seeking to understand *why* there is a difference of opinion. Why do these two people or camps have such trouble getting along? Why does this same issue keep presenting itself? Ask questions early and often. The *opportunity* presented by conflict is one for deeper understanding. If there's a lack of trust or respect, why? What can be done? How might people achieve more self-awareness and transformation through seeking to build up trust? If you discover that conflict has arisen from a lack of clarity, then once the leader provides that clarity, the subordinate can buy in, and the level of conflict can be reduced.

When you explore the root of conflict and ask the hard questions, you choose to mine the conflict for its usefulness. Areas of dysfunction can be exposed. People can experience profound personal growth and increased self-awareness. Ideas can be challenged and improved. Psychological safety can be strengthened.

That's the goal: to manage conflict in a way that aligns with the goals and needs of the individual *and* the organization. This often requires that you devote real time, effort, and thought towards resolving the conflict. However, when done productively, your organization and your people will be in a better place as a result.

FOUNDATIONAL ELEMENTS FOR PRODUCTIVE CONFLICT

Dennis O'Neil narrates

The other night, my wife and I went out to dinner with one of her close friends. As often happens with this woman, the conversation veered towards politics. My wife's friend began expressing her opinions decisively and quizzing me on my own—which she knew were very different from hers.

Finally, I said, "I need to be honest—I really don't enjoy talking politics with you. I don't think it's healthy for the wonderful relationship that we all have. When we talk politics, I often feel like you're trying to convince me that I'm wrong and you're right, rather than sharing your ideas and seeking to understand mine better. Would it be okay if we tried to avoid this topic for a while?"

The woman thought about it and then said, "Okay."

My wife was mortified that I had the gall to suggest that we shouldn't talk about politics at dinner anymore. But I knew that if I wanted to maintain a good relationship with my wife's close friend, I needed to acknowledge this source of frustration. When I really thought about why this particular conflict stirred up such strong feelings in me, I realized that it was because I felt like my own views were being invalidated. It was like we were in a zero-sum game, where one of us had to be wrong if the other one was going to be right. Until we both decided to really hear each other out and respect our different perspectives, there was no way to engage in productive, meaningful dialogue.

My goal at that moment was to preserve the health of this relationship. If I hadn't spoken up, I would likely have just made an effort to avoid this person—and, for my wife's sake, I didn't want to do that. But I also didn't want to pummel her with my own opposing views and invalidate *her* opinion. So instead, I did my best to point out the existence of the conflict and make a plan for us to move beyond it.

When there's conflict that is emotionally charged based on personal beliefs—religious, political, or otherwise—preventing the conflict before it starts might actually be the best strategy, particularly if you have the goal to maintain a healthy relationship with that person. But other conflicts may have a direct impact on the work that gets done; those *do* need to be addressed head-on. What's important is that those points of conflict get addressed in a productive, healthy manner. There are six "prerequisites" for productive conflict. Taken together, these six elements will help set you up to manage conflict in a way that is productive, not harmful.

1. RECOGNIZE THAT THERE *IS* A CONFLICT.

The first step in managing conflict well is to recognize that there *is* a conflict. Rather than ignoring the existence of disagreement and hoping it will go away by itself, recognize that the difference of opinion exists.

There's a book called *Crucial Conversations*[51] which provides three defining characteristics of a "crucial conversation"—i.e., the type of conversation that could easily lead to conflict if not handled with care:

1. There are two or more differing opinions.
2. There are emotions involved.
3. The outcome matters.

How often do we have conversations where those three components are present? Most likely, all the time, every day. We have them with our spouses, our children, our co-workers—even customer service phone reps. When you realize that these three elements are present, register for yourself that this is a difficult conversation, an emotional conversation, a *crucial* conversation. Whatever adjective you prefer, the basic essence is that it's a conversation that's important. The conversation's outcome will impact the relationship, which means it's time to make a game plan.

Then, take a pause. If you have a knee-jerk reaction to a disagreement, the conflict will likely stir up strong emotions rather than move towards a thoughtful, productive end. In that pause, put in the work required to manage it positively. Ask the right questions, consider why this disagreement exists, and determine your goal. (And by all means, don't engage these difficult conversations by email or text!)

2. STEP BACK AND DETERMINE YOUR GOAL.

The most important thing you can do when you recognize that you're in a conflict is to step back and reflect on *what you want* in this situation. Get clarity in your mind about what your goal is during this conversation before you fully engage.

Suppose you don't have clarity in your mind about the outcome that

---

51   Kerry Patterson, Joseph Grenny, Ron McMillan, and Al Switzler, *Crucial Conversations: Tools for Talking When Stakes Are High* (New York: McGraw-Hill, 2012).

you want. In that case, it's extremely likely that you're going to be emotionally hijacked during the conversation and unintentionally take it to an unproductive place. For example, your heated emotions might lead you to focus all your energy on proving the rightness of your position and the wrongness of *their* position, when actually, the most productive strategy might be to work out a compromise that would require listening well. Going off on tangents is another unproductive reaction that can happen during conflict when there's no clear goal in mind: "Oh yeah, you think my behavior was an issue today? Well, let's talk about what you did two years ago!" Neither of these routes will take you on a positive trajectory to handle conflict in a healthy way.

Instead, keep track of what you're working towards. After realizing that you're in a crucial conversation, pause to evaluate: What do I want for myself? What do I want out of this relationship? What do I want for this other person or other people? How am I going to drive the conversation if these are truly the results I want to get? Keep your eyes on the prize. If you know what your goal is, you'll operate with greater focus and intention.

One of the greatest tools you have as a leader is your prefrontal cortex: your analytical, thinking brain. Remember: Between the emotionally triggering stimulus and your response, *there is a space*. Use that space to move from your "fight or flight" reptilian brain to your thoughtful, reflective brain. Consider the outcome you want for your team, department, organization, relationship. If that's the outcome you want, how do you need to respond to move closer to your desired outcomes?

The challenge, of course, is that you're only able to control half the conversation. The other person or people that you're speaking to may not be committed to working towards a productive goal. However, you still have the ability to focus your half of the conversation around the issues at hand. Your calm, focused responses and your efforts to promote respect and safety for others will do a lot to quiet the emotions that might be stirred up.

In sum: When you recognize that you're in a conversation with two or more opinions and strong emotions, and the outcome of the conversation matters, then quickly get clarity in your mind about your goal for that conversation. What do you want to happen as a result of this dialogue? Then, engage the conversation in pursuit of that goal.

3. SEEK TO LEARN RATHER THAN WIN.

In any conflict, or "crucial conversation," you are far more likely to achieve your desired outcome if you don't enrage the other person. You can do this by seeking to *learn*, rather than win.

To manage conflict productively, seek to increase your shared understanding, what the authors of *Crucial Conversations* call "the pool of shared meaning."[52] Use this communication strategy we discussed in Chapter Seven: listen generatively. Try to get a fuller understanding of where each person is coming from so that you can better appreciate why each person sees the world the way they do. Then, emphasize that you want to explore those ideas so that you can all make better decisions, achieve better quality outcomes, and secure buy-in. In doing so, you may just manage to find common ground.

To manage conflict productively, seek to increase your shared understanding.

There's an incredible benefit to engaging conflict with a learning attitude: *you actually learn.* You will genuinely come to understand something new when you listen generatively, instead of listening passively or reactively. It's likely you'll be able to fully appreciate why someone else sees the world differently from you and that others will understand your views better. You'll be able to temper your strong opinions and perhaps even improve them.

---

52   Patterson et al., *Crucial Conversations.*

Don't listen to rebut; don't argue to win. Instead, actively engage in listening in a way that seeks to explore and understand.

4. BE WILLING TO PURSUE CHANGE.

For conflict to be productive, you must be willing to pursue change. Our "fight or flight" mode, often activated during conflict situations, can make this hard. Rarely can we think rationally in that mode; we'd rather double down on our position and respond with our preferred conflict engagement strategy: fight or flight. But you can choose to rise above these more primal instincts if you open yourself to change.

The researcher Thomas Kilmann developed a well-known resource describing conflict dynamics profiles, which illustrates the different ways people tend to respond to conflict based on two factors: your level of assertiveness (i.e., your pursuit of your interests) and your level of cooperativeness (i.e., your concern for the interests of others).[53]

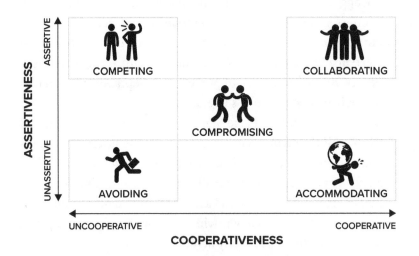

Depending on your level of assertiveness and cooperativeness, you will tend to respond in one of the following ways:

---

53   "Conflict Styles, Tool 37," Multi-Stakeholder Partnerships, Wageningen University and Research, 2012.
      http://www.mspguide.org/tool/conflict-styles.

- If you are *unassertive* and also *uncooperative*, your conflict response will be **avoidance**. You do everything possible to simply avoid the conflict—and other people as well. In this response, no one's needs get met. (This is the "flight" response.)
- If you are *assertive* and *uncooperative*, then you will **compete**. You will attack conflict head-on in a combative way, pursuing your interests above the interests of others, looking to "win" and make them "lose." (This is the "fight" response.)
- If you are *unassertive* and highly *cooperative,* your response to conflict will be to **accommodate**. In other words, you will forfeit your interests for the sake of others, accommodating their preferences even if it means that you suffer.

None of these conflict response profiles seem to strike a healthy or productive balance—yet. However, Kilmann's final two conflict dynamics profiles start to point us toward a better way:

- By striking a *balance* on the assertiveness spectrum: not passive, not aggressive, but *assertive*. And also a *balance* on the cooperativeness spectrum: not uncooperative and not accommodating, but *cooperative*—you can achieve **compromise**. In this mode, you consider your interests with equal weight as the interests of others. As a result, you can pursue an acceptable solution that partially meets everyone's needs.
- If you are *assertive* and also highly *cooperative*, then you can cultivate **collaboration**. This conflict response is ideal: it means you're using everyone's ideas to achieve a better outcome than anyone had predicted. It goes beyond compromise, implying that everyone must "give in" a little to "get" a little. Collaboration, instead, pursues a win-win situation for all, ensuring that everyone's interests are fully achieved.

Take note: There's a major common denominator in the final two productive conflict dynamic profiles: *the willingness to change one's own position as well as a determination to fully understand another's position.* By opening yourself to compromise, and even better, collaboration, you can help lead conflict towards a productive outcome.

A willingness to pursue change flows naturally out of listening generatively. If you are genuinely listening to learn from someone, your mind will be opened to new ideas. You'll be positioned to collaborate and explore new alternatives.

However, as a leader, it's not enough to stop there. Simply arriving at a good solution that works for everyone is worthless without follow-through. Once you've determined healthy steps to take, lead your team in taking them. You're not just opening yourself to change; you're initiating it, holding others accountable to it, and actively pursuing that healthy change.

5. SEEK OUT NEEDED RESOURCES.

Throughout this book, we have made the premise that leaders have two fundamental responsibilities at every level: set priorities and allocate resources appropriately. When managing conflict, those same two responsibilities apply. But what does it look like to allocate resources in managing conflict?

Sometimes, those resources will be *tangible.* We knew of a medical team that was short on PPE—personal protective equipment—at the start of the COVID-19 pandemic. One of the medical leaders decided to give the doctors the limited PPE, even though it meant the nurses wouldn't have enough. Obviously, that didn't go over well with the nursing staff, who spent more time with sick patients than the doctors did. The limited resources and the inequitable allocation created a major conflict among this team at a critical point when they needed to work together. We would put that initial decision about resource allocation in the "poor conflict management" category.

This particular conflict was ultimately resolved after the leaders asked the medical staffers for help in coming up with a solution. One of the nurses came up with the idea to use one of the unit's steriliza-tion machines to clean the limited PPE after every shift. That's what they did: at the end of every shift, all of the used PPE was put into a room, and the sterilization machine disinfected everything so that it was clean and ready for use the following day. That's an example of productive allocation of tangible resources. When tangible resources are in short supply—whether that's *funding, material, space*, and so on—this can be an area where people easily butt heads. As a leader, it's your responsibility to allocate equitably, find creative solutions, and/or drum up more resources.

But what about the intangible resources, which may be even more important? Sometimes, the resource needed is *attention* or *acknowledgment*. A department might feel frustrated with their senior leadership because their hard work is never recognized; they need the intangible resource of acknowledgment. Sometimes, the resource needed is *time;* deadlines need to be adjusted, or import-ant conversations need to get scheduled. Often, the chief resource allocated in conflict management is the *leader's willingness to address the issue* and devote the time needed to resolve it fully. When the demands of an organization seem urgent, and there are different needs from different parties which seem to be incompatible—often, the leader might simply force a solution, even if it leaves one or more groups with the short end of the stick. In those conflict scenarios, the resource most immediately needed might simply be the leader's willingness to thoughtfully engage the conflict.

Related to this is the need for *cognitive resources*. Arguably, the most common resources required during conflict are related to cognition: it's the ability to be thoughtful, creative, analytical, collaborative, and calm. Human beings possess amazing brains, and two brains are better than one. If a leader makes a point to invite these cognitive resources, they can get the best ideas out on the table and achieve a win-win solution. In the example of the nurse coming up with the brilliant idea to stretch the PPE supplies by cleaning them with the sanitizing machine, that solution came about because the leaders made space for cognitive resources. If a leader allows for diverse points of view to be shared, they can make room for compromise, thoughtful resolutions, and even creative problem-solving that could make up for constrained resources.

Leaders should also consider whether or not the need is for *emotional resources*. One of the three defining elements of a crucial conversation is that "emotions are involved," so you can trust that people have lots of significant feelings in a disagreement. Remember the analogy of the driver sitting on the elephant, where the large, powerful elephant is equivalent to our emotions. Emotionally fraught people need to be heard: the elephant in the room (that large, emotional one) must be acknowledged.

A positive, constructive response to conflict involves expressing one's emotions. In identifying what you're feeling, you are able to integrate your cognitive and emotional responses—it's like getting the small driver and the big elephant to talk to each other. As soon as you can take a negative emotion like anger, sadness, or frustration, and you *name* it, then you stop *being* it. By naming an emotion—"I feel angry"—people are able to move from their primal reptilian brain to their prefrontal cortex. Naming the emotion also causes the emotion to weaken in its intensity. Rather than *embodying* that emotion via a raised voice, harsh language, aggressive body language, and so on, you're filtering that emotion through your cognitive process, which enables you to *manage* it.

You can help other people do this same thing by naming—and therefore validating—their emotions: "I can tell that you feel really frustrated by this." "You seem upset." "You seem sad. Can you help me understand why?" If you as a leader are engaged in a conflict with someone who needs emotional resources, acknowledging their feelings can be significant. It will help them feel heard, validated, and opens the door for empathy and understanding.

Equally important to being able to name and tame our emotions is making sure that you don't invalidate or disrespect what others are feeling. Many a conflict has gotten far worse when one of those involved in the conflict says, "You shouldn't feel that way." This invalidates the other person's feelings and, by extension, the other person as a whole. It will exacerbate the negative feelings, most likely causing the other person to double down on their argument. You'll make greater progress by recognizing and naming what the other person is feeling.

6. SHOW RESPECT TO THE OTHER PERSON THROUGHOUT THE PROCESS.

Demonstrating respect for others is paramount if you hope to manage conflict effectively. In fact, the only way to recognize that conflict *could* be positive requires that you acknowledge there's more than one side that has merit. If a leader says, "Anybody who disagrees with me is negative. It's my way or the highway," that leader is not allowing for any difference of opinion, from anyone. There's no mutual respect in that scenario; there's only authoritarian leadership. Nevertheless, respect must exist if conflict is to be addressed and engaged to a productive end.

Even though this point is listed last, respect should be maintained throughout the conversation. In fact, *Crucial Conversations* makes the point that conflict should be stopped entirely if it starts to veer into a place of disrespect or a lack of safety. When Dennis was engaging with his wife's friend over dinner, he recognized that the conversation was veering into disrespectful territory. At that point, the best next step was to simply halt the conflict entirely. However, if at all possible, do what you can to maintain a respectful tone so that the conflict can be seen through to a productive end.

Remember the *value* of conflict: When people feel safe to share differing opinions, you can get to better ideas. You can achieve a greater level of commitment from all those involved and build momentum towards a common direction. You can help avoid mistakes. However, none of those benefits can come if a leader does not respect their people during times of disagreement. When leaders assume that they are the only source of truth, the potential for productive conflict is lost, and, in fact, the entire organization is jeopardized.

How can you show respect, even when you disagree with someone? Regardless of whether or not you find another person's views illogical, they have *reasons* for holding those views. If you want your own views to be understood as valid, then appreciate and respect that their perspective is *also* valid. Valid doesn't necessarily mean "right," but it means that this person has arrived at their point of view through their reasoning. Even if you disagree with their view, you can learn to appreciate their reasoning. However, if you start by saying something along the lines of, "You're an idiot, and your ideas are idiotic," you're only going to cause them to create defenses and stop listening to you.

When going into a "crucial conversation," accept that the other person (or people) has a valid point of view, which they have reasons for believing. Seek common understanding—that pool of shared meaning—so that you can pursue a shared goal. Others might see the solution differently from you, and that's okay. Allowing safety for other opinions to be heard allows the problem to be fully explored and help protect yourself against making mistakes. You will increase psychological safety and increase buy-in when a solution is ultimately agreed on.

If you hope to minimize harm and maximize the usefulness of a conflict, then respect is required. To paraphrase Theodore Roosevelt, your employees won't care how much you know until they know how much you care.[54]

---

54 "Home," Theodore Roosevelt Center at Dickinson State University, accessed June 28, 2021, https://www.theodorerooseveltcenter.org/.

HOW TO LEAD CONFLICT MANAGEMENT

We've shared foundational requirements for moving conflict in a productive direction. Most of these requirements assume that you are directly engaged in the conflict. But what about when the conflict is between your subordinates? If you find yourself in the role of conflict mediator, we have these recommendations.

CONFLICT AMONG SUBORDINATES: DOS AND DON'TS

There are two common paradigms managers use to try to resolve conflict among subordinates. Most often—though not always—these paradigms would fall into the "don't" category:

Don't Intervene to Solve the Problem Without the Input of the People Involved

We sometimes see leaders with the attitude, "If there's a problem, I need to be the one to fix it. No one else can fix it better than me because I'm the smartest person in the room, and my solutions will be right." That *is* a technique—but it doesn't fit the criteria of minimizing the harm and maximizing the value of conflict. If you step in and solve every problem, you're not empowering people to operate independently of you. The goal is to make sure your subordinates are so thoroughly acquainted with your intent, objectives, and organizational goals, that they can be empowered to work through their conflict with those objectives to guide them. However, the opposite response is also a "don't"...

Don't Expect Your People to Solve All Conflict Issues Without Your Involvement

We see other leaders who say things like, "That's your issue, not mine. I don't want to hear about your problems unless you're also coming to me with a solution. If you don't know how to work through this, look up some solutions on YouTube or Google. But I'm not interested in this nonsense." Responding in this way communicates a lack of empathy or a lack of respect for the emotional impact on the subordinate. This approach isn't going to do your organizational trust any favors. It's also likely to exacerbate the conflict's potential harm rather than minimize it. It's not realistic to expect your subordinates to resolve their own challenges when you're not providing any tools, resources, or support in doing so.

While these two practical "don't do" strategies can be quite helpful, we also have a few "dos" to offer that we have found great utility in. These three "do" strategies can help team members manage conflict as effectively and constructively as possible:

Do Offer Guidance and Support by Seeking Out the Root Cause of the Issue

For example, is this a conflict over a scarce resource? Is someone frustrated by a lack of access? Is it a conflict between two people? If so, seek out the issue: Is it a personality difference, a difference in world views, or just a negative interaction pattern? Once you identify the root cause, arrange for appropriate resources and tools to work through the conflict. Remember that resources may be tangible or intangible. Sometimes, a workplace drama can be substantially calmed by simply just allowing someone to express their emotions and be heard. Other times, a conflict may impact the organization's goals; in those scenarios, your active involvement will be especially important in resolving it.

Do Provide a Super-Ordinate Goal

In other words, a goal that is big enough to require a higher level of collaboration and cooperation among your people to get it done. Not only will this ambitious goal require your people to work together, but it also will help provide needed clarity and direction to your subordinates. Lack of clarity is often a trigger for conflict, so this super-ordinate goal will help resolve conflict in more ways than one.

Do Create Space for People to Talk About the Conflict They're In

So often, in conflict situations, people get used to tip-toeing around the proverbial elephant in the room. As your team's leader, you're going to name that elephant and give people a safe place to share their perspectives respectfully. What are the needs that are going unmet? What systems are breaking down and causing unnecessary stress? Where have there been instances of inappropriate conduct? Through exploring these questions in a safe, respectful environment, you and your team will arrive at answers you wouldn't have been able to find any other way. That's the value of productive conflict management. Creating space for that conversation, providing the time, and establishing a safe atmosphere are key ways to contribute towards effective conflict resolution.

Remember: effective conflict management aims not to eliminate it, but to reduce the harmful effects and maximize the useful effects. Instead of saying, "This is a conflict that only I can fix," or alternately, "I don't want to hear about your fighting, go away," seek the middle ground. Ask: "What is the most helpful way for me to manage this conflict?" You don't have to solve it, and you don't have to ignore it; instead, you can address it in a healthy way. Reduce the harm and increase the good.

CONFLICT WITH YOUR SUPERVISOR: DOS AND DON'TS

We've provided recommendations for managing conflict among subordinates and with people on the same level—but what do you do when you have a conflict with your boss? We find that many senior leadership teams have very driven leaders who advanced and were promoted because they got hard things accomplished. However, sometimes these same drivers are less concerned about relationships and making sure others are being heard and feel valued. If you work for a leader who is overly demanding, unreasonable and makes it difficult for you to work with, what can you do?

We know of a leader whose direct reports were interviewed by another consultant and all those employees talked about how this leader made them feel overly disrespected. Several employees were young mothers, yet their boss would think nothing of scheduling a Zoom call at 7:00 a.m. or sending them a text asking for something at 7:30 p.m. or on the weekends. When some of his direct reports saw his number and name appear on their phone, they became emotionally distraught. This boss had no sense of boundaries, and as a result, his employees were desperate to jump ship.

Leaders should take warning from that story: as labor markets continue to get tighter and great employees have lots of opportunities to work other places, it is a strategic imperative for leaders to create workplaces that establish strong mutual respect and have boundaries regarding time off. Your employees may tolerate your toxic behavior for a time, but they will look for an exit as soon as possible.

Our hope is that more employees will feel empowered, when their bosses are violating boundaries, to raise those issues in ways that are heard and which leads their leadership to take appropriate actions. This can be hard to do. When facing down an intimidating boss who seems to have authority over your career advancement, the temptation is often to avoid conflict and simply bear it. However, it is vital to engage the conversation with your boss. A conflict with your superior, left alone, will not get better with time. However, any boss worth their salt will recognize the value of your input, provided you approach the matter strategically with some of these "don'ts and dos."

Don't Avoid Your Boss

They may drive you crazy, but it's a failed strategy to simply avoid them altogether. They're likely to *lose* trust in your abilities, which means they'll pull you in closer for direct supervision (i.e., micromanagement). If you want to get to a healthier relationship with your boss, you actually need *more* time with them, not less. You can seek that out in whatever way makes the most sense for your context and your boss—emails, brief check-in conversations, scheduled meetings, Friday happy hour, phone calls, or some other option.

Don't Tell Them They're Wrong

No one likes to be told they're wrong, and you're not going to help your career by engaging in direct personal conflict. Instead, keep your angry venting limited to your journal or a private conversation with a friend who's removed from the situation.

Do Seek to Appreciate Your Boss's Goals

As we have written previously, ironically, people don't typically get promoted because they're great leaders; they get promoted for being great followers. Recognize that learning how to be a great follower is an important element of your success. That doesn't mean you "suck up" to your boss, but it does mean that you should seek to fully appreciate their goals. Those you work for probably have a wider view of what's going on across your organization. As a result, most supervisors will have a broader understanding than you of the constraints, demands, and challenges posed in their efforts to achieve their goals. If you can understand those challenges with greater clarity, you'll have more understanding of the daily struggles your boss experiences and perhaps have even greater appreciation for why your boss can be challenging at times.

Do Understand Your Boss's World and Help Them Be Successful

Once you fully appreciate your boss's goals, you can play an active role in helping them achieve those goals. That will help increase their trust in you and—ideally—will lead them to give you greater autonomy in your work. For example, if you have a control freak boss, overwhelm them with data and details. Eventually, they'll realize, "I guess this person is on top of things. I'll go control someone else." Or, if your boss is an introvert and tends to be hard to access, seek out time with that boss in small doses. In doing so, you're trying to understand their world and their goals so that you can be as aligned with them as possible. They should experience you as someone who fully supports their aspirations and vision for the organization.

Do Seek Common Ground

Maybe you've got a clear sense of why your boss is pursuing the route that they are—but you still disagree with it. Once you've got a clear understanding of your boss's goals, then you can ask the question, "Can I share my thoughts on this?" If you have fully come to appreciate your boss's strategic plans and goals, then you can pitch your strategy in a way that can address their values. It's also appropriate to say something like, "I can sense that we have slightly different perspectives on this point, but the last thing I want to be is in opposition to your goals. At the end of the day, you're the boss, and I'm going to do everything I can to support your success. Because I am so committed to our success, can I share a few ideas that I believe could make us even more successful?" Even if your boss doesn't go with your idea, this type of conversation will still work to build their long-term trust in you as you demonstrate your understanding of their goals and your own thoughtful strategies.

Do Look Further Down the Road

It can be easy to struggle with a boss over their communication style or behavioral patterns—but try to raise your eyes above those daily frustrations and take the long view. In the future, you're likely to want more space to operate independently. Therefore, in the immediate future, you need to invest in your boss's needs so that they decide you are worthy of their trust. Seek to find their best rhythms: How many cups of coffee do they need before they're primed for interaction? Do they prefer email communication, text, in-person chats, or a phone call? Do they like lengthy sit-downs or quick check-ins? Do they need data and research to be convinced of the legitimacy of your ideas? Identify their goals and needs and do what you can to meet those needs in the near future so that you can enjoy a better future down the road.

If you work for a truly toxic individual, it might be the healthiest thing for you to pursue employment elsewhere. However, many difficult leaders can become more amenable when they see that you are as passionate as they are about achieving their goals. If possible, build mutual respect with your challenging boss and try to come to joint solutions.

FROM A PRISON CELL TO THE NOBEL PEACE PRIZE

Human history is fraught with leaders who did not change altitude effectively enough to draw in the perspectives and opinions of others—especially when those views were in opposition to their own. But those who did were capable of extraordinary leadership.

When Nelson Mandela took over leadership of South Africa after the abolishment of apartheid,[55] he had to find a way to bring together deeply divided groups of people. The white South Africans, who had long benefited from the system of apartheid, had a great deal to lose in the new, more just, system of government. The black Africans and "coloreds" had been brutally oppressed and stigmatized for decades—a fact which could easily have led to rage, boiling over in violence. Somehow, Mandela had to bring them together towards a more unified South Africa.

Mandela did this through modeling the behavior he needed his fellow South Africans to embrace. During his twenty-seven years as a political prisoner, Mandela did not fester with thoughts of revenge. Instead, he worked on his bitterness towards his captors so that he could eventually show goodwill to all. He learned the history and language of his oppressors so that he could effectively communicate with them. He was willing to connect not only with his allies but also with his former enemies. By modeling such a powerful personal transformation, he was able to credibly ask the people of his country to undertake a transformation as well. His own humility and

---

55 Apartheid in South Africa was a legalized system of discrimination against black Africans and "coloreds" (people of mostly Middle Eastern descent). The legal apartheid system was finally ended in 1994, when Nelson Mandela became president of South Africa.

persistence to rise towards a greater good inspired a willingness in his people to work with their former enemies—resulting in a largely peaceful transition towards a more just South Africa.

Ultimately, leaders get paid to make decisions—but those decisions should not be made in a vacuum. The best decision in any scenario will be informed by the richness of diversity around the table—a wide variety of perspectives that can dissent and debate freely in order to arrive at the best solutions. The more you can create a psychologically safe environment where people feel respected and valued, the more you can engage in this *productive* conflict. Out of the stirring of ideas, the organization can strengthen; the team can grow; you'll get higher levels of engagement and commitment from all; and you'll arrive at the best decisions possible. *That's* what we consider maximizing the value of conflict.

ACTION STEPS

1. Identify a recent "crucial conversation" in your life, where there were two or more differing opinions, emotions were involved, and the outcome mattered. Evaluate yourself in how you engaged that crucial conversation. Did you recognize it as a conflict? Did you pause to consider your goal and then engage in the conflict with that goal in mind? Did you seek to learn rather than win?

2. What would you identify as your conflict dynamic profile? (Avoidance; aggressive; accommodating; compromise; collaboration.) How can you personally make a shift to pursue greater collaboration when you engage in a conflict?

3. Review the foundational elements of productive conflict. Which element(s) do you need to work on the most?

4. Is there a conflict among your subordinates that needs your guidance? What specific steps can you take to provide guidance without solving the problem for them or forcing them to solve it completely on their own?

5. Are you experiencing conflict with your leadership? What specific steps can you take to improve your alignment with that leader's goals, understand their world, and build their confidence in you?

CHAPTER ELEVEN

PARADOXICAL LEADERSHIP

THE IMPORTANCE OF HOLDING COMPETING INTERESTS IN TENSION— ESPECIALLY DURING A CRISIS

"The ultimate measure of a man is not where he stands in moments of comfort and convenience, but where he stands at times of challenge and controversy."

—DR. MARTIN LUTHER KING, JR.

BRUTAL FACTS WITH UNWAVERING FAITH

Greg Hiebert narrates

In Chapter Four, I mentioned that I'd had the privilege to learn from former POWs during my college years. As a junior in 1979, West Point sent me to the Naval Academy to study for a semester. At that time, there were a number of former POWs who served in positions of leadership at the Naval Academy—some as professors, some as battalion tactical officers, and even the Superintendent, Admiral

William Lawrence. One regular presence at the Academy, Admiral James Stockdale, had been the highest-ranking POW in Vietnam and awarded the Medal of Honor for his extraordinary leadership while in captivity. He had recently retired from the Navy and often visited the Academy.

Jim Collins, author of *Good to Great*, also had the chance to learn from Admiral Stockdale and discusses interviewing him in his book.[56] Collins, knowing that Stockdale had made enormous personal sacrifices to protest the deaths of several of his colleagues during torture, was interested in Stockdale's perspectives on leadership.

When Collins interviewed Stockdale, he asked, "Who were the people that didn't make it out of the camps?"

Admiral Stockdale answered immediately. "That's easy," he said. "It was the optimists." He explained that the optimists leaned on false hopes. They would pick an arbitrary date and claim certain rescue by that date: "Clearly, the Americans will rescue us by Christmas." Then, Christmas would come and go. The optimists would pin their hopes on another date, claiming rescue by Easter, and then the Fourth of July, with no basis for their expectations other than extreme optimism. When those dates kept passing them by, month after month, they ended up giving up hope entirely. Stockdale summed up their fate: "They died of a broken heart."

At the other end of the spectrum, Stockdale explained, the pessimists also struggled. They lived in a constant state of despair, saying things like, "We'll always have these daily beatings. Life will never get better. There is no hope to get out of this." Stockdale argued that the people who survived—and not only that but those who ended up coming out of the POW camps whole and hopeful—were the ones that faced the brutal and harsh realities of today, without losing hope

---

56 Jim Collins, *Good to Great: Why Some Companies Make the Leap and Others Don't* (New York: HarperCollins, 2001).

that the future could be better. This concept came to be known as the Stockdale paradox.

When a crisis hits, false optimism is easy. So is despair, for that matter. At the start of the COVID-19 crisis, we spoke with a number of senior healthcare leaders who would repeat over and over, "Well, we're going to get past this in another month or two" without having any science or logical reasoning to substantiate their optimism. And yet, giving in to despair and doing nothing would have been even more catastrophic for those healthcare leaders. They had to learn to embrace Stockdale's paradox—to maintain hope, even while facing the brutal realities of their current environment.

LEADERSHIP PARADOX #1

1. The Stockdale Paradox: You must maintain unwavering faith that you can and will prevail in the end, regardless of the difficulties, and at the same time, have the discipline to confront the most brutal facts of your current reality, whatever they might be.

A paradox can be defined as the co-existence of two or more things which, logically, should not be able to co-exist—and that's exactly what I'd encountered. Paradoxes like these are not uncommon in the task of leading others, when there are rarely "right answers," but only "better alternatives." Hopefully, the stakes of your workday are not life-threatening, but there's no question: the stakes are still high. In a chaotic and high-stakes environment, when so many priorities are competing for your attention, how do you lead well?

That's what this chapter is all about.

BOTH, AND

We're going to discuss crisis leadership during this chapter, but it doesn't take a crisis to know that our world is volatile, uncertain, and complex—even on a good day. The world we live in is constantly changing and highly dynamic. In a paradoxical environment, we must often respond with paradoxical leadership, holding competing priorities in *tension* to maintain balance and seek the best outcomes.

Effective leaders operate in that state of flux by maintaining close attention to the situation at hand. They are always scanning the field to make sure that they have great clarity of what's really going on, right now in the organization. They have a strong sense of where they need to spend their time, where they need to focus people's attention, what their people need to be successful, and how they need to move to optimize the outcomes for their team and organization.

They need to move. When we think about this notion in terms of physical movement, the necessary paradoxes of leadership become vivid: leaders must step back and consider their direction, evaluating whether or not recalibration is needed. They must move in, asking questions of their staff and listening closely to their team's honest feedback. They need to increase their altitude to consider the big-picture ramifications of certain decisions. They need to decrease their altitude to understand what's happening on the ground level of the organization. There's enormous movement, versatility, and dynamism required to lead well.

This versatility lies at the heart of effective leadership. Strong leaders must know when to change and when not to change—and *what* to change, and *what not* to change. There's enormous fluidity and movement required in order for the leader to see and understand many different vantage points—to see widely and also see deeply—and not just see, but also act. Embracing the paradoxes is required.

Remember Viktor Frankl's quote: "Within the stimulus and the response, there is a space."[57] Leaders must use that space—that

---

57   Viktor Emil Frankl, *Man's Search for Meaning: An Introduction to Logotherapy* (New York: Houghton Mifflin Harcourt, 2000).

pause—between the stimulus and response to evaluate what is going on in a volatile, uncertain, complex, ambiguous world and choose a response that will best suit the needs of the organization *and* your people. It's not one or the other; it's "both, and." The challenge is to find the balance in between those two competing interests and hold them in tension. That's leading paradoxically.

COMPETING VALUES FRAMEWORK

Dennis O'Neil narrates

There's another definition of paradox we reference often, describing the term as a "competing values framework." The definition implies a scenario when there is moral value in two competing and contradictory actions. It emphasizes the point that leaders must often make quick, difficult decisions with imperfect information, in a challenging environment, when there are competing values at play. In those moments, you simply have to do the best you can to discern quickly and decide well.

I've experienced this personally. In Chapter Nine, I described an intense day of combat I experienced in Mosul in 2009. On that day, as I stood on an elevated street above an alley, three hand grenades were thrown in my direction. Fortunately for me, the three explosives fell short.

It was in that next moment that I had to make one of the hardest decisions of my life. When the hand grenades went off, I pulled up my M4 carbine, flipped the safety off and looked through the site with my hand on the trigger, hunting to kill whoever had thrown them. Immediately, I found three people. I aimed carefully and took the slack out of the trigger. They were standing just down the alley, a grenade throw's distance away—a soccer ball at their feet.

And not one of them appeared to be more than twelve years old.

Were these the individuals responsible for the three hand grenades? Or were they just three kids playing soccer in the wrong place, at the wrong time?

I eased off of the trigger and chose to let them live.

I still question whether that was the right decision—most likely, those kids were responsible for throwing the hand grenades, and I probably should have killed all three of them. But I didn't want to be wrong with that decision. That was a decision I knew could not be taken back.

I also had more compelling threats to deal with, so I shifted my attention to those. We were still being shot at by a sniper at the exact same time, and all my Iraqi counterparts were under fire. My team, along with our partners, had to maneuver our position to clear the adjacent buildings, return fire to the sniper, secure the first responders, and evacuate the wounded.

It was a moment that required both offense and defense; both self-preservation and protecting others. Many things all needed to happen at the same time, and if they didn't, lives would be lost. There was no obvious right or wrong answer; there was only guesswork in the interest of optimizing outcomes. Even my enemy refused to fit neatly into the category of "terrorist"—because maybe those three kids were the very people I'd been called to protect.

To sum this moment up as a "competing values framework" trivializes it, but essentially, that's what it was. There were profound moral implications on either side of my decision. I confronted this paradox on the battlefield—but I'm certain this wasn't the first time. Most of us first encounter a competing values framework as a child.

For example, imagine a second-grader whose dad has always taught her, "If somebody hits you, hit them back. Don't tolerate being picked on." At school, some bully hits the second grader, and she wallops them back, following her dad's advice. Afterward, the principal tells her, "Hitting is never right. Violence is not the solution to any problem." This little second-grader has just confronted a huge paradox. She's been given one moral framework from her dad—"Hit 'em back!"—and another moral framework at school: "Hitting is wrong." How does she balance those competing frameworks? That's the earliest essence of paradox.

There's value in these moments. Over time, these paradoxical moments help us hone our moral compass. Our values help us define our "true north" in a way that ultimately allows us to embrace the complexity of the wide array of scenarios the world throws at us and navigate those paradoxes.[58] There are very few times when there's a clear right or wrong answer. Leadership is about choosing better outcomes, navigating areas of gray, and maximizing the potential opportunities based on the environmental circumstances.

The well-known professor and author, Robert Quinn from the University of Michigan, explored this concept in his model of leadership called the "Competing Values Framework."[59] His model identified four dominant things that leaders needed to do—all of which compete with one another:

1. Do things first: create.
2. Do things fast: compete.
3. Do things right: control.
4. Do things together: collaborate.

In doing things first, leaders *create*; they break through with innovation. In doing things fast, leaders *compete*; they drive, they get things done, they score some goals. In doing things right, leaders *control*; they need

58 Bill George, *Discover Your True North: Becoming an Authentic Leader*, 2nd ed. (Hoboken: Wiley, 2013).

59 The Competing Values Framework was created in 1983 by Robert Quinn and John Rohrbaugh.

to manage continuous improvement. And in doing things together, leaders *collaborate*; they facilitate connections and cooperation.

Quite obviously, these different domains can easily clash! But good leaders must integrate their decisions into those paradoxes, determining *when* it's more important to do things fast, versus do things right. Sometimes, you must maintain control, and other times, you must be flexible. There are times when you need to be internally oriented, and other times when you must shift very quickly to be externally oriented.

Another paradoxical leadership model that we use often is Jim Collins' "Level Five Leadership." Collins, once again the Gallup CEO, described Gallup's research of over 1,400 companies. They looked for the organizations which sustained extraordinary results, ultimately identifying eleven companies that fit those criteria. We've already discussed Gallup's findings on employee engagement at length, but equally as important was what they discovered related to senior leadership. Those eleven companies—the organizations that truly embodied this "good to great" movement—all had senior leaders that embodied two seemingly contradictory characteristics: a deep, professional will and personal humility.

The deep, professional will is the consistent, passionate pursuit of goals, the kind of driving attitude that says, "We're not going to stop until we've climbed this mountain." This professional will is sometimes described as a "hunger."[60] But the personal humility is

---

60 Jim Collins, *Good to Great: Why Some Companies Make the Leap and Others Don't* (New York: HarperCollins, 2001).

the attitude that gives credit to others, the attitude that says, "The reason we were successful in climbing this mountain is because of the incredible effort and determination that *all of you* demonstrated in getting us here." Professional hunger must be balanced with personal humility. It's the passionate drive towards goals that still recognizes the needed contribution of others and expresses gratitude for them. In fact, when Collins and the Gallup researchers looked more closely at the eleven CEOs leading "good to great" organizations, they were relatively obscure figures. These leaders had tempered their egos and were happy to get themselves out of the way; still, they never lost sight of the goals, direction, and urgent needs of the organization, leading their people to focus their efforts in achieving their objectives.

LEADERSHIP PARADOX #3

3. Collins' Level Five Leadership: Balance professional hunger with personal humility.

What does this Level Five Leadership look like, in action? We work with a fantastic CEO who has this driving professional will: he gets up every morning with a hungry dissatisfaction with the current status quo. He's a change agent, always driving for more. But recently, one of his leaders was diagnosed with cancer. The love, concern, and compassion that he demonstrated for this man was palpable. He is a leader who demands the best from his people and holds them to extremely high expectations. But he also demonstrates genuine care for them; as a result, his people are ready to follow him anywhere.

Can you think of any more leadership paradoxes? We can.

LEADERSHIP PARADOXES #4-10

4. Be flexible and rigid: flexible enough to let go of outdated paradigms and inefficient models when needed; rigid by maintaining control, establishing routines, and holding to systems.
5. Be soft and hard: soft in demonstrating care, concern, and compassion for your employees; hard by holding people to extremely high standards, holding people accountable when they fail to meet those standards.
6. Hold fast to your vision and know when to change your mind.
7. Be engaging and reserved.
8. Be humble and confident.
9. Be decisive and discerning.
10. Be accommodating and directing.

The trick with knowing which side to lean on with all these paradoxes often comes down to the *when*. There is a time to add value to a conversation by speaking up; there is a time when you need to simply shut your mouth and listen. The challenge is being able to identify which time it is: time to speak, or time to listen? We're going to devote the second half of this chapter to discussing strategies that can help you navigate these paradoxes and determine the "when."

Leading paradoxically is not easy. In fact, it *shouldn't* be easy. If leadership feels easy, then you're not leading paradoxically. A leader who is always right is not doing it right.

With that in mind, we're now going to make everything feel twice as difficult and talk about leading during a crisis.

THE KEY TO CRISIS LEADERSHIP

Here's the good news about crisis leadership: there's a built-in need for change. In "normal" times, this need for change may be less obvious, both to the leader and to their teams. That can make direction less clear and motivation less urgent.

We spent a large portion of Chapter Eight detailing strategies for leading change, exactly because knowing the "how," the "what," and the "why" can be challenging. Under normal circumstances, leading change can feel like pushing a wheelbarrow up a hill while trying to convince your people to hop *out* of the wheelbarrow and help you push! Not so in a crisis. In a crisis, there is an urgent, obvious need for change which can provide clear direction and strong motivation to accomplish that change quickly. Forget the wheelbarrow; a crisis drops everyone into a rollercoaster and presses *GO*.

Here's the bad news: The stress we experience during a crisis can make us inclined to revert to our "default mode" and bad habits. All the tendencies of an organization—both good and bad—will be accelerated or exacerbated in times of crisis. Your people will be less inclined to adhere to the team norms they all agreed on, because they'll be stressed, tired, and cranky. You'll be less inclined to practice the new habits of leadership you've learned to change altitude successfully, and instead will want to simply do the things that feel most comfortable.

But don't! "Between stimulus and response, there is a space." Between the crisis and your subsequent action, you can *choose your response*. And the key to crisis leadership is leading paradoxically. You must deliberately consider the competing needs, discern when to prioritize each one, and lead your people in each next step.

> The key to crisis leadership is leading paradoxically.

Let's take a closer look at how to take advantage of the "good news" in a crisis, and how to mitigate the "bad news" of our stress response tendencies.

THE GOOD NEWS: A COMPELLING NEED FOR CHANGE

Remember the elephant and the driver analogy we shared in Chapter Eight, from the book *Switch*, by Chip and Dan Heath?[61] The elephant represents our "emotional" brain, the fight or flight brain. The diminutive driver sitting on top represents the "thinking" brain which—ideally—will direct the elephant in a productive direction. The elephantine emotional brain has all the power; the analytical driver needs to get that power moving in the direction it wants.

This analogy can also extend to your organization: your team and all of its collective power represents the elephant. You, the driver, are only one person, but you direct that powerful force.

When a crisis hits, that elephant is ready to *move*. The built-in resistance to change which would normally characterize your team will evaporate, because people will see the compelling need to go somewhere else, fast. That's good news, provided you know where you want to direct the elephant. Get ahold of that elephant!

How do you do that? You lead paradoxically. In this case, you need to innovate and change things up, while also providing stability to your team with clear directions. Put differently, you take an abstract future state, and then anchor it to a methodical plan of how to get there. You can do this well, via the Comprehensive Change Model we discussed in Chapter Seven. Leading change in a crisis means that everything speeds up, but the essential steps to direct the elephant remain the same. Here is a review of how the Comprehensive Change Model can lend itself to crisis leadership, with a few tweaks:

Direction comes first: Given all the information you currently have about the crisis you're in, identify a better future that you could realistically move towards. This may need to be short term: determine what needs to be the focus for the next several weeks and create a plan for needed steps to move in that direction. Don't assume everyone

---

61   Chip Heath and Dan Heath, *Switch: How to Change Things When Change Is Hard* (New York: Penguin Random House, 2010).

understands what your intended vision is; don't offer something complicated and vague. Spell out your future vision in razor-sharp terms. It should be articulate, communicated explicitly, and universally understood so that everyone can see the direction you want to move in.

Then, calm that elephant down. Give reassurance to your team: "We're going to get through this, and we're going to be okay. We've got to carry on." Normally, steps two and three of the Comprehensive Change Model are providing motivation and inspiration to your team, but in a crisis, those two features are already there: the elephant is ready to bolt. Instead, what you want to do next is **alleviate fear**. When people are in a crisis, their instinctive negativity bias is amplified. There's constant reinforcement of all the things to be fearful of. If your elephant is going to move forward productively, you need to get it to stop ramming into palm trees as it runs in panicked circles. Stressed out, fearful people will not be able to make productive headway. Give your team the reassurance that you have a plan and you have clarity about your direction; then, provide them with a roadmap to get there. In order to fully buy in, your people need to agree that these targets are reasonable, feasible, realistic, and anchored in the goals of the organization.

That's when you reference steps four and five of the Comprehensive Change Model: **navigation** and **activation**, aka, the "how" and the "what." Map out milestones, targets, metrics, and any other relevant means through which to manage the journey forward. Align resources towards a common goal. You may be confronted with certain rules and regulations that inhibit moving with flexibility and speed; if possible, do what you can to amend those regulations to streamline processes. Recognize the barriers standing in the way of your team's success by scanning your environment. Do your best to remove those barriers or find a way around them. Identify the other numerous stakeholders at play, both internally and externally. Communicate your direction and focus to those other stakeholders so that, as much as possible, there's alignment in resources, understanding, and focused effort.

You're going to innovate and you're also going to stabilize. You're going to direct and you're also going to collaborate. You're going to be inspirational and also pragmatic. You're going to describe a hopeful future while also recognizing the current brutal realities. That's paradoxical leadership—and it's the key to leading during a crisis.

But what about the bad news? What about the fact that you may not do this incredible balancing act very well, especially if you're stressed and scared and exhausted? When you'd really just rather crawl under your desk in your office and hide? What if *you* feel like the elephant ramming against palm trees, and not the analytical driver?

There's no denying the personal challenges that a crisis can impose. But there's a key to navigating that too: self-awareness.

THE BAD NEWS: YOUR OWN CHALLENGING BIOLOGY

Here's what happens to our bodies when we confront a stressful stimulus:

- The stressor gets the attention of the thalamus in the brain which acts as an alarm clock.
- The thalamus activates our reticular activating system, which is like the switchboard saying, "Here's what's coming in!"
- Our endocrine system starts producing adrenaline for long-term action, and our electrical system jolts us into immediate "fight or flight" action.
- The end result: increased blood pressure, increased heart rate, perspiration. Blood is pumped to our extremities so that we can run fast and fight hard, and as a result, *less* blood is pumped to our brain.

Did you catch that? When we experience high stress, there's less blood flow to our brains, which means *it's harder to think clearly.*

However, by having the self-awareness that this is what's happening to your body, you can manage it.

Here's how: Under extreme stress, *insert a pause*. Often, we assume (wrongly) that we are always in possession of our focus and attention, but that's simply not the case. Stress changes things. By having the self-awareness to know that your rational analysis is compromised during stress, you can willfully take a step back, observe the environment, oxygenate your brain with some deep breathing, and regain your ability to have cognitive clarity.

The power of self-awareness under stress can take you even further than that. Understand that in a crisis, you are much more likely to fall back on your natural tendencies—i.e., your biology—rather than execute complex thinking. That means you'll default to your strong preferences. If you're a natural driver who's had to work hard to extend patience and understanding towards your subordinates, then in a crisis, that patient understanding will go out the window. You'll drive and you'll drive harder. However, by *knowing* your gravitational pull, you can acknowledge it as a tendency and a preference. You'll have the self-awareness to admit it's not simply the only way to operate in a crisis, and maybe not even the right way to respond in a crisis—it's simply the way *you* respond in a crisis. That clarity is going to enable you to self-correct quickly, particularly when using some of the strategies we'll soon discuss.

We began our book discussing the importance of "knowing thyself," and there's a good reason why. Self-awareness is powerful in nearly every facet of leadership, but especially needed during times of crisis. The whole premise behind "changing altitude" is the idea that leaders have to move, but deep stress and pressure causes people to become less mobile.

If you want to increase your physical mobility, you exercise and you stretch. Self-awareness is the cognitive equivalent of increasing your flexibility; it's like yoga for your mind. The tools we've recommended already in this book—the 360-Assessments, the personality assessments, and so on—will help you mitigate your response to stress and maintain greater versatility.

How? With self-awareness, you can set up safeguards for yourself ahead of time. For instance, if you tend to be a spontaneous and sometimes disorganized leader, you can establish systems and checklists around you to help force your organization. Under stress and pressure, those systems will help you stay focused and manage your natural tendency to be disorganized.

Self-awareness also is going to help you maintain greater clarity about how your team is doing. We can't be objective about others until we're objective about ourselves. Similarly, when we have an unbalanced view of ourselves ("I am always right"), it's difficult to have a balanced view of somebody else ("They are always wrong"). By increasing our objectivity about ourselves, we will have more accurate insights of others, enabling us to better understand their differences. We have needed clarity to identify gaps in workplace relationships, clearly evaluate people's performance, and maintain more positive interactions. In times of high pressure or crisis, this clarity is particularly invaluable.

Self-awareness can even help you in the heat of the moment. We work with a talented pediatric orthopedic surgeon who has a profoundly strong set of preferences. Under stress, she can often default towards being intense and rigid. However, she's also developed a tremendous amount of self-awareness about these preferences. She has a well-developed filter that enables her to catch her intensity and rigidity before she passes it along to others. When we asked her how she'd learned to catch herself with such consistency, she acknowledged that her self-awareness had largely been illuminated during a time of real personal struggle. In working through her struggles, she had gained an invaluable understanding about her tendencies under stress.

Take some encouragement from this story: if you've concluded at any point during this chapter that you won't be able to meet the challenges of paradoxical leadership—don't worry. We weren't always able to meet them either. But just like this pediatric surgeon, we learned a thing or two from our struggles.

TIMES WHEN WE WERE REALLY BAD AT THIS

Greg Hiebert narrates

In the summer of 1980, when I was still a cadet at West Point, I was sent to Panama to lead a rifle platoon in an infantry battalion. The Army in 1980 was still struggling to recover from its Vietnam failures, so there were tremendous drug issues and discipline problems. The unit I was a part of was a mess. To make matters more challenging, my platoon sergeant had severe narcolepsy. Shortly after arriving, I was told that one of my first official acts was to inform one of my soldiers that his father had committed suicide. After I notified the young soldier of the news, his response was, "Good. I hated the son of a bitch anyway." I knew it would be an interesting leadership experience. Talk about stress.

On one of the first weekends, I went to the beach and got brutally sunburned. If I had been in the United States, I would have gone to the hospital, but as it was, I did my best to manage the blisters and carry on. Still—the pain did not help my level of stress, nor did it do any favors for my cognitive capacity.

The day after I'd gone to the beach, I had to take my unit to the field for training. The platoon sergeant couldn't go along because of his narcolepsy, and my subordinate leaders were squad leaders who clearly hated each other. As I was trying to get my soldiers to space out tactically, preparing to go into the jungle, the two squad leaders started screaming obscenities at each other. My brilliant way of handling that was to yell even louder, in front of the entire platoon, "Shut the hell up!"

They shut up. But it was not my finest moment.

That night, we had to create defensive positions in the jungle, and I ordered everyone to dig foxholes. Sadly, I dug my foxhole under a fire ants' nest. Hundreds of fire ants fell onto me, crawled into my clothes, and began stinging my blistered, sunburned body. Given that today I am deathly allergic to bee and scorpion stings, I am certain the level of toxins would have killed me if it had happened to me today, but thankfully, as a young man, I got through it.

My platoon thought it was the funniest thing that had ever happened. For days afterward, they would recall the hilarious sight of me ripping off my clothes, whacking the ants off my sunburned body, and crying out in pain. It was a pretty humbling experience. But it also was a game-changer in my relationship with the platoon—the experience endeared me to them and ended up bringing us much closer. Things got better. Thankfully, I never resorted to screaming obscenities at my platoon again, nor did I feel the need to.

Initially, my stress caused me to double down on an authoritarian strategy. In the face of my shouting squad leaders, I just shouted louder. Ironically, that wasn't the leadership moment that earned me respect with my platoon. That came later—thanks to my own pain and humiliation—which led to opportunities for growth, influence, and relational trust.

CRISIS LEADERSHIP PARADOX #1

1. Greg's Fire Ants Paradox: Exert confident authority and express personal humility.

I see the paradox now: the goal was to exert authority and also express personal humility, acknowledging that I was human and could make mistakes. I might have led a lot more gracefully if I had embraced that paradox from the beginning. But, thanks to a sunburn, narcolepsy, dueling squad leaders, and a whole lot of fire ants—I got there.

Dennis O'Neil narrates

When I was a new leader in the Army, I led a group through six weeks of training at a huge complex called the National Training Center out in the middle of the Mojave Desert. It's a vast area between Los Angeles and Las Vegas with incredible open space where the military carries out full-size maneuvers. For those six weeks, I worked with my team doing offense, defense, and movement-to-contact with an invented enemy. By the time the training wrapped, we were all exhausted. It had been continuous combat operations in the middle of the desert, day in and day out, for weeks on end.

At the end of the six weeks, each group was supposed to get all their equipment ready to either return to the National Training Center, or load onto the railway to send back to their home station. I was responsible for ensuring that all of my group's equipment was present and accounted for—which turned out to be a tall order. For the last six weeks, we'd been maneuvering all over the Mojave, and some of the equipment had gotten misplaced. My First Platoon sergeant, a wonderful non-commissioned officer named Thomas Cobb with two decades of experience, told me, "Our guys are tired, they need to slow down. We'll get it all done. We just need to give them time."

I should have listened to him—but I didn't want to slow down. I wanted it done in twenty-four hours. And after all, I was the boss in charge, with a sum total of six months of experience.

I gave my group the order: "I want to see one hundred percent of our equipment here within twenty-four hours. I don't care how you get it done, just get it done."

It turns out, that's one of the worst things you can ever say as a leader. The level of interpretation for *how* subordinates should "just get it done" is pretty broad. When I told my soldiers that all equipment needed to be present and accounted for within twenty-four hours, and that I didn't care *how* it got done—they were faced with a moral dilemma. Where were they going to obtain the things that they'd lost? Faced with my demand, they got creative. Most of the missing equipment was "found" in a neighboring motor pool. (In other words: stolen from other soldiers.)

After his years of experience, Sergeant Cobb understood the paradox: "You have to slow down to go fast." Unfortunately, I was unwilling to recognize the sense of that. I didn't want to cater to my soldiers' fatigue and stress, which meant that I asked them to do more than they could feasibly—or responsibly—accomplish. My subordinates did exactly as I asked: they came up with one hundred percent of everything we were supposed to have—just not in an honest way. But then again, I hadn't specified that honesty was a requirement. I had just said, "Get it done." Another great soldier, Len Rosanoff, expanded on this lesson later in my career by showing me that, in combat, "Slow is smooth, smooth is steady, and steady is fast." The notion of "ready, shoot, aim" rarely gets the results we need.

Looking back now, it's obvious to me that this was simply a moment of failed leadership. I was too prideful to listen to the experience of my platoon sergeant; I was impatient and wanted to drive hard to get it done my way; and I failed to provide clarity and guidance to my subordinates about the right way to do things. The outcome of my failed leadership was some pretty questionable decision-making on the part of my subordinates. But who set them up for that failure? It was me.

Still, out of that failure came a few key lessons that helped put me on a path towards better leadership. I learned to listen better—particularly to people who have years of experience. I learned to view my subordinates as human beings with limitations; sometimes, it was my job as a leader to push them beyond their perceived limitations, but sometimes it was my job to acknowledge and heed those limits. I learned to communicate more clearly and establish better parameters. I got a good dose of humility—and thoroughly internalized the paradox, "You have to slow down to go fast."

CRISIS LEADERSHIP PARADOX #2

2. Slow is smooth, smooth is steady, and steady is fast.

LEARN FROM YOUR FAILURES

We can laugh about these failures now because we've found some worth in the learning that came out of them. Each experience cast a spotlight on our preferred tendencies when the stress was amplified, and that's been invaluable information for us to understand in all the stressful moments that have occurred since then. That self-awareness enabled us to better mitigate our unhealthy default strategies during crisis.

Remember what we discussed about post-traumatic growth in Chapter Four: the term describes the decision to grow *out of* trauma. Rather than letting problems, failures, and difficulties define your daily experiences, you learn from them so that you don't repeat them.

Leading paradoxically is difficult; most certainly, you will fail to strike the delicate balance at times. But even those failures can be sources of growth. In fact, we could identify that as another paradox: failures can lead to greater future success—provided you seek out the lessons within them.

3. Failures can lead to future success.

However, even if occasional failure is inevitable, we hope it's the exception, rather than the rule. We're going to give you some strategies now to help guide you in the challenging call of leading paradoxically.

STRATEGIES FOR PARADOXICAL LEADERSHIP

There are a few key steps you can take to deliberately set yourself up for paradoxical leadership. You can think of these strategies as river-banks, channeling your energy in a productive direction by ensuring you don't "flood" into your default preferences when times get rough.

TEAM OF RIVALS

One of the first things that Abraham Lincoln did after being elected president was to create a "team of rivals" in his cabinet. Rather than surrounding himself with a bunch of "yes men," he chose to do the opposite. He put three of his chief political rivals into key roles within his administration. Edwin Stanton—the incredible trial lawyer who once insulted Lincoln by calling him a "hairy ape"—was made his secretary of war. William Seward was a distinguished, well-educated New Yorker who had run a highly competitive campaign against Lincoln during the Republican primary; the new president appointed this rival to be his secretary of state. Edward Bates, once the pre-ferred Republican candidate named by the Republican National Committee, was appointed as Lincoln's attorney general.

In each of these three cases, Lincoln and his appointees had to swal-low a bit of their egos in order to move forward. However, Lincoln emphasized to the men that he simply couldn't lead without them. Rather than using his position of power to sabotage his rivals and prevent them from posing a future political threat, he chose to direct their abilities towards the service of a bigger purpose. Lincoln told them that they had gifts, strengths, and talents that he didn't have, and that he needed their voices to help inform his administration. The general opinion of modern historians is that Lincoln would have indeed floundered without them.

Part of successfully changing altitude is surrounding yourself with people who see angles of a situation that you don't see and will tell you the truth that you may not want to hear. Excellent leaders will create an environment with the psychological safety required for people to give honest feedback. If you want to take an example from Lincoln, that feedback won't just be allowed; it will be an obligation and responsibility of your subordinates and colleagues to provide. These dissenting voices will help you see the side of the leadership paradox which may not be obvious at first. These "rivals" will help you identify the best path forward.

One of the best things you can possibly do to excel as a leader is to surround yourself with people whose strengths complement your weaknesses. If you know that you excel in generating ideas and vision, but struggle with the nuts and bolts of deadlines and organization—surround yourself with some detail-oriented people. Enlist their help with forming your schedule and plotting out strategy for your organization. Get them to double-check your work. There is a tremendous amount of literature written about leadership which makes the point that you will make more progress by honing your strengths, rather than trying to fix your weaknesses. We recommend that you lean into your strengths, *understand your weaknesses* so that you can appropriately mitigate them and compensate for them, and let other people with natural talents in your areas of weakness fill in your gaps.

Imagine paradoxical leadership as two sides of a teeter-totter or seesaw in perfect balance. You're looking to put equal weight on either side so that you can quickly and easily shift from one priority to another when necessary. For example, imagine that a teeter-totter has "slow down" on one side and "move fast" on the other, two sides of a leadership paradox. Now, if a gung-ho young leader were to be on that teeter-totter by himself, he might only weigh down the "move fast" side and wouldn't enjoy much movement. But with a rival perspective balancing the other side, "move slow," he's suddenly more agile. That balanced weight would enable him to lean on the side of slowing down when appropriate, and then spring back towards charging full steam ahead when it was time to go, go, go!

Take note of the areas where you are heavily biased on one side—both in the areas of your strengths and your beliefs. Then, make deliberate moves to create more balance with the help of the people around you. By surrounding yourself with a "team of rivals" who can offset your perspectives and complement your areas of weakness, you can make paradoxical leadership shifts quickly. You'll give yourself more agility, flexibility, wisdom, and speed.

REAL NEEDS, RIGHT NOW, RESPOND ACCORDINGLY

On September 11, the terrorist attacks on the World Trade Center threw the United States into one of the greatest crises it has ever known. On September 12, the world was different. We knew it was different. Leaders had to focus on that difference as they moved forward.

Crises can have no foreseeable end date. That was the case for Admiral Stockdale and the other Americans in the POW camp; that's been the case during the COVID-19 pandemic. But whether a crisis has a defined date or is prolonged indefinitely, our response to crisis as leaders can be guided by taking the same three steps:

- Determine the **real needs**.
- Identify what needs to be done **right now**.
- **Respond accordingly**.

Start by evaluating the **real needs** of what's happening. Seek to understand your current environment as fully as possible. Consider: What, if anything, is *not* working right now? Recognize where your organization may have fallen into patterns; it's easy to rely on the strategies that you've always done, but a crisis might require new strategies. If the only tool you have is a hammer, then everything looks like a nail. If your crisis is clearly more complicated than a nail, seek out some new tools to attack it with from the wealth of material written about leadership science. What do your people need? What does your organization need? What tools do you require to meet those other needs?

Then: Consider what is needed **right now**. Although you may feel urgency to make changes, ironically, this step requires you to slow down and think strategically about what most needs immediate attention. One of the mantras of the US Army Special Forces is "Slow is steady; steady is smooth; smooth is fast." Slow down, steady the ship, and clarify your next steps. If the answer isn't obvious, clarify the focus by considering what *will be needed* in the future. If you know you need to get to point B by next week and you're currently at point A—what needs to happen today?

Another way to think about this question is "What do we need to change?" Here are some examples of some fundamental areas of change to consider:

- Is immediate change needed *within* your organization, i.e., making smaller changes within a department? Or is change needed *across* your organization, refiguring its systems, culture, processes, etc.? If a change is needed within the organization, what department most needs attention today (i.e., sales, engineering, marketing, research and development, etc.)? If change is needed across the organization, what systems and frameworks need to be adjusted?
- Do you need to empower your subordinates? Often, this step can be a game-changer in an effective crisis response. Align your

planning towards a common vision and goal, provide parameters, and then give your people the space to pursue that goal with as much flexibility and speed as needed. In the military, we call this centralized planning and decentralized execution.

- Do you need to reassure your people and provide clarity? It's possible that balls are getting dropped in your organization simply because people are panicked and there's a lack of clear, consistent communication. In a crisis, your staff will need your clear communication even more than they usually do.

- What kind of influence strategy might you need to use to get your people's buy-in and trust? Often in a crisis, an authoritarian approach feels most comfortable, but a coalition approach might actually be the best way to ensure everyone's alignment with a new direction. When people feel scared, they're not going to do things just because you said so, because the stakes are too high. Instead, they need to be shown that you are worthy of their trust, and that you trust them. Be thoughtful and deliberate about the best strategy to influence your people to get the results you need.

We recently spoke with a surgeon who was helping to lead her hospital through the COVID-19 crisis. She was acutely aware of the real needs of her staff. She told us on the phone that her people were getting nervous; their ICU was at capacity; everyone was stressed and exhausted. We asked her, "What's important *now*?"

She said, "I think what's probably most important to do now is to do some sort of visual assessment of my people so that I can take stock of how they're doing during this difficult time."

We said, "Perfect. How are you going to do that? What will that practically look like?" The conversation continued until she had a clear idea of her next steps. By taking a moment to slow down and consider the pressing *real needs* of her organization—namely, the well-being of her staff—then, considering what she could do *right now* to support them, she was able to arrive at a clear response.

And that's your next step as well: **respond accordingly**. Here are some possible responses you could take:

- Consider how to utilize, develop, and deploy new tools to make necessary changes.
- Get people aligned with the organization's direction, set the priorities, then allocate the appropriate resources.
- Implement a process that will lead your organization towards improvement and change.
- Constantly evaluate, monitor, and provide guidance; demonstrate your commitment to utilizing the available resources.

In other words, take the action steps most obviously indicated by the "real needs, right now" considerations.

As you respond, remember to lead paradoxically. Acknowledge the hurt and pain that your people may be experiencing, while still expressing hope. Show your employees that you care about them, even if you need to make hard staffing changes. Maintain the balanced tension of leading a caring organization, while still holding your people to rigorously high standards.

Real needs, right now, respond accordingly: these three considerations are always important—not just in a crisis, but *especially* in a crisis.

FROM FEAR, TO CONTRIBUTION

Greg Hiebert narrates

When the COVID-19 pandemic began, my initial, knee-jerk response was similar to many other Americans: I stocked up on toilet paper and ramen noodles. I obsessively read the news and shared every scary news story on social media. I walked around in dread, constantly waiting for the other shoe to drop.

Eventually, I woke up to the fact that I was living in a place of unbridled anxiety, which was not a great place to be. In the spirit of changing altitude, I determined that I needed to get to a better place. "What is needed now?" I asked myself. I decided I had better get proficient at using Zoom. I needed to manage my news intake. I decided that I could put more faith in the supply chain of my local grocery store and not stockpile food. By taking a step back, taking a longer view, and realizing that I had more resources at my disposal than my initial fear had let me believe, I was able to move from anxiety to a place of productive learning.

From there, I began to realize that I had the ability to make a contribution within the pandemic. My new question became, "How can I make this time meaningful?" I moved from a focus on my own learning, to a place of seeking to serve others and contribute something beneficial to the world.

During a crisis or in times of high stress, we have a natural tendency to become myopic. We focus on putting out individual fires, solving the urgent but neglecting to give attention to what's actually important. We don't take the time needed to truly understand the environment, determine the important priorities, and then empower others to take them on.

But in case you haven't already heard these words enough, I'll repeat once again the wisdom of Viktor Frankl: "Between the stimulus and response, *there is a space.*" Within that space, choose your response. Whether you're reeling in the midst of a crisis, or simply struggling in the midst of a stressful workday—take yourself from here, to contribution.

First, recognize if you're in a place of disproportionate fear. Name it, analyze it, choose to move on from it. Focus next on learning:

what can you change? How can you learn? What's most important? Finally, look to contribute. How can you serve others? What might you be able to offer to the world that will help it thrive?

WHAT IS NEEDED, NOW?

There's an amazing photograph taken during World War II that shows a milkman carrying his tray of milk bottles through the catastrophic Battle of Britain in 1940–1941. Dressed in a crisp white jacket, the milkman climbs over the debris and rubble from London's blown-out buildings. His stoic expression conveys focus and determination: he had customers in need of milk, and he had the milk to deliver, so by God, he was going to deliver it.

The image is a paradox in and of itself. The idea that a milkman should attempt to deliver milk in the midst of such chaos is almost ludicrous, and yet this was a person doing what he could, with what he had, where he was at. That is also your task as a leader: do what you can, with what you have, where you're at. The charge is simple, but its execution is hard. The many paradoxes of leadership emphasize how complex this challenge truly is—yet still a challenge worth engaging, like crossing bombed-out rubble to deliver milk to hungry people.

The best move will not always be the same move. The foundation of effective leadership is the ability to recognize the nuance of a situation and understand the best strategy to address it. What *is* that best strategy? It depends on the moment, the situation, the time, the person. It will often require that you hold two competing priorities in balance as you seek to answer: what is needed, now?

In this book, we've spoken to leaders who have recently changed altitude—going from one level of leadership to another. But we've also discussed changing altitude in terms of its requirements as different needs arise. If you're looking out of a cockpit into fog, you might change altitude to get more clarity—either up or down. You might increase your altitude to get a better bird's eye view of your trajectory. Or, you might take the plane all the way to the ground to "look up" and get a clearer idea of what your team experiences. If you run into turbulence, the need to change altitude might arise again. Your role as a leader requires that you assess your environment, consider your people, focus on your goals, and make hard decisions that honor all of the above.

This requires boldness and courage. It requires vision to take your people to a better place. This requires collaboration, as you seek to utilize the strengths and talents of the people around you. This requires trust in your team. This requires your self-awareness, to know when you need to set aside your own biases and preferences. This requires slowing down in order to be steady and ultimately go fast.

So, lean into those paradoxes. Learn from your failures. Build self-awareness. Consult that team of rivals. Consider the real needs, right now, and respond accordingly.

That's your mission—and it's one you're capable of. You can fly through the storm. You can thrive in changing altitude.

ACTION STEPS

1. Of the many leadership paradoxes we discussed in this chapter, is there one in particular you want to focus on? What action can you take to better balance both sides prescribed by this paradox?

2. Review the Competing Values Framework. Between creating, competing, controlling, and collaborating, what do you see as the most pressing need for your organization, now? What can you do to prioritize that need?

3. What are your default preferences when you're under great stress? What are some lessons you have taken from your failures?

4. If you were to form a "team of rivals," who should be on it? Consider whether or not you should make staffing changes to create this team of rivals around you.

5. What are your organization's real needs, right now? What resources are needed to make necessary changes? What barriers need to be removed or addressed? Taking all that into consideration, what is your next step in addressing these urgent needs?

CONCLUSION

Katie was not looking for a promotion. After decades of working for the same consulting company, Katie was settled and content in her role running the service team. But when an unanticipated leadership change occurred at the executive level, Katie suddenly found herself thrust into a new altitude of leadership. Overnight, she went from running one department of her organization to running the whole organization.

A CHANGING ALTITUDE SUCCESS STORY

Katie's long employment with the company might have been considered an asset—but in her case, she had the self-awareness to realize that the longstanding company culture she'd gotten used to, a culture of "harmony over honesty," was the opposite of what was needed. Her employees weren't ready to be fully honest about what was going on, which made it difficult for Katie to get a clear sense of what was happening across the organization. Katie's long tenure posed other challenges: many of her colleagues were used to seeing her as a peer, not as a leader, and she had a reputation for advocating hard for her own service unit, which made employees worry that she would show favoritism.

There were other organizational issues. People generally worked independently in their own siloed units; there was no synergy across the organization and even less integration with their parent company. Katie could also see that the company wasn't structured for radical growth, which was what they needed. In particular, their consulting arm was struggling and basically leaderless.

On top of these preexisting issues, Katie found herself at the helm as the economy bottomed out due to the COVID-19 pandemic. If that wasn't enough, she was the one gripping the wheel when turbulence picked up surrounding social unrest. She knew the company would resist taking an honest look at how they were perpetuating racial inequity. Although the company had made some small steps towards greater inclusivity and diversity, Katie knew they still had a long way to go.

The deck was stacked against her, and Katie recognized all these challenges almost immediately. Early into her tenure as CEO, one of the unit leaders quipped to her, "I'm glad it's you and not me, Katie." Her position was not enviable.

But Katie got to work—and we were privileged to witness her efforts as we coached her along the way. One by one, she started tackling the problems that she saw. She announced that they were going to tackle the diversity issue head-on. She initiated conversations about the issue and stressed the importance of being open, honest, and candid. She led an HR team through a process of rewriting their hiring practices and promotional standards so that more people of diverse backgrounds had the opportunity to advance.

Katie bolstered the struggling consultant team by realigning the sales and service unit so that it could organizationally support the needs of the consulting team. She initiated more cross-collaboration among departments, looking for opportunities to build natural synergy—not an easy thing to do, as everyone was working remotely due to the pandemic. In addition to breaking up the siloed units, she also increased the organization's alignment with their parent company so that the two were more truly integrated and her organization was set up to grow. Over eight months, during some of the most turbulent times, Katie was able to break through the chaos and determine the company's top priorities—the things they were going to focus on doing exceptionally well. And she did this not by autocratically making all the decisions herself, but carefully engaging not only her direct reports but a wide gathering of formal and informal leaders throughout the organization. She got them involved and diligently heard their perspectives and ideas.

So much of Katie's success in changing altitude came from her embrace of many of the concepts we've discussed in this book. She had commendable self-awareness and made conscious efforts to correct her biases. As CEO, Katie made the conscious effort to set aside her preference towards her old service unit in order to become a trusted leader for all departments. She also had the humility to seek out perspectives that were different from her own. She was known for seeking out the most peripheral people in the organization—individual consultants, individual intelligence people—so that she could "lie on the ground, and look up," to achieve a better understanding of the organization from different levels.

She knew what her strengths were and she leaned into them. In her former role, Katie had developed close-knit connections with her people. She knew how to make them feel valued, seen, and build a culture of trust. In her new role as CEO, Katie expanded that culture of trust across the organization. She increased approachability across all levels by creating regularly scheduled "skip level" meetings, where a person met with a boss two levels above them. Instead of engagement just between supervisors and their direct reports, these skip level meetings went beyond the basic modes of hierarchal structure to enhance communication, collaboration, and alignment in the organization. In her leadership, Katie made it easy for people to tell her the truth. That helped shift the company's "courtesy over candor" culture towards greater honesty.

Katie's natural intelligence also made her secure enough to question her own view of reality. She was open to differing points of view and eager to enhance her own understanding of the multifaceted challenges she faced. She listened well. Katie also had the humility to admit when she was wrong, and sought to learn from her mistakes. These practices meant that Katie made decisions that were thoughtful, not reactive.

Her leadership hasn't been perfect, and the road certainly hasn't been easy. In terms of "changing altitude," Katie had to take her initial "head pilot" flight through one of the most challenging storms we can imagine. But she's done so with self-awareness and humility; with concern for others and a clear focus on organizational priorities; with attention to healthy team norms and utilizing potent influence strategies. She has led change effectively, often leaning into the necessary paradoxes of leadership, and she's done so with agility and resilience. Needless to say, we're enormously proud of her.

Katie is an exemplary leader—not because she's a natural superstar, but because of the *actions* she took and the *choices* she made based upon her willingness to engage her organization at multiple levels. Those are actions and choices we've outlined for you in this book so that your own story of changing altitude can also be a soaring success.

THE HEART OF CHANGING ALTITUDE

This book was written for any leader who has recently seen a rapid expansion in their responsibilities. We've tried to do two things to help you navigate that journey: we tried to get you to ask new questions and then provided you with tools to answer them.

Your first question might have been what led you to pick up this book in the first place: "My style of leadership worked well in my old role—so why is it not working anymore?" Even great natural leaders can only get so far on their instincts. If you've realized that leadership is more complicated than you initially thought, then you possess a healthy level of self-awareness and a readiness to engage.

We sought to capitalize on that engagement as you read this book, prompting you to ask new questions, questions that may have been informed or inspired by the prompts in our "Action Steps" sections. Questions like: "How can I be more thoughtful and reflective in how I understand reality and engage with the people around me? How can I create a culture where people not only feel safe, but are also encouraged to speak up and dissent when needed? How can I collect a wider pool of information from my people so that I can get better ideas? How can I secure even deeper commitments from the people who are responsible for putting my ideas into action? How can I better maintain my personal well-being so that I can perform at my best? How do I make sure my team members are aligned, cohesive, connected, engaged, and appreciative of one another's differences?"

If we prompted you to consider some of these new questions, or think more deeply about the complexities of leadership, then the first goal of this book has been achieved. Great leadership requires the humble courage to challenge your own mindset and belief systems. A willingness to ask the hard questions signals a greater preparedness to engage with not what you *want* to hear, but what you *need* to hear. That's how great leaders make key decisions.

But we didn't want to abandon you there—we wanted this book to serve as a primer for your change in altitude, providing you with tools to answer your questions. Again and again, we reminded you of Viktor Frankl's wisdom, that between the stimulus and the response, there is a space. In that space, we urged you to be thoughtful. We outlined a process to help you—a leader in a new role—organize your thoughts and actions in a higher, more effective, and accelerated manner. In other words, a process for you to successfully *change altitude*, covering it all chapter by chapter.

In quick summary:

- **Know Yourself**: We don't see the world as it is; we see the world as we are. In this chapter, you were guided to form a clear idea of your leadership philosophy, your values, and your "big picture" strengths and weaknesses, empowering you to lead with greater objectivity and efficacy.

- **The Seven Critical Characteristics of Leadership**: The practice of leadership is a science which has been refined over thousands of years. You learned seven characteristics based on that science, ones that produce excellent leaders: inspire engagement; advocate for excellence; plan and implement; drive for results; lead change and innovation; influence others; practice teamwork and collaboration. You were prompted to evaluate your competency in each area and learned the importance of aligning your "Say/Do Ratio."

- **The Importance of Feedback**: Candid, honest feedback can be a catalyst for growth. Like the gauges in an airplane's cockpit, feedback serves as a clarifier about your current performance and provides information about what changes need to be made. You learned about how to implement the 360-Assessment tool, the "After-Action Review," and the benefits of walking with a mentor—all of which provide invaluable feedback for improvement.

- **Optimal Altitude**: We are the most productive, creative, innovative, and collaborative when we function in a positive frame of mind. This chapter gave you tools to function at your best: energy management, protective boundaries, a clear hierarchy of work priorities, and self-care. By maintaining "optimal altitude" in a rapidly changing world, you are equipped to respond effectively to its uncertainty and complexity. You also will have the energy to fully engage with the strategies for effective leadership.

- **Form and Live Collective Values**: Organizational culture and group dynamics are largely informed by what a leader emulates and tolerates. You learned the importance of leading by example and building a culture of shared respect. We walked you through how to develop a formalized covenant that would clearly identify positive values for your team to commit to. These covenants can help teams better align with an organization's mission, ensure healthy workplace culture, lead to better understanding of individual preferences, and help increase employee engagement so that your people and organization can thrive.

- **Communication and Active Listening**: Effective communication and listening not only enables us to learn, grow, and improve; it also enables us to improve the quality of our workplace dialogue so that we can better explore all opportunities in front of us. You learned that communication begins with your accessibility as a leader. It continues with your practice of generative listening and respectful engagement with your people.

- **Leading Change and Exerting Influence**: Leadership is the process of influencing human behavior to accomplish the goals and outcomes of the organization. By employing the Comprehensive Change Model, you can provide clarity, motivation, and clear next steps for your team as you lead them towards positive change. Then you can effectively take your organization on a journey from its current state to some better future state by using the *currency* of leadership: influence. This chapter described a variety of influence strategies that can be used to secure your employees' appropriate level of commitment and buy-in.

- **Empowering Others**: When you empower your people to lead, it's like turning on new jet engines that have the power to rocket you forward. In order to do this well, you need to lead in a way that is "tight, loose, tight." Provide clear communication and remove any barriers for your employees' empowerment (tight); secure their buy-in and alignment with your objectives, then give them flexibility to carry out their goals (loose); and promote a healthy culture of accountability (tight). In doing so, you not only empower others to accomplish their tasks, you also empower their growth and development as future leaders.

- **Understand the Environment**: Agile leadership requires a thorough awareness of your environment. By reading environmental proxies, you can anticipate needed moves and identify opportunities. We taught you the five steps to evaluate your environment and provided you with a cultural assessment tool so that you can fully understand how best to act within your environment.

- **Conflict Management**: Conflict is inevitable, but it can be healthy and productive, provided you manage effectively to minimize the harm and maximize its value. This chapter overviewed the foundational elements for productive conflict to maximize its value in any context. When mediating conflict between your subordinates, provide guidance, but still push for their involvement in the resolution. When engaging in conflict with your leadership, ensure your alignment with their goals and seek to understand their world before gently pushing your agenda. Conflict, used productively, can accelerate the growth of your team and align your people towards a common vision of success.

- **Paradoxical Leadership:** Leading others in a complex, volatile, changing world often requires that you hold conflicting aims in tension; for instance, allowing space for innovation and creativity, while also implementing effective controls against risks. This chapter gave you strategies to grow in paradoxical leadership by creating a "team of rivals" and by considering the real needs, right now; then, respond accordingly.

Within these pages, we've sought to provide you with the essential tools you need to successfully change altitude, but the conversation doesn't need to stop here. As you continue on your journey of leadership, we invite you to connect with us and use the resources available on our websites. You can find a complete 360-Assessment at www.3ELeadershipGroup.com, along with a number of other resources. You can also reach out to either one of us at www.leadershipforward.com, our coaching website.

At face value, changing roles and looking at things from a different perspective doesn't seem like it should be incredibly difficult—but in reality, it really is. Every situation, every individual, and every organization is different. Without a framework and process to reference, leaders can find themselves essentially flying blind.

But *with* the systematic approach we've provided in these pages, we've tried to give you all the tools you need to achieve clarity, conviction, capability, and courage in your new phase of leadership.

These steps are all ones you can take on your own, in your individualized context. The process we've outlined has the power to accelerate your change in altitude so that you can fly with greater agility, speed, and alignment with the targeted direction of your organization.

This process isn't just for you. This approach is set up to help develop the growth of *everyone* on your team. These steps will not only make you a better leader; they will also make you a better person, and they'll guide you towards bringing out the best in all the people around you. As you empower your people to grow, develop, and eventually lead, you usher others towards their own experience of changing altitude.

SOAR

Tomorrow morning your alarm will go off. You'll slowly sit up; eventually you'll stand. Then you'll begin the first motions of your day. Perhaps you'll exercise; perhaps you'll meditate. Coffee or tea might be involved, and hopefully there's some food as well. Then—either when you log on to your computer, open your email, or walk through the doors of an office—work will begin.

When it does, this is what we hope for you:

We hope you are inspired to be open and honest about your personal strengths and areas of struggle. We hope you can view your struggles not as failures but as opportunities for growth—experiences that will ultimately help you assist others in their own development.

We hope that you are less frustrated by the challenges of your new role, and instead, feel ready to embrace them with openness and enlightenment about what is possible.

We hope that you seek to understand reality with greater insight, and that you will build a team diverse with perspectives, inclusive as a community. We hope you seek to better understand how others see the world and to value that difference just as much you value your own perspective. We hope you listen to learn, and that you listen well.

We hope that the investment you made in the purchase of this book turns into a huge accelerator of your own potential, something that you want to share with every other person you know who gets promoted.

We hope you are empowered to be thoughtful and reflective about the requirements of each situation set before you. We hope that in your tasks and decisions, you take advantage of *the space* between the stimulus and the response to consider the nuance and complexity of the task at hand. We hope you recognize that, often, the answer starts with, "It depends"—and that even in being able to recognize that, "it depends" is an act of courage.

We hope that the tools and principles we have shared provide you with the means to be a more effective, profound, and capable leader. We hope these evidence-based strategies give you a richness to draw from and will serve as powerful upward drafts.

Ultimately, we hope they will lead you to soar.

ABOUT THE AUTHORS

DR. DENNIS O'NEIL is a prominent thought leader and subject matter expert on executive coaching and leadership development. He has over thirty years of practical leadership experience at the highest levels of Fortune 500 Companies, the White House, the military, and as a Professor of Strategic Leadership. In addition, he has been a trusted executive and advisor providing strategic and analytical guidance to public and non-profit boards, CEOs, senior government and military officials, and multi-national organizations. An accomplished executive coach and leadership development expert with leadership*Forward* and 3ELeadership Group, Dennis' training methods inspire individuals and teams to deliver top-tier performances through one-on-one coaching and team engagements. Dennis lives in Virginia with his wife, Noreen. They have raised four tremendous children together, and he is honored to be a grandfather.

GREG HIEBERT is the co-founder of leadership*Forward*, a leadership education and consulting company. His commitment to profound change in people and organizations comes from long service as a leader and mentor. With an eclectic span of experiences—including West Point, the United States Army, Harvard Business School, Egon Zehnder International, BellSouth and McKinsey & Company—Greg's coaching approach incorporates deep levels of authentic and courageous dialogue to create conditions for personal and organizational transformation. Greg resides in Atlanta, Georgia, with his beloved wife Claudia, and is a proud father and grandfather.

GREG'S ACKNOWLEDGEMENTS

As the last several years have been challenging ones for so many of us, the greatest treasure of my life is the continued love, support, and partnership I have with my wife of over forty years, Claudia. While our economy was shut down and I had to come off the road where I had probably traveled a good forty-eight weeks a year, it was so wonderful to be with the love of my life. I'm so thankful that we can get through any storm and difficulty that we might face together.

Every year I go through a ritual where I reflect on all the people who have not only blessed my life, but who have affirmed and reminded me that there is a lot more good in me than I certainly think of myself. And amazingly, when I reflect on people who may have tried to "rain on my parade" and disrespect or mistreat me, I come up completely empty. Maybe it's because I have a terrible memory or have learned to forget the bad things that have happened in my life. However, I choose to believe for reasons beyond my comprehension that my life has been filled and blessed by literally hundreds of family, friends, colleagues, and clients—far too many to acknowledge, so I will highlight just a few.

I will always be thankful for and grateful to my late parents, Don and Pat Hiebert, who loved me unconditionally. Despite my rebellious ways, they taught me that a person's character and virtue really matter.

I acknowledge my oldest brother, Don (Dee) Hiebert, who died far too young in a B-52 crash in 1983 and continues to be an enormous inspiration and role model for me. My passion for leadership really started because of conversations we had, in addition to observing him lead others with tremendous virtue, humility, and purpose.

I have also been enormously blessed to have two other brothers and two sisters, who are all amazing, as are their partners in marriage: Theresa and Paul Horne, Tom and Kate Hiebert, Tim and Lori Hiebert, and Julie and Scott Hodsden. They are all exceptional leaders, parents, spouses; and I am blessed to have them in my life as they continue to inspire me to be a better man.

I also acknowledge my wonderful adult children for continuing to teach me about unconditional love: Emily, Erik, Katie, and Molly. I also celebrate my four amazing grandchildren: Judah, Estelle, Rowan, and Lucie. Thank you for continuing to teach me about joy.

I have also been truly blessed as well over the years by my colleagues at leadership*Forward,* especially Paul Litten and Michelle Ruiz. It continues to be a great joy and privilege to work with you. It is hard to believe that we are close to celebrating our twentieth anniversary! You continue to help me be a better colleague and human being. Thank you for continuing to help me achieve my dreams.

Writing a book by yourself can be a challenging journey. Writing it with a colleague and friend has the potential for disaster. However, writing this book with Denny has actually been easy and extremely fulfilling. Certainly, we disagreed at times but always worked through to common ground where we both felt heard and appreciated. In the end, our friendship and partnership could not be stronger. I am also grateful to everyone on our publishing team at Scribe who have been extraordinary to work with. Greta Myers, in particular, has been a superstar, and I am most grateful for her amazing patience, thoughtfulness, thoroughness, and persistence. This book could have never been done without her.

As this book shares many client stories, Denny and I have deliberately changed the names of many of the people to protect their confidentiality, while also making sure that they were comfortable with the stories we did share. Ever since I started leadership*Forward* and have coached, taught, mentored, and developed client leaders for the last twenty years, my life has been enormously purposeful, positive, productive, and profound. And at the heart of that work have been the incredible clients I have had the privilege to serve and support.

Finally, throughout my military, academic, corporate, and consulting careers, I have been greatly blessed by some amazing bosses and leaders who were always trying to strike the right balance between mission accomplishment and taking great care of the people who had to accomplish that mission. This book could not have been written without the great examples I have observed over the years, such as General Tom Needham, General Dan McNeill, General John Wattendorf, Jeff McNally, and two of my very first bosses, Mark Pentecost and Jim Jarvis, and countless other truly exceptional people in the US Army, including the staff and faculty at the United States Military Academy, the Harvard Business School, McKinsey & Company, BellSouth, and Egon Zehnder.

DENNIS'
ACKNOWLEDGEMENTS

To say that this book was written by Dennis and Greg would be a gross understatement, to say the least.

First and foremost, I want to share my gratitude for those to whom I've dedicated this book: my family, who enabled me to write it and have taught me the greatest leadership lessons in life—Noreen, Nora, Katie, Megan, and Owen. I love you all. I also want to acknowledge Chris, Hunter, Ellie, and all my future family members. I thank all my brothers and sisters for the love and support they've given me throughout a lifetime, including Mike and Jenny, Chris and Lisa, Aiden and Joanne, Preston and Mary, and Jack and Lori. No one has had a greater influence on me than my wonderful parents, Pat and Linda, who first taught me leadership, honor, trust, and that hard work and perseverance will pay off. I also express deep thanks to my loving in-laws, Jack and Josephine, for their years of unwavering support to me and for always being the rock of our family.

Many of the lessons I have included in this book come from my two-plus decades in uniform. I'm eternally grateful for all the soldiers, noncommissioned officers, and officers that I've had the pleasure of serving with, especially my teams in Iraq and Afghanistan—for the good laughs and the camaraderie during rough days. Many of my colleagues have become both dear friends and peer mentors, including Joseph Kopser, Shannon Sentell, Eric Weis, Chip Daniels, Ken Robbins, Jim Tuite, Todd Woodruff, Len Rosanoff, Marc Wehmeyer, Thom Sutton, and many others at the White House, West Point, the Command and General Staff College, and National Defense University. I also thank the numerous examples of great strategic leadership that I had throughout my career, including Martin Dempsey, Bob Cone, Ray Odierno, George Casey, and Norty Schwartz. Four specific mentors that have been instrumental to my leadership study and development are Tom Kolditz, Mark McGuire, Pat Sweeney, and Michael Endres. A special thank you to my dear friends who have always helped me translate my military career into civilian success, including Larry Olsen, Charlie Hooker, Dave O'Connor, and Jerry Elliott.

I thank all the staff, faculty, and students at Duke University who took a chance on me and taught me not only good research but how to be a better person as well, including Phil Costanzo, Blair Sheppard, and my cohort team.

Next, I would like to thank all my colleagues in business at Alcoa, Arconic, and most recently leadership*Forward*. To my business partner, co-author, mentor, and longtime friend Greg Hiebert and his wife Claudia: none of this would have been possible without your love and support over the past 30 plus years. And to the rest of our team at leadership*Forward*, including Paul Litten, Jennifer Daniels, Carole Moran, Nora Anderson, Michelle Ruiz, and many others along the way, thank you for contributing to my successes every day.

I am profoundly grateful to all the people who help research, write, and publish this book, including Greta, Christine, Mickey, Zach, Rose, and numerous others who assisted behind the scenes at Scribe.

Finally, I would like to thank all our clients, especially in healthcare, who have given so much of themselves these past few years during very difficult times. You are an inspiration to us all.

CPSIA information can be obtained
at www.ICGtesting.com
Printed in the USA
LVHW032158121121
703161LV00001B/3

9 781544 525631